CW00786696

EZEKIEL

ECSTATIC, VISIONARY PROPHET

Sotirios Christou

Books by Sotirios Christou

The Priest & The People Of God – 2003
Revised as Images Of Formation – 2009
Evangelism & Collaborative Ministry – 2004, 2012
The Unsearchable Riches Of Christ – & Paul – 2006
Informed Worship – 2007, Revised 2010, 2014
The Psalms – 2010
Messianic & Intimate Psalms – 2010
The Psalms, Intimacy, Doxology & Theology – 2011
Breathtaking Authority – 2013
Esther – 2013
Ruth & Esther – 2014
David, Jonathan & Saul – 2016
Models Of Evangelism – 2016
Elijah & Elisha – 2016
Ezekiel – 2017

First published in Great Britain by Phoenix Books.
18 Bullen Close, Cambridge CB1 8YU
christousotirios@hotmail.co.uk

The right of Sotirios Christou to be identified as the author
Of this work has been asserted to him in accordance with the
Copyright, Designs and Patents Acts 1988.

All rights reserved.
No part of this publication may be reproduced or
transmitted in any form or by any means, electronic or
mechanical, including photocopy, recording or any information
storage or retrieval system, without permission
in writing from the publisher.

THE TEN COMMANDMENTS
EXODUS 20: 2-17

I am the Lord your God, you shall have no other gods besides me.

You shall not make for yourself a graven image or any likeness of anything that is in heaven above or that is in the earth beneath, or that is in the water under the earth. You shall not bow down to them or serve them: for I the Lord your God am a jealous God.

You shall not take the name of the Lord your God in vain: for the Lord will not hold him guiltless whotakes his name in vain.

Remember to keep the Sabbath day holy. Six days shall you labour and do all your work, but the seventh is a Sabbath to the Lord your God. For in six days the Lord made heaven and earth, the sea, and all that is in them and rested on the seventh. Therefore, the Lord blessed the Sabbath day and hallowed it.

Honour your father and your mother, that your days may be long in the land which the Lord your God gives you.

You shall not kill.

You shall not commit adultery.

You shall not steal.

You shall not bear false witness against your neighbour.

You shall not covet your neighbour's house, you shall not covet your neighbour's wife, or covet anything belonging to your neighbour.

ACKNOWLEDGEMENTS

I am pleased to give permission to Sotirios to use my late husband's painting 'Let There Be Light' for the cover of his book on Ezekiel.

My husband always believed that his paintings, although based on Bible stories, were nevertheless universal in their truth.

He said of his work: 'My paintings are not concerned with the surface appearance of people or things, but try to express something of the fundamental spiritual reality behind this surface appearance. I try to express in visible form the oneness and unity of this invisible power binding all things into one whole.

I do not illustrate stories literally as I am not interested in the place or the people, but try to express what I feel is the deeper significance of each story for every individual throughout all time.'

Not long before John passed on, a book was published of fifty of his recent paintings entitled, 'The Painted Word – Paintings of John Reilly' – which also includes the Bible passage that inspired each painting. John's book, also, prints can be obtained from theJohnreillygallery.co.uk or from the Amazon website.

Jill Reilly

CONTENTS

PREFACE   9

CHAPTER ONE
INTRODUCTION

CHAPTER TWO
EZEKIEL'S PROPHETIC CALL
1:1-3:27

CHAPTER THREE
PROPHECIES OF JUDGMENT
4:1-7:27

CHAPTER FOUR
ORACLES AGAINST ISRAEL
8:11:12:16:17:19:21:22:24

CHAPTER FIVE
HOPE FOR ISRAEL
33:34:36:37

PREFACE

Ezekiel has made important contributions to Christian symbolism and the history of Christian art. The man, the lion, the ox, and the eagle, traditional symbols of the four evangelists, Mathew, Mark, Luke and John respectively, appear first in that order in Ezekiel 1:10, 10:14, Rev. 4:7. The illuminated Bury Bible in Corpus Christi College, Cambridge (c.1135) contains an eloquent illustration of this, showing Christ enthroned beside a rainbow (Ezek. 1:28) and surrounded by the 'four living creatures' (Ezek. 1:5), which represent the evangelists, with the prophet Ezekiel in the foreground looking on. In traditional iconography, the Seraphim got their six wings from Isaiah Ch. 6, and the Cherubim got their four faces and their four wings from Ezekiel 1:26, 10:21. Ezekiel's extraordinary vision of the throne of God apparently resting on four wheels and four creatures, known to art historians as the tetramorph, is far less well developed in Christian tradition than it is in Judaism. Jewish writers since Jesus Ben Sirus (c. 180BC, Sir 49:8) know it as the merkabah 'chariot' which subsequently provided the central motif of a major trend in Jewish mysticism. But there are a few Christian versions of the scene as well. Notably a small painting by Raphael in the Pitti Palace in Florence (c. 1518), showing the deity above the clouds, riding on winged creatures, in a scene more reminiscent of classical mythology than of anything biblical, and William Blake's powerful 'The Whirlwind' – Ezekiel's Vision of the Cherubim and Eyed Wheels (c. 1803-1805).

More often than not, however, for Christians 'Ezekiel's Vision' refers to the valley of dry bones, so dramatically depicted in the Dura Europos Synagogue frescoes (c. 200 ce), but also a favourite theme of Christian artists. Signorelli's fresco in the chapel of San Brizio in Orvieto Cathedral (1499-1502) is one of the most impressive, although without any explicit reference to Ezekiel, and another with the prophet very much in evidence, is by the Spanish painter Francisco Collantes in the Madrid Prado (1630). It also appears on a number of early Christian sarcophagi, including a fourth-century child's sarcophagus in the Vatican Museum, showing Christ bringing the dead back to life with a wand while Ezekiel looks on. One of the many other examples of the influence of Ezekiel's striking language and imagery on Christian tradition, there is the mark (Hebrew *tau*) on the forehead of those to be saved on the day of judgment – Ezek. 9:4 cf. Rev. 7:3, 9:4, 14:1. This was interpreted from the beginning as the sign of the cross since in the ancient Hebrew script *tau* was written as a cross. The so called Tau cross especially associated with St. Francis of Assisi is derived from the Greek letter *tau* and can therefore trace its origins back to Ezekiel as well.[1]

There is an element of mystery about Ezekiel as we know so little about him, and yet he is one of the most fascinating prophets due to his visions of God and his ministry that is marked by his symbolic sign-acts. 'With respect to force and awesomeness, no theophany in the OT matches Ezekiel's inaugural vision.'[2] Hence the Book of Ezekiel primarily points to the Lord. Once his visions of God reach a climax with the 'appearance of the likeness of the glory of the Lord,' the message he subsequently reveals to Ezekiel, is God's covenant wrath in His relationship with Israel. Key to understanding the Lord's judgment on his people in the Book of Ezekiel is the Covenant the Lord made with the Hebrews when He brought them out of Egypt. (The details of the Covenant are recorded in Exodus 19-20, Leviticus 18-20 and Deuteronomy 28-30). In these passages that are essential reading to interpreting Ezekiel, the Lord promises to bless Israel on the condition they are obedient in keeping his commandments and laws, while failure to keep them will incur God's judgment and the curse of the Covenant. (To understand the book of Ezekiel it is also helpful to read 2 Kings 21-25 and 2 Chronicles 33-36).

Ezekiel's character was determined by his training to be a priest and his subsequent call to be a prophet. We do not have any other details about him other than he was the son of Buzi, and was married. The defining characteristic of Ezekiel was seeing the appearance of the glory of the Lord's presence, along with his experience of being animated and energised by God's Spirit. 'The role of the Spirit in Ezekiel's experience is described as, *wattabo bi ruah,* 'and the Spirit entered me' – 2:2, 3:24. Here the power of the Spirit is demonstrated by raising the prophet on his feet, *he emid al-raglay,* as on six occasions Ezekiel is swept by the Spirit to another location – 3:12, 14, 8:3, 11:1, 24, 43:5. Ezekiel's prophetic role is also dramatically represented by the divine coercion formula, *watthei alay yhwh* – 'the hand of the Lord came upon me,' which occurs 7 times. This describes the overwhelming pressure the Lord exerts on Ezekiel, as he asserts complete control over him that at times transports him back and forth to distant places – 8:1, 37:1, 40:1. Equally, the divine inspiration formula, *wattippol alay ruah yhwh,* 'the Spirit of Yahweh fell upon me' – 11:5a, represents a spiritual variation.'[3] Ezekiel's encounters with God's Spirit are an integral aspect of his ministry and is memorably associated with the symbolic signs he enacts and the oracles he announces. His ministry was also marked by confinement to his home and considerable hardship and suffering.

Ezekiel the younger contemporary of Jeremiah was also the contemporary of Daniel, Hannaniah and Azariah, who were also taken captive to Babylon, and these four young men stood out as exceptional men of faith in the Lord. As these three young men were chosen to learn the letters and language of the Chaldeans and to be educated for three years – Daniel 1:4, Ezekiel like other leaders from Jerusalem taken into exile, may have also been educated in a similar pattern of learning that made him familiar with Babylonian culture, their deities and mythology. As the Babylonian's policy was to take the leaders and skilled workers from the nations they defeated and bring them to Babylon and train them to serve the empire.

Ezekiel's prophetic ministry in Babylon spans two periods and the first between 593-587 that focused on judgment is recorded in chs. 1-24. The second period between 587-571 that is centred on hope is recorded in chs. 33-48 (in between chs. 25-32 are oracles to the surrounding nations). Ezekiel's call as a prophet was to proclaim the word of the Lord to his people – a word of judgment due to Israel's rebellion against God's commandments and laws, and because of the peoples' abominations due to their idolatry and apostasy – Ezek. 5:5: 6:1-10, 8:5-17, 16:15-22, 20:30-32. These texts of Scripture record Israel's rebellion of setting up altars in high places and sacrificing to other gods and idols, and carrying out these abominations in the temple itself and worshipping them. Their rebellion also involved sacrificing their children on the altars of these gods and idols. And they also made alliances with the Assyrians and Egyptians described as 'harlotry,' with Israel as an adulterous and unfaithful wife – 16:23-34. Because of these things the Lord declared his severe judgment, and the first 24 chapters of Ezekiel contain one of the most sustained and vehement declarations of judgment to be found anywhere in the prophetic literature of the Bible. Walter Zimmerli says, 'The radical corruption of Jerusalem is illustrated in a surprising use of historical elements from the ancestry of the city – 16:3: 'From your origin and your derivation you are from the land of the Canaanites. Your father was an Amorite and your mother a Hittite.' It is in agreement with this insult about its Canaanite origin that the sin in Ezekiel 16 is not seen to lie in the political sphere, but in the cultic and cultural spheres. In another way chs. 15 and 22 give expression to the radical corruption of Jerusalem.'[4]

Yet while the Lord informed Ezekiel that his audience the house of Israel were impudent, stubborn and rebellion 2:4-6, after the fall of Jerusalem – 33:30-35, the census reveals that when the Lord stirred up Cyrus to build him a house in Jerusalem – Ezra 1:1 and he gave permission to the Jews to return to their homeland to rebuild the house of the Lord in 538, just over 40,000 returned – Ezra 2:64. While it is speculative, this dramatic spiritual renewal may have reflected the long term effect of Ezekiel's ministry, as his colleagues were among the first among the exiles to recognise him as a true prophet after the fall of Jerusalem – 33:33.[5]

Ezekiel's vision of seeing the appearance of the glory of the Lord – Ezek. 1:1-3:27, is different to Isaiah's, yet both hear the Lord speaking to them. While Isaiah responds to God's voice saying, 'Here am I send me' – Isaiah 6: 8, Ezekiel is stunned into silence as he is overwhelmed by the visions of the Lord, and his message concerning the rebelliousness of Israel that he is to address as the Lord's spokesman. The Hebrew for being overwhelmed is *masmim* –'to be desolate, appalled.'[6] Ezekiel is stunned and reduced to silence and disturbed by the Lord's message of judgment on his people. His encounter with God and his call to preach a message of judgment to an unresponsive audience, emotionally and psychologically left Ezekiel embittered – 3:15, probably because he was aware it was a difficult and thankless task. A task that caused Jeremiah his contemporary extreme grief and now was his calling too.

Ezekiel's famous vision that combines elements of the storm theophany and the throne theophany in Ch. 1 are drawn in part from ancient Israelite traditions.[7] Storm, cloud, and fire are in the OT, regular elements of a storm theophany. A literary tradition that was basically derived from mythological descriptions of the storm or war god in ancient Near Eastern religious contexts.[8] But Ezekiel's description of the four headed, winged cherubim would have been familiar to any inhabitant of ancient Mesopotamia surrounded by great statutes of tutelary deities, guarding temple entrances and other sky bearing creatures with multiple forms that supported the thrones of deities. Ezekiel's vision transforms the static Mesopotamian imagery mainly by the addition of wheels, hands, eyes, and the prevailing Spirit of Yahweh, into a dynamic portrayal of the sovereign, roving freedom of Yahweh. God's presence, power, and glory were in Babylon, and could take on and yet transcend Babylonian symbolism: and could be even more overwhelming in effect, than all the Babylonian statuary put together.[9]

Yet we must not overlook the significance of the cherubim in the OT, as in Exodus 25:17-22 Moses is commanded by the Lord to fashion two cherubim out of hammered gold and to place one at each end of the lid of the ark of the covenant, facing each other with their arms outstretched. Cherubim were also woven into curtains for the tabernacle and later the temple (Ex. 26:1, 31:2, 2 Chron. 3:14). For the temple Solomon had two cherubim made of olive wood ten cubits high and overlaid with gold, and they were also placed in the Holy of Holies with the ark. Solomon's temple also had cherubim carved on the walls of both the Holy Place and the Holy of Holies and on the doors – 1 Kings 6:29-35. Cherubim were also carved all around the eschatological temple Ezekiel saw in a vision – 41:17-20, 25. The cherubim in the Holy of Holies over the ark served as God's throne the place of his majestic presence. In addition the cherubim David planned Solomon to build for the temple, whose wings were spread and covered the ark of the covenant of Yahweh are said to be God's chariot – 1 Chron. 28:18. 'The picture that the OT presents is that wherever God's heavenly throne and majesty are revealed or described in detail the cherubim always attend him. They are either the throne of his majestic presence, as in the Holy of Holies, or they attend his presence, to serve and enhance the Lord's glorious presence and to sing his praises.'[10]

The Book of Ezekiel has left its mark on the Book of Revelation with significant traces of the influence of Ezekiel. The vision of the chariot from heaven with the four living creatures (Ezek. 1:5-10) becomes the heavenly throne room with four living creatures surrounding Christ (Rev. 4:1-8). The prophet is bidden to eat the scroll (Ezek. 2:8-9) as is John the seer (Rev. 5:1, 10), and both Ezekiel and Revelation end with the vision of a new temple (Ezek. 40-48, Rev. 21-22).[11] The image of Jesus as the good shepherd (John 10:11-18) has its inspiration in the prophecy about the shepherds and the sheep (Ezek. 34). Also, John's vision of the river of life (Rev. 22) springs from the river flowing in the temple (Ezek. 47).[12] The resurrection of Christ is a symbolic fulfillment of Ezekiel's vision of the dry bones and the promise of Israel's resurrection.

In God's providential will and sovereign purpose, the Lord chose and consecrated Ezekiel to be a prophet and spokesman. His background as a young man training to be a priest and his familiarity with God's laws and temple procedures, were the foundation that the Lord used to equip and prepare Ezekiel to serve him. However, so controversial was his task and in effect so confrontational, as it challenged the religious beliefs and the false confidence and inviolability the people had in Jerusalem as God's chosen nation, that the Lord's call on Ezekiel's life as a prophet was reinforced in a number of ways in his inaugural vision. The Lord took hold of Ezekiel through his visions of the chariot throne in heaven and the appearance of the likeness of the glory of the Lord. And he was spectacularly enlisted into his service through the overwhelming visions the Lord gave him of heavenly realities completely outside of his experience.

A striking characteristic of Ezekiel's ministry is clearly the symbolic sign-acts the Lord instructs him to perform. Daniel Block says, 'In my view, no other prophet is so creative in his presentation of his message, and none is so forceful. The rhetorical strategies reflected in this collection are both visual and aural, all designed to penetrate the hardened mind of his hearers.'[13] Although the symbols involved images that were not real, they were used to communicate God's message to his people about events that really did exist or will really occur.[14] Joseph Blenkinsopp has a catchy heading for Ezekiel's symbolism, 'Prophetic Theater of the Absurd.' He especially attributes this to chapters 3–4 which he sees as:

> Embodying an extraordinary form of communication, one that risked bringing upon the prophet the charge of eccentricity, if not insanity. They illustrate the truth that prophetic ministry is not exhausted in the mandate to speak, especially in situations of extreme crisis.[15]

Sotirios Christou Cambridge October 2017

CHAPTER ONE

INTRODUCTION
EZEKIEL'S HISTORICAL CONTEXT

Paul Joyce in 'Ezekiel'–The Library of Hebrew Old Testament Studies says, 'The Book of Ezekiel is one of the most interesting and compelling books of the Hebrew Bible, and simultaneously it is one of the most difficult perplexing books.'[1] And it is difficult because of its length, 'rich language frequently hyperbolic, and often with strange images remote from ordinary experiences, that are at times repellent.'[2]

Ezekiel the younger contemporary of the prophet Jeremiah, was among those who were exiled to Babylon in 597 BC, before Jerusalem fell in 587. His prophetic ministry took place amongst the exiles and much of this evolved around issues concerning the temple and Jerusalem. He was born into a turbulent world where the major nations on the Near Eastern ancient stage were switching roles and the smaller nations disappearing. For centuries, the neo-Assyrians were the dominant power in the region that at times stretched as far as Egypt. By 627 BC, at Ashurbanipal's death, they had over-extended themselves with the Babylonians waiting in the wings. In 604 BC, there was a decisive battle at Carchemish (Jer. 46:2), and the Assyrians were driven off the map by the Babylonians never to be heard of again, and their allies the Egyptians were forced to retreat with their tails between their legs. Nebuchadnezzar 11, (605-562) led the Babylonians in their spectacular victory at Carchemish. From this time onwards, the affairs of Judah were destined to become inter-twined with those of the Babylonians.[3]

In 2 Kings 21:1-18 and 24:3-4, Manasseh (687-642) is described as the worst king in David's line, and Judah never recovered from the spiritual apostasy and degradation he inflicted on the nation. After 45 years of royal court paganism, apostasy was so deeply entrenched in the nation the sweeping reforms of Josiah (640-609) attempted to address this. He sought to purge the nation of pagan cult objects, divination and magic, centralised public worship in Jerusalem, reinstituted the Passover and extended his campaign against idolatry into the northern kingdom – 2 Kings 23:2, 2 Chron. 34. A short time after Josiah's death, Pharaoh Necho placed Josiah's eldest son on the throne, who he renamed Jehoiakim as an act of sovereignty – 2 Kings 23:31-37. Sadly, he managed to undo the effects of most of Josiah's reforms.[4]

In 605 after Nebuchadnezzar had consolidated his power in Babylon his army returned to Palestine to fight against the Egyptians who were driven out of Judah and Jehoiakim became a vassal of Babylon. In 597 and again in 587 Judah suffered crushing defeats at the hands of Nebuchadnezzar, and in 597 a significant proportion of the population was taken captive a thousand miles to Mesopotamia. The leading citizens, including Daniel and his friends and vast amounts of treasure, along with the temple treasure were taken to Babylon.

Nebuchadnezzar installed Josiah's youngest son Mattaniah as king, whom he renamed Zedekiah – 2 Kings 24:17-18. On several occasions with his neighbours Zedekiah tried to throw off the Babylonian yoke and in 589 with Tyre and Sidon launched an open revolt. Consequently, Nebuchadnezzar invaded Judah and Jerusalem was put under siege for more than a year after which the walls were finally breached. Zedekiah fled but was soon captured. Nebuchadnezzar had his sons executed before him, his eyes were gouged out, and he was taken to Babylon in chains – 2 Kings 25:1-21, Jer. 52:9-11. Nebuchadnezzar then reduced Jerusalem and the temple to a pile of rubble.

The Assyrians' exile policy differed from the Babylonians. They took large numbers of people and resettled them in small groups in different parts of their empire. The policy of divide and conquer broke up old alliances and rendered their defeated enemies unable to mount any resistance. They lost their original ethnic identity and become assimilated into the Assyrian culture. In effect, as a political entity, the northern kingdom of Israel was dispersed and destroyed. However, the Babylonians policy differed. They took leaders and skilled workers from the nations they defeated and brought them from the margins of the empire, to the centre in Babylon to serve the empire and allowed them to retain their own ethnic identities.[5]

Unlike the deportation of inhabitants of the Northern Kingdom of Israel by the Assyrians in the eighth century, the exiles from Judah were not scattered but were placed in ghetto-like settlements in Babylonia, such as Tel-abib (Ezek. 3:15). They seemed to have enjoyed freedom to socialise as the elders are depicted gathering at the house of Ezekiel (8:1, 14:1, 20:1). 'The letter to the exiles' in Jeremiah 29 certainly indicates an expectation that the exiled community will enjoy the liberty to, 'build houses and live in them: plant gardens and eat what they produce: take wives and have sons and daughters' – Jer. 29:5-6. Despite the tolerable conditions the anguish and bitterness against Babylon is reflected in Psalm 137:9 – 'By the waters of Babylon, there we sat down and wept, when we remembered Zion. On the willow there we hung up our lyres.'

The years leading to the fall of Jerusalem in 587 are part of the background to the prophecies in the book of Ezekiel that began in 593, five years after he was exiled to Babylon. His ministry was to the exiles although he also predicts the fall Jerusalem, and the arrival of a messenger among the exiles bringing news of the fall of Jerusalem (anticipated in Ezek. 24:27 and realised in 33: 21-22).[6] 'Although the physical events of destruction and exile were devastating, the other disaster lies in the psychological and emotional impact: and the theological dimension of this trauma is crucial for understanding the Book of Ezekiel. For within just a few years Judah was robbed of all the main elements in her theological system: land, chosen people status, city, temple and monarchy. The events of defeat and exile at the hands of the Babylonians and the theological questions that they posed are the essential key to understanding Ezekiel and his tradition.'[7]

THE STRUCTURE OF EZEKIEL

The book of Ezekiel stands out in a unique way from other prophetic books in Scripture as it is ordered in almost perfect chronological sequence, and Ezekiel attaches dates to many of his oracles, some of which are at pivotal points in his ministry. The Book of Ezekiel can be divided in the following way:

*   1:1-3:27:   Ezekiel's call as a prophet.
*   4:1-24:27:   Oracles of doom on Israel/Judah
                                 prior to the fall of Jerusalem in 587.
*   25:1-32:32:   Oracles of doom on the nations.
*   33:1-48:35:   Oracles of hope after the fall of Jerusalem
                                 between 587 and 571.

The first chapter of Ezekiel serves as a prelude to the entire book, and chapter 33 in which news reaches the prophet that Jerusalem and the temple have fallen, is the turning point after which Ezekiel's oracles turn from judgment to hope. The Book of Ezekiel broadly divides into two major sections. The longest being the first in chapters 1-33, contains oracles and visions of judgment about the fall of Jerusalem – 33:21. Ezekiel's call to be a watchman comes in this section – 3: 16-21, and also in 33:1-9. This section also contains a three vision cycle that unifies the prophecy of Ezekiel – 1-3, 8-11 and 40-48, with a number of features linking these passages. Firstly, all three are dated to the day, month, and year – 1:1, 8:1, 40:1. Secondly, all three have the title 'visions of God' – *mar'ot 'elohim* – 1:1, 8:3, 40:2. Thirdly, in all three passages the expression 'the hand of the Lord/Sovereign Lord was upon me' occurs – 1:3, 3:14, 8:1. The common feature that these three visions share is Ezekiel's encounter with kabod – the divine glory of the Lord. In the first vision in Ezek. 1-3, Ezekiel encounters the glory of the Lord in exile. The second vision in chs. 8-11 depicts the departure of the glory of the Lord from Jerusalem. In the third vision in 40-48, Ezekiel sees the glory of the Lord return to the temple – Ch. 43.

    The chronological order of Ezekiel's prophecies complements the broader structure of the book as his ministry covers two specific phases. His prophecies cover the first five years between his call and the fall of Jerusalem, and the remaining fifteen years afterwards. Chapters 1-24 are from the first period and are predominantly oracles of judgment, indicating the imminent catastrophe justified on the accumulated rebellion of Israel. Chapters 33-48 are from the later period, and the dominant theme of Ezekiel's oracles are now full of hope for the future through God's promise of restoration. The remaining chapters 25-32 are recorded prophecies against foreign nations most of which were delivered during the siege of Jerusalem, or shortly after the destruction of the city. The structure in Ezekiel reflects not only the his chronological career in its two distinct phases, it also reiterates the central biblical truth that judgment precedes grace.[8]

We read in Ezekiel 1:1-3, 26: 'In the thirtieth year, in the fourth month, on the fifth day of the month, as I was among the exiles by the river Chebar, the heavens were opened and I saw visions of God. On the fifth day of the month (it was the fifth year of the exile of King Jehoiachin), the word of the Lord came to Ezekiel the priest, the son of Buzi, in the land of the Chaldeans by the river Chebar: and the hand of the Lord was upon him there…And above the firmament over their heads there was the likeness of a throne, in appearance like sapphire, and seated above the likeness of a throne was a likeness as it were of a human form…Such was the appearance of the likeness of the glory of the Lord. And when I saw it, I fell upon my face, and I heard the voice of one speaking.'

Although the word worship is not used, the scene around the throne of God pulsates with divine worship. In the climax of Ezekiel's vision a vast crystal expanse sparkled with awesome brightness. Through and above this transparent crystal he saw a throne in a brilliant rich blue constructed from one of the most precious stones of the ancient world – lapis lazuli. And on the throne with all the added brilliance of contrasting fiery amber was a figure like that of a man. 'His vision involves a fascinating reversal of the concept of 'image of God.'...Here in anthropomorphic reversal God appears in the likeness of a human being albeit in glowing fiery splendour, that anticipates the transfiguration of the incarnate Son of God himself and certainly provided the imagery for John's great vision of the heavenly throne in Revelation 4...This is none other than Yahweh himself very much alive and still on the throne...Nothing will ever be more significant for Ezekiel than this encounter with the living God.'[9]

Lying prostrate Ezekiel's submits to the revelation of God's glory. Christopher Wright perceives that God's glory reveals his transcendence and the cosmic exaltation of the Lord pervades the worship of Israel – and he warns worshippers against any *'chummy familiarity.'* The glory of the Lord also reveals his sovereignty and the image of a throne itself speaks of authority and power. It also manifests God's omnipresence because of the very location of the vision. God has arrived in Babylon in all his glory.[10] The vision of the Lord, a vision of divine heavenly reality, announces from God's perspective the reality of things as they are on earth. The Lord has taken the initiative to reveal that he is God and that he is in control of history. What he has seen speaks into the very depths of Ezekiel's soul even though initially no words are spoken.

In chs. 1-3, the vision of the glory of God is followed by the vision of the glory of God returning to his land, people and temple in chs. 40-48. Also, Ezekiel's commissioning to be a prophet occurs during the first vision and comes again in Ch. 33. The dates of the first five years of his ministry come between his call in 593 BC and the beginning of the siege of Jerusalem: 1:1, 1:2, 87:1, 20:1 and 24:1. The dates linked to his oracles against foreign nations come between chapters 25-32, 26;1, 29:1, 29:2, 29:17, 30:20, 32: and 32:17. The two final dates, concern news of the fall of Jerusalem 3:21, and the date of his vision of the restored city, land, and temple 40:1. These dates ground Ezekiel's prophetic utterances in unmistakable historical time. So there could be no accusation, he had merely interpreted history after the events had occurred. 'The word of God through Ezekiel comes well in advance and his carefully dated file of messages could prove it. Thus not only was he eventually vindicated as a true prophet, according to fulfillment criteria, but also the sovereign power of Yahweh to predict, control, and interpret events was demonstrated.'[11]

EZEKIEL'S MINISTRY

Ezekiel is a prophet among the exiles and the Hebrew name Ezekiel – *yehezqel* can be interpreted either as an affirmation of faith, 'God strengthens/toughens' or as an appeal of faith, 'May God strengthen you.'[12] Ezekiel was a priest, the son of Buzi – I:3 although we know nothing else about his family except that he was married. He was probably born in 622 BC if we assume the phrase, 'In the 30th year in 1:1 refers to the 30th year in his life. Born into a family of priests this was a favourable year to be born, as it was the year when the book of the law was discovered in the temple in Jerusalem, at a time when Josiah had already begun his reforms. Jeremiah called to be a prophet in 627, had begun his ministry in the 13th year of Josiah's reign, about five years after he had begun his reforms. 'The whole of Ezekiel's education throughout his childhood and youth into his young adult years, would have been thorough his training for the day when he would enter on all the varied professional duties of Israel's priesthood…These included the responsibility to teach and administer the law – Israel's Torah.'[13]

Christopher Wright discerns other important elements in Ezekiel's priestly worldview that are significant in understanding him as a prophet. God was at the centre and the defining fact of Israel's life and existence, and Ezekiel's life was equally focused on God with an uncompromising passion for him.

> Absolutely everything in his life and understanding
> was dominated by Yahweh as God: the mighty hand of
> Yahweh: the word of Yahweh: the Spirit of Yahweh:
> the name of Yahweh: the holiness of Yahweh: the
> presence (or absence) of Yahweh, and especially the
> glory of Yahweh.[14]

Walter Eichrodt perceives that Ezekiel's life was filled
with strain and tension between the priestly tradition he
inherited and his calling as a prophet. As a member of the
Zion priesthood familiar with the traditions of being a priest,
whose conception of God had a deeply spiritual character,
involved expounding and interpreting the law. His intellectual
training involved being acquainted with the history of Israel
and its political and spiritual development, as well as understanding the religious and political beliefs of the neighbouring
nations.[15]

As a priest, Ezekiel was training to serve in the temple but
his priestly worldview involved an abrupt disorientation, and
the enormous reorientation from being brought up as a priest
to being called as a prophet. The disjunction between the
two was both professional and theological. While Ezekiel's
training as a priest made an invaluable contribution to him as
a prophet, he experienced a profound shock reflected after his
response to visions of God in 1:1-3:15, when he sat by the
river Chebar overwhelmed for seven days, *'in bitterness in
the heat of my spirit.'*[16]

Ezekiel's famous vision combines elements of the storm
theophany and the throne theophany in Ch. 1, and are drawn
in part from ancient Israelite traditions.[17] Storm, cloud, and
fire are in the OT, regular elements of a storm theophany. A
literary tradition that was basically derived from mythological
descriptions of the storm or war god in ancient Near Eastern
religious contexts.[18] But Ezekiel's description of the four
headed, winged cherubim was familiar to any inhabitant of
ancient Mesopotamia, surrounded by great statutes of tutelary

deities, guarding temple entrances and other sky bearing creatures with multiple forms that supported the thrones of deities. Ezekiel's vision transforms the static Mesopotamian imagery mainly by the addition of wheels, hands, eyes, and the prevailing Spirit of Yahweh, into a dynamic portrayal of the sovereign, roving freedom of Yahweh. God's presence, power, and glory were in Babylon, and could take on and yet transcend Babylonian symbolism: and could be even more overwhelming in effect, than all the Babylonian statuary put together.[19]

Ezekiel's call is singularly described to him by the Lord when he says, 'Son of man, I have made you a watchman to the house of Israel: whenever you hear a word from my mouth, you shall give them warning from me' – 3:17, 33:7. The role   of the watchman in Ezekiel's day was as a sentry who was stationed in the lookout towers on the walls of the city or towers outside the city, whose responsibility was to monitor the enemy's movements and sound the alarm – blow the trumpet to give his colleagues warning of danger or an imminent attack. However, the shocking truth the Lord gave to Ezekiel was that as a watchman he had to warn the people that the Lord himself was the source of danger and in effect their enemy. This was to counter the false notion that the Lord would rescue his people from their enemy the Babylonians, whereas in fact the real enemy was the Lord himself who was going to execute his judgment on the nation. 'Yahweh, who poses as the enemy, also dictates the nature and timing of the alarms – warnings. Many in Israel would have found this notion shocking.'[20]

Ezekiel's style of ministry is unique due to his prophetic experiences and symbolic actions and messages derived from his encounters with God. 'He is a man totally possessed by the Spirit of Yahweh, called, equipped, and gripped by the hand of God. Ezekiel is a sign, a portent, carrying in his body the oracles he proclaims.' Unsurprisingly, due to the erratic nature of his acts and speech, he has been the subject of

numerous psychoanalytical studies, and the concentration
of so many bizarre features in one individual is without
precedent. For example, lying bound and naked, his muteness,
digging holes in walls of houses, emotional paralysis due to
his wife's death, images of strange creatures, hearing voices
and the sounds of water. E. C. Broome, a German theologian
concluded, 'Ezekiel was a true psychotic, capable of great
religious insight, but exhibiting a series of diagnostic
characteristics.' Daniel Block counters this as he says,
'He fails to recognise the symptoms of authentic prophetic
experiences, may often resemble what uninitiated folk
diagnose as a fundamental pathology.'[21]

At the same time, certain features of Ezekiel indicated
physical affliction or suffering. For example, shocked numb-
ness during the entire week of his call – 3:15, occurrences of
the loss of speech–3:26, 24:25-27. Ezekiel is also commanded
by the Lord to perform another sign act, 'to eat bread with
quaking, and drink water with trembling and with fearfulness
– 12:17-18. The words chosen to describe shaking are striking
and commonly associated with the earth quaking and also
being anxious. Ezekiel is also forbidden by Yahweh to mourn
the death of his wife – 24:15-17. Reflecting on these experiences, Walter Zimmerli believes, there are few passages
that reveal Ezekiel's own feelings and that as a rule his
feelings are forced into the background in his prophetic
office.[22]

He says, 'A distinctive feature of Ezekiel's visions lies in
the fact the prophet himself is, in large measure, active and
shares strongly in the event itself…To this drama, in which
the prophet himself shares, and in which he not only sees the
vision, but acts within it, we must add the prominence given
to the prophet's symbolic actions and gestures. Symbolic
actions, in which the preached message may itself be
anticipated as an event being symbolically enacted before-
hand, is also found in earlier prophecy, both before Amos,
and then from Hosea through Isaiah to Jeremiah. In Ezekiel

we find such actions are much more prominent than in Jeremiah...All this betrays an unusually strong, and even physical participation of the prophet in the experience of receiving his message in vision and word.'[23] For example, while Jeremiah says, 'Your words were found, and I ate them, and your words became to me a joy' – Jer. 15:16, in Ezekiel's experience, this saying is changed into an event at his call. He eats the scroll given to him by the Lord with the divine message and it becomes in his mouth sweet as honey – 3:1-3. There are a number of independent and similar examples in Ezekiel that indicate he was a prophet with a particular sensitivity and dramatic power, for whom a metaphor could become a fully experienced event, however strange it might be. We see such drastic examples in the pictures of the Last Day (Ch. 7), of the Shepherd (Ch. 34), of the unfaithful wife (Ch. 16), that are elaborated with unusual visionary power, right down to the small details.[24]

In Ezekiel's ministry, there is a focus on the Lord's divine jealousy, but it is important not to interpret this from a human perspective. Although the word '*qin'a* – jealousy,' only occurs ten times in Ezekiel, it expresses an underlying motif in his ministry. In the OT, *qin'a* is aroused when a legitimate and wholesome relationship is threatened by interference from a third party, and as a marriage metaphor expresses Yahweh's covenant love for Israel. As Yahweh's relationship with Israel has been violated the Lord's jealous love is aroused. Ezekiel challenges the peoples' perception of their relationship with the Lord by exposing their delusions of innocence. Prior to the fall of Jerusalem, Ezekiel's prophecies contain harsh words of judgments on the people for their apostasy and faithlessness to the covenant, and about their relationship with the Lord that is ruptured. As a result, the people are sent into exile. After 586 the tone and content of Ezekiel's prophecies change and bring a message of hope and restoration in the future.[25]

Ezekiel's message of judgment followed Jeremiah's, but in contrast to Jeremiah's suffering as a prophet and the empathy he felt for his people, 'Ezekiel's preaching has a bitter harshness, which only quite exceptionally reveals his personal feelings. Nowhere does he betray any of his compassion for the fate of the house of Israel, even where he lies personally bound. Or when he quakes at eating his food, or when he is stunned by the death of his wife. Only the cry at the departure of the destroyer into the city – 9:8, 11:13, appears to break through this harsh reserve…Ezekiel's preaching of the coming judgment remains hard and fearfully 'objective.' What undoubtedly permeates all his preaching is above all a knowledge of the majesty of the God of Israel, who has been so humiliated by the actions of his people, that his harsh judgment for the sake of the holiness of his divine name becomes unavoidable.'[26] The Lord's judgment not only concerns the sin of Israel but also encompasses the whole breadth of their rebellious history – Ezek. 2:3-4: 'And the Lord said to me, 'Son of man, I send you to a people of Israel, to a nation of rebels who have rebelled against me: they and their fathers have transgressed against me to this very day. The people are also impudent and stubborn.' Only in Ezekiel, do we find such a comprehensively severe verdict upon Israel's history.

Ezekiel's initial ministry as a prophet was to proclaim the word of the Lord to his people that He spoke to him – a word of judgment due to Israel's rebellion against God's ordinances, and because of the peoples' abomination due to their idolatry and apostasy – 5:5 – 6:1-10, 8:5-17, 16:15-22, 20:30-32. These texts of Scripture record Israel's rebellion of setting up altars in high places and sacrificing to other gods and idols, and equally doing these things in the temple itself, and worshipping them. Their rebellion also involved sacrificing their children on the altars of these gods and idols. Moreover, they also made alliances with the Assyrians and Egyptians described as 'harlotry,' with Israel as an adulterous and unfaithful wife – 16: 23-34. Because of these things, the Lord declares his severe judgment when he says – 5:13-17: 'Thus shall my anger spend itself, and I will vent my fury upon them and satisfy myself: and they shall know that I, the Lord have spoken in my jealousy, when I spend my fury upon them. Moreover, I will make you a desolation and an object of reproach among the nations round about you and in the sight of all that pass by. You shall be a reproach and a taunt, a warning and a horror, to the nations round about you when I execute my judgments on you in anger and fury, and with furious chastisements – I the Lord have spoken – when I loose against you my deadly arrows of famine, arrows for destruction, which I will loose to destroy you, and when I bring more and more famine upon you, and break your staff of bread. I will send famine and wild beasts against you, and they will rob you of your children: pestilence and blood shall pass through you: and I will bring the sword upon you, I, the Lord, have spoken.'

Zimmerli says, 'The radical corruption of Jerusalem is illustrated in a surprising use of historical elements from the ancestry of the city – 16:3: 'From your origin and your derivation you are from the land of the Canaanites. Your father was an Amorite and your mother a Hittite.' It is in agreement with this insult about its Canaanite origin that the sin in Ezekiel 16, is not seen to lie in the political sphere, but in the cultic and cultural spheres. In another way chs. 15 and 22:1ff give expression to the radical corruption of Jerusalem. Ezekiel Ch. 15 uses the metaphor of the vine, which had a place of honour in Israel's religious language. The prophet in an unexpectedly new direction asks a question about the value of the wood of the vine. As a piece of burnt vine wood (the event of 597), he deduces directly from this metaphor the essential uselessness of Israel. Like a burnt vine wood, it is suitable only for burning. Ch. 15 is frightening in its directly ontological judgment about the essential uselessness of Jerusalem.[27]

LITERARY FEATURES

One striking characteristic feature of Ezekiel's ministry is the inclusion of symbolism that the Lord instructs him to use. Although the symbols involved images that were not real, they were used to communicate God's message to his people, about 'events that really did exist or will really occur.'[28] Jospeh Blenkinsopp has a catchy heading for Ezekiel's symbolism – *'Prophetic Theater of the Absurd,'* he especially attributes to chapters 3-4. He sees them as:

> Embodying an extraordinary form of communication, one that risked bringing upon the prophet the charge of eccentricity, if not insanity. They illustrate the truth that prophetic ministry is not exhausted in the mandate to speak, especially in situations of extreme crisis.[29]

Joel Biwul perceives, 'Ezekiel leans on the Jewish prophetic tradition of symbolic expression to develop his extended sign-acts because symbolism is a notable characteristic of the prophetic literary tradition in Jewish society. Prior to Ezekiel's use of symbolic acts, Isaiah and Hosea had already utilised them.'[30] Ezekiel's older contemporary Jeremiah, also often used symbolic sign-acts in his ministry. For example, wearing a soiled loincloth – Jer. 13:1-7, publicly smashing a jar of clay – Jer. 19, and wearing a wooden and then iron yoke on his neck – Jer. 27-28. Both Ezekiel's and Jeremiah's symbolic sign-acts were not merely illustrative or visual aids. 'Their purpose was to enhance the force of the spoken word, to make possible the more intense kind of identification which successful theatre can achieve.'[31]

The use of the symbolic sign-acts in Ezekiel as a form of preaching is reminiscent of earlier prophetic tradition. For example, in pre-classical prophecy, Ahijah of Shiloh hands the kingship over the ten tribes of Israel to Jeroboam in the ten parts of his torn cloak – 1 Kings 11:29-32. Elisha enables Joash to gain victory over Syria by means of the arrows of Yahweh's victory, which Joash shoots through the open window towards the east and with the arrows with which he strikes the ground – 2 Kings 13:14-19. Also in classical prophecy in both Hosea and Isaiah, the prophet's message has a visible form in his children and their names that convey messages – Hosea 1, Isaiah 7:3, 8:1-4. 'Sign-acts are best interpreted as dramatic performances designed to visualise a message and in the process to enhance its persuasive force, so that the observer's perceptions of a given situation might be changed and their beliefs and behaviour modified.'[32] Walther Zimmerli says: 'The purpose of the prophet's sign-actions is to set forth in a visible action, the event announced by Yahweh as something already begun...These symbolic sign-acts establish the character of the prophetic word as event. By this action, which is more than mere symbolism the prophet prefigures as an event what he proclaims through his word. More precisely the event is brought into effect by the prophet and is commanded to happen. By accomplishing this action, the prophet guarantees the coming event.'[33]

Walther Eichdrodt suggests a symbolic action is an independent means of preaching. It can take the place of the word and contributes to the effective delivery of the message. The compelling power behind the prophet's symbolic activity is because the Lord has commanded it and receives its meaning from him, and because the prophetic action carries his authority. It is a sign of what God intends to do in the future and the revelation of his will. 'The prophet's symbolic action is itself an integral part of his preaching. As the anticipatory representation and actualization of a real event, it guarantees, establishes, or serves to indicate that God acts.'[34] 'Ezekiel's tradition presents a unique pattern of symbolic sign-acts because the prophet himself is told to function as 'a sign.'[35] Horace Hummel highlights that Ezekiel uses extended allegories to drive home his points, and that his use of striking *'action pro*phecies' parallel his words.

This provides a sort of Word-Sacrament synonymity. These are often called *'symbolic actions'* or considered a sort of street theatre as a teaching aid. Such labels are perhaps not entirely inappropriate, but they are all too weak: 'sacramental' and 'performative' are much better. Other prophets use such acted-out prophecies too, but none as often as Ezekiel, nor as bizarre as Ezekiel's often are, especially in chapters 4-5.[36]

The Lord forewarned Ezekiel that his audience the house of Israel were rebellious, impudent and stubborn – 2:3-4, so these symbolic sign-acts were the equivalent of parabolic visual aids to get their attention about God's judgment and the fall of Jerusalem, because encouraged by false prophets the people cherished the expectation their exile would be short lived and that the Davidic monarchy would be restored in Jerusalem. Ezekiel was to counter the exiles' false hopes of an imminent return to Jerusalem that made them resistant to his preaching, and their belief in the inviolability of Jerusalem and the temple. At times, Ezekiel uses evocative language that includes the sign-acts in an attempt to penetrate the peoples' hardened hearts. In chapters 6, 16 and 23, his oracles are couched in potent sexual language, due the peoples' abhorrent apostasy and idolatry that is described as harlotry. 'His verbal proclamations and performed communication are often intentionally shocking, to wake the audience to the reality of their state'[37]

Joel Biwul identifies four categories, Ezekiel's symbolic sign-acts fall into. (1) d*ietary symbolism:* (2) g*estures symbolism:* (3) *objects symbolism* and (4) *speech symbolism.*[38] It is striking to note, Ezekiel uses numerous major symbols and it is staggering to contemplate the demanding nature of carrying out the symbolic sign-acts the Lord commanded to do. *Dietary symbolism* is found in the following texts: eating the scroll – 2:8-3:3, signifies Ezekiel's obedience and submission to the Lord, by way of contrast to Israel's rebelliousness and stubbornness. Eating rationed food and drinking rationed water cooked on human excrement – 4:9-17, eating and drinking with trembling in a horrifying psychological manner – 12:18-19, indicates the literal scarcity of food and starvation in Judah during the final siege of Jerusalem. This also symbolises the defiled food the Israelites would eat in a defiled land as they face the difficulty of observing ritual laws of purity in Babylon. These sign-acts were intended to shock his audience to take seriously Jerusalem's collapse.[39] There are four signs in the *gestures symbolism* – lying on his left side for 390 days, then on his right side for 40 days – 4:4-8: striking his hands and the sword and stamping his feet – 6:11, 21:14-17, eating food with trembling and shuddering – 12:18-19, and beating his breast and smiting his thigh – 21:12, that refer to Jerusalem, and indicate punishment and imprisonment in the exile. And 'The binding aspect with ropes so Ezekiel is unable to alternate his lying position until the completion of the specified period, is a figurative representation of the unalterable and inescapable siege and demise of Jerusalem.'[40]

Objects symbolism is to be found in the following texts: drawing a picture of Jerusalem on a clay tablet and laying siege to it 4:1-3: setting up a signpost for the king of Babylon to come – 21:19-23: the vision of the valley of dry bones – 37:1-14, and the joining of two sticks representing Judah and Israel – 37:15-28. Laying siege to Jerusalem and setting up a signpost for the king of Babylon depicts the military operation of the king against the city and its downfall and defeat. Biwul observes, 'Herein lies a clear example of the intended effect of symbolism in prophetic tradition.'[41] Ezekiel's message points to the attack and the hostility that will take place and to the destruction of the city. There is no ambiguity for those who witness these sign-acts as they are self-explanatory, and Block describes this when he says, 'By a series of disturbing but rhetorically powerful sign-acts, Ezekiel is to address head-on the inevitable fate of Jerusalem.'[42] The joining of the two sticks represents the Northern and Southern Kingdoms that were once united but are now in 'exile in national, political and religious ruins.'[43] Joining the two sticks points to the future restoration of the people of Israel into one nation again: and the vision of the valley of dry bones graphically portrays the revival of Israel and the dawn of a new era, by a sovereign act of God's power.

There are three signs in *speech symbolism* – dumbness, Ezekiel's loss of speech – 3:26-27, sighing with breaking heart and bitter grief before their eyes – 21:6-7: keeping silent and not mourning the death of his wife – 24:15-27. There is an enigmatic element in interpreting Ezekiel's dumbness when the Lord says – 'and I will make your tongue cleave to the roof of your mouth, so that you shall be dumb and unable to reprove them: for they are a rebellious house. But when I speak with you, I will open your mouth, and you shall say to them, 'Thus says the Lord God…'' As we seek to interpret Ezekiel's silence, it is important to remember the context is the first sign-act the Lord imposes on him, when he is tied up with cords. This takes place at his initiation as a prophet and a spokesman for the Lord, and he will only speak when the Lord commands him to. As Ezekiel has been tied up there is a physical binding as well as the binding of his speech. This is a divinely imposed restriction on him to prevent him calling the people to repentance or interceding for them. Those observing Ezekiel as he was bound and speechless would have perceived that the hand of the Lord was responsible for the prophet being in-capacitated, and grasped that when he was set free and spoke, his messages were from the Lord. Ezekiel's second speech, a symbolic sign-act, sighing with breaking heart and bitter grief before their eyes – 21:6-7, is a response to the Lord's word against the sanctuaries and the land of Israel, which comes in the form of the Lord drawing forth his sword to execute his judgment against them – 21:2-5. Ezekiel's breaking heart and bitter grief, reflect a deep agonising, excessive pain and sorrow that conveys the pain and grief the exiles will feel when Jerusalem falls to the Babylonians. The devastating impact of Ezekiel's prophetic oracle was that the Lord's judgment in the form of a sword had already been unleashed from its sheath. The Lord informs Ezekiel that when the people ask him about the meaning of his sighing he is to say, 'Because of the tidings. When it comes, every heart will melt and all hands will be feeble. Every spirit will faint and all knees will be weak as water. Behold it comes and it will be fulfilled,' says the Lord God – 21:7. Ezekiel's third speech sign-act – keeping silent and not mourning the death of his wife – 24:15-27, at the command of the Lord, is not an enacted symbolic sign-act, it is an experiential reality. This is truly extraordinary as he is commanded not to observe the cultural conventions of mourning the death of his wife: wearing sackcloth, sprinkling ashes or dust on his head, shaving his beard and hair, and going about barefoot. Instead, he is to wear sandals and put on his festive turban. While it is reading in between the lines, the devastating tragedy of his wife's death is sudden and appears cruel and vindictive, as the Lord acknowledges to Ezekiel that his wife 'is the delight of your eyes' – 24:16. Christopher Wright says, 'We have here, in a few short verses, one of the most poignant moments in the rich history of Israel's prophets – comparable to, but possibly surpassing, the heartbreak of Hosea, and the loneliness of Jeremiah…this heart wrenching personal tragedy would be the ultimate sign. It would quite literally be the last thing he could give or do that would convince those capable of being convinced that Yahweh was serious in his intention to destroy Jerusalem and the temple. But the sign would not consist merely in the death of his wife, but in the reaction he was to display to it in public.'[44]

A unique feature among the prophets is the care Ezekiel takes to date many of his oracles that reflect his awareness of the significance of the events. Although the oracles are autobiographical in style, on only six occasions does he express his personal feelings at his response to the Lord's incomprehensible actions. 'What we see is a man totally under the control of the Spirit of Yahweh: only what God says and does matters.'[45] There are a number of reasons that indicate Ezekiel was involved in the writing of his book, and while prophetic messages were preserved for contemporary and future generations, he encountered specific problems. Because of false prophetic opposition and a lack of response to his ministry, a record of his prophecies was important as evidence they were fulfilled, and also as proof that events took place specifically in fulfillment of his oracles. Especially, as many of his prophecies of judgment were issued many years before Jerusalem fell. A number of criteria indicate the possibility that Ezekiel's own hand left its mark on his book. * The hardness of heart of his audience indicates it is unlikely that any of his hearers took him seriously enough to have recorded his pronouncements, and his reclusive nature rule out the probability of using a secretary to dictate his messages to. * All his prophecies are recorded in the first person autobiographical style suggesting they were based on his personal memoirs. * On occasions, Ezekiel is instructed to record the oracle he receives from the Lord – 24:2, 37:16. The inscribed scroll in 2:9 – 3:3, Ezekiel is instructed by the Lord to eat anticipates preserving a written record of his oracles. * We can discern that Ezekiel's emotional response left its mark on the confused and erratic shape of some texts. This makes it 'difficult to reconcile later reworking of the text unless the editors were stylistic or literary bunglers.' * Ezekiel's conflict with false prophets and his hardened audience, heighten the need for written records of his oracles. * For Ezekiel the transcription of his oracles was necessary to prove a true prophet had been in their midst.[46]

There is a noticeable repetition of style in Ezekiel's oracles, and some of these are unique to him while others are common among the prophets. He usually refers to Yahweh with the full title *adonay yhwh* 217 times, of which 208 come in introductory and concluding markers of divine speech. This double title emphasises God's personal name and his title as Lord, and also his own authority, and alludes to Israel's rebellion.[47] The formula 'and you' or (they) shall know that I am the Lord, occurs 54 times in Ezekiel in its basic form and over 20 more times with minor variations.[48] There are fourteen references to the 'divine' name in Ezekiel and the primary motivation of the dramatic initiative of the restoration of Israel is for the 'sake of the Lord's name' – 36:22. On five occasions, the Lord is acting for the 'sake of his name' 20: 9, 14, 22, 44, 36:22. The Lord has 'concern' for his name – 36:21: 'to sanctify his name' – 36:23: 'to make known his name' – 39:7: 'to be jealous for his name – 39:25. It is of particular importance that the verb with which the 'divine' name most frequently appears is *'halal'* – *'to profane.*[49] The Lord never addresses Ezekiel by his own name, but constantly as *ben-adam* – literally 'son of man.' This title occurs nowhere else in the OT except in Daniel 8:17, and highlights Ezekiel's humanity, and emphasises his human status in contrast to God's divinity.[50]

A number of features distinguish Ezekiel's oracles. One that stands out is the extended prophetic narratives. For example, visions – chs. 1, 8-11, 40-48 and allegories – chs. 16, 23. There is a somber tone in Ezekiel marked by the absence of words for petition or praise, and Zion referring to the temple mount is absent. Also missing are words for 'to trust' – 'to redeem' – 'to bless' – 'salvation' – 'grace' – 'love' – 'covenant faithfulness.' Ezekiel's language is influenced by the Priestly writings and the Holiness Code (Lev. 17-26) and the Mosaic Torah – especially his pronouncements of judgment on Israel based on the covenant curses of Lev. 26 and Deut. 28.[51]

A main feature of Ezekiel's oracles are framed within the formula, 'The word of the Lord came to me saying' – which occurs more than 50 times, especially in 11:14 – 39:29. Apart from 1:3, this formula always introduces divine speech as an objective reality that highlights the divine source of revelation. The phrase *koh-amar adonay yhwh,* 'Thus has the Lord declared' referred to as the messenger formula, occurs around 120 times in Ezekiel. In the OT prophetic books, this highlights the prophet's role as a herald whose voice represents God's voice. In 2:4 – 3:11, God's commissioning address to Ezekiel, the Lord explains to him the reason for this formula which is to authenticate him as a prophet.[52] The variations of, *ne'um adonay yhwh* – 'the declaration of the Lord Yahweh' occur 365 times in the OT and is found 85 times in Ezekiel and 175 times in Jeremiah. This formula adds solemnity to the prophetic announcement by pointing to the divine source of the oracle.[53]

Ezekiel's prophetic role is dramatically represented by the divine coercion formula, *watthei alay yhwh* – 'the hand of the Lord came upon me,' which occurs 7 times. Metaphorically, this describes the overwhelming pressure the Lord exerts on Ezekiel as he asserts complete control over him that at times transports him back and forth to distant places – 8:1, 37:1, 40:1. Equally, the divine inspiration formula, *wattippol alay ruah yhwh,* 'the Spirit of Yahweh fell upon me' – 11:5a, represents a spiritual variation.

Also, the role of the Spirit in Ezekiel's experience is described as, *wattabo bi ruah,* 'and the Spirit entered me' – 2:2, 3:24. Here the power of the Spirit is demonstrated by raising the prophet on his feet, *he emid al-raglay,* as on six occasions Ezekiel is swept by the Spirit to another location – 3:12, 14, 8:3, 11:1, 24, 43:5. Although a milder guidance formula uses forms of *hebi,* 'and he brought me,' *holik,* 'and he led me,' *hosi,* 'and he took me out,' and *hesib,* 'and he brought me back.' Daniel Block says:

> Ezekiel is a man seized by God. This extraordinary divine physical control over the prophet distinguishes him from his professional colleagues more than any other quality. It accounts for his mobility and immobility, the apparent lunacy of some of his actions, and his stoic response to rejection, opposition and grief.[54]

As we consider the literary features in the Book of Ezekiel, once we move beyond Ezekiel's ecstatic visions in chapter one, the dominant theme in chapter two and three is the content of Ezekiel's message as a prophet. In these two foundational chapters of his call and commission as a prophet, the Lord tells Ezekiel that his ministry involves 'being sent' to a rebellious nation and to declare the word of the Lord, as and when the Lord reveals it to him. Integral to his commissioning in chs. 2-3 the Lord speaks specifically to Ezekiel about his ministry.

In 2:3-5, 7 we read: 'And the Lord said to me, 'Son of man, I send you to the people of Israel, to a nation of rebels, who have rebelled against me: they and their fathers have transgressed against me to this very day. The people are also impudent and stubborn. I send you to them, and you shall say, 'Thus says the Lord God.' And whether they hear or refuse to hear (for they are a rebellious house) they will know that a prophet has been among them...And you shall speak my words to them, whether they hear or refuse to hear, for they are a rebellious house.' The privileged title 'the house of Israel' has now changed to the shameful 'house of rebellion,' whose rebelliousness can be traced all the way back to their ancestors. Such is the seriousness of their sin as throughout their history they refused to submit to the sovereignty of God: refused to submit to his commandments and laws, and became apostate and turned to idols and made alliances with other nations. In his eyes, the Lord unequivocally states the spiritual malaise of his people to ensure there is no ambiguity about this, and that Ezekiel is in no doubt whatsoever about his audience from the Lord's perspective. Zimmerli says, 'From the words of the canonical prophets it becomes increasingly clear that the fact of being sent by God forms the basic authorisation of the prophet...The use of the messenger formula, 'Thus says the Lord' as an introduction to a prophet's speech also shows that the title 'sent one' best fits the prophet's consciousness of his office. It is therefore entirely to the point that the first divine word to Ezekiel should contain the statement of sending.'[55]

When the Lord instructs Ezekiel to speak he is to say, 'Thus says the Lord.' This will confirm that 'he stands in a line of prophetic proclamation in Israel.'[56] 'Thus says the Lord' is the authentic proclamation that is recognised by the audience as the prophet representing God's word to them. The phrase *koh-amar adonay yhwh,* 'Thus has the Lord declared' referred to as the messenger formula, occurs around 120 times in Ezekiel.[57] Whether they hear or refuse to hear God's word, Ezekiel has an obligation to declare it as he proclaims the oracles when the Lord speaks to him.

The Lord specifically speaks to Ezekiel and has an unusual and unique command for him – Ezekiel 2:8-3:3: ''But you son of man, hear what I say to you: be not rebellious like that rebellious house. Open your mouth and eat what I give you.'' And when I looked, behold, a hand was stretched out to me, and, lo, a written scroll was in it and he spread it before me: and it had writing on the front and on the back, and there were written on it words of lamentation and mourning and woe. And the Lord said to me, ''Son of man, eat what is offered to you, eat this scroll, and go, speak to the house of Israel.'' So I opened my mouth, and he gave me the scroll to eat. And he said to me, ''Son of man, eat this scroll that I give you and fill your stomach with it.'' Then I ate it, and it was in my mouth as sweet as honey.'

Zimmerli mentions that the preaching of the prophets was frequently recorded and the collected words of Jeremiah that he dictated to Baruch to be inscribed on a scroll that appeared ten years earlier, was without doubt known to Ezekiel and revered as a record of divinely authorised prophetic speech. In this context, the written scroll given to Ezekiel symbolised that he had been entrusted with God's word to his people, and its authority was not dependent on any feelings or opinions he had. 'The scroll expressed the way in which revelation takes place through Ezekiel as a theory of prophetic inspiration.'[58] Zimmerli says, 'The more consciously a prophet felt his responsibility, the more he needed a conviction, stronger than that of his predecessors, of the objectivity of the word with which he had been entrusted as something other than, and distinct from, his own inward feelings. Jeremiah was therefore assured that the word of God was being imparted to him by God's hand touching his lips. While Ezekiel received a similar assurance through the delivery of a handwritten scroll, containing words already inscribed there without his knowledge.'[59] As the scroll was spread-unfurled before Ezekiel, he read the contents and saw that the consequences the Lord's words would have were words of judgment, lamentation, mourning and woe.

Zimmerli further clarifies the relevance and significance the scroll probably would have had for Ezekiel that constituted his ordination as a prophet. His obedience in eating the scroll was the prophet's preparation for preaching and so he is filled with the divine message. By this symbolic act, Ezekiel became an obedient servant in contrast to rebellious Israel. While the concept of the scroll may sound strange, we find in Jeremiah Ch. 36 that Baruch read the words of Jeremiah he had dictated to him on a scroll in the temple, in the ninth month of the fifth year of Jehoiakim's reign at about the turn of the year 603/604. A good four years before the first deportation and Ezekiel may well have been present with the priests when this took place. Eating the scroll symbolised for Ezekiel being entrusted with God's word, along with his complete subordination to the word of God.[60] As a visual representation for Ezekiel, the scroll was an over-powering image. Moreover, he is not to alter or modify the contents of the scroll. He is to faithfully declare the oracles he receives from the Lord and as the scroll had writing on the front and back, this indicates a well-defined complete message. Eating the scroll symbolises that Ezekiel is filled, nourished and empowered by the divine word, and the scroll represents the divine speech that he will declare which is composed in a fixed an unalterable form.[61]

Once Ezekiel has eaten the scroll, the Lord says to him, ''Son of man, go, get you to the house of Israel and speak my words to them…Son of man, all my words that I shall speak to you receive in your heart, and hear with your ears. And go, get you to the exiles, to your people, and say to them, 'Thus says the Lord God,' whether they hear or refuse to hear'' – Ezek. 3:4, 10-11. The Lord forewarns Ezekiel not to proclaim his own insights or perceptions as a prophet about Israel's present situation or about their future. He emphasises the importance of only declaring the words that the Lord gives to him. He is not to be selective about the oracles from the Lord he declares. He is not given the freedom to choose or edit the Lord's word. 'The Lord calls for a verbatim repetition of the message that Ezekiel received from him. The prophet is forbidden to add or to subtract from the words he receives from the Lord.'[62] This anticipates Ezekiel's dumbness when his own voice is silenced. 'Accept in your heart and listen with your ears,' reiterates and symbolises the earlier eating of the scroll, and the prophet's commitment to transmit the Lord's undiluted word, regardless of the response of his audience. It also demands that Ezekiel remains open and receptive to receiving God's word in the future as and when the Lord speaks to him: and in the following chapters, Ezekiel will speak repeatedly of receiving God's word. The oracles Ezekiel was going to declare to God's people were messages of judgment. They were not going to endear him to the people or make him popular, and so to avoid the danger and temptation of watering down God's word, or saying that Israel was protected because of the Covenant God had with her, the Lord ensures Ezekiel comprehends and grasps the nature of his prophetic calling.

As I have thought about Ezekiel's call to declare God's word to his people exactly as he received it from the Lord, I believe this is an important principle of truth that has enormous significance in the life of the Church. Especially as we consider the Lord's command to Ezekiel to faithfully declare the words the Lord gave him to his people. To reiterate, God's word did not depend on any feelings or opinions Ezekiel may have had. God's word was the objective truth he had been entrusted with, and he is not to proclaim his own insights or perceptions. Neither is he to be selective in what he declares. He does not have the authority or freedom to selectively edit God's word, and he is forbidden to add or subtract from the word of the Lord he receives. Horace Hummel says,

> Likewise, the Christian pastor is called to proclaim the full counsel of God in his Word, 'whatever' that Word contains. The avoidance of doctrines or teachings because they are distasteful to the pastor or his hearers is not an option. Neither should the pastor adjust his message depending on 'whether they listen or do not, for they are a rebellious house' – 2:7. Catering to what people want to hear is a sure route to apostasy – 2 Timothy 4:3 as 'user-friendly' worship services may easily be so...All preachers face the perennial temptation to be 'user friendly' by softening, providing altogether those aspects of the Divine Word their listeners find offensive. But Ezekiel is commanded not to adapt his message to his audience's preferences. To do so would be to rebel against God – 2:8.[63]

As we consider God's word, what inexplicably stands out is that the Ten Commandments are virtually redundant in The Church of England, as they are never included verbatim in public worship: neither have ministers in the Church promoted the Ten Commandments in the life of the nation. Also, contemporary worship is at the mercy of the selective preference of its clergy, as ministers aim for accessibility in their worship. In the misguided concept of seemingly making worship more accessible, for example the Ten Commandments are omitted. Equally, corporate confession is usually reduced to a simple prayer of saying sorry, with no meaningful scriptural content preceding it to prepare our hearts. Leading up to the confession, there is no mention of the commandments that in a Communion Service includes the two major commandments to love the Lord and our neighbour.

Even in Communion Services, in Common Worship 2000, that are scripturally based on the authority of the Church of England – much of the content of Communion Services or the Service of the Word, is selectively ignored or omitted because of the preference of the clergy, or the informal culture of the congregation. As a result, has contemporary worship lost the sense of awe and reverence for the Lord, with the emphasis on being informal? Has contemporary worship that is at the mercy of the selective preference of its clergy, with its emphasis on being accessible, informal and selective, inadvertently forfeited the overwhelming glory of the Lord described in 2 Chronicles 5:13-14 and 7:1-3?

CHAPTER TWO

EZEKIEL'S PROPHETIC CALL
VISIONS OF GOD – 1:1-3

'In the thirtieth year, in the fourth month, on the fifth day of the month, as I was among the exiles by the river Chebar, the heavens were opened, and I saw visions of God. On the fifth day of the month (it was the fifth year of the exile of King Jehoiachin), the word of the Lord came to Ezekiel the priest, the son of Buzi, in the land of the Chaldeans by the river Chebar: and the hand of the Lord was upon him there.'

Jehoiachin was 18 years old when he became king, and he reigned for 3 months before surrendering to Nebuchadnezzar in 597, who carried off all the treasures from the house of the Lord, and the king's house, and cut in pieces all the gold vessels in the temple that Solomon had made. Nebuchadnezzar carried to Babylon all the princes, all the mighty men of valour, 10,000 captives, all the craftsmen, and only the poorest remained behind – 2 Kings 24: 8-14. Although he was not yet ordained as a priest, Ezekiel was amongst the ruling class of the leaders and priests from the temple carried into captivity to Babylon. The exile had significant theological implications, as this signalled the end of God's people in their homeland.

Ezekiel began his prophetic ministry in the fifth year of Jehoiachin's exile – 593, when he was 30 years old, and from this we can deduce that he was 25 years old when he was taken captive with the exiles to Babylon. In v. 1, his auto-biographical account records the date when he reached thirty, which was a significant date, as it was the age when he would have been ordained priest in Jerusalem. But Ezekiel was far from God's presence in the temple at Jerusalem, 'leading a shadowy existence in a lost world where there was not even the faintest hope of liberation: all that must have weighed heavily upon the heart of the young priest...'[1] Ezekiel with the other exiles found himself at the river Chebar, one of many branches of an elaborate canal system that distributed water from the Tigris to the Euphrates throughout the city and to its outlying regions.

It was at the river Chebar the heavens were opened and Ezekiel saw visions of God. What is striking and unusual about the expression, 'the heavens were opened' is that nowhere else does this appear in the OT.[2] There are more visions in Ezekiel than in any other OT book, except for Daniel, and than in any NT book except Revelation. As a result, Ezekiel has an un-shakable confidence the indescribable visions do not originate within himself, but emanate from God 'introducing him into a new dimension of reality, a strange sublimity that far trans-cends all that is imaginable to man.'[3]

Ezekiel experiences out of this world, divine supernatural realities, surrounded by a dazzling brightness and a radiant brilliance. There is an 'awesome loftiness' to his vision of the throne room of heaven and the appearance of the glory of the Lord, to which there is nothing similar in the OT.[4] Although Isaiah's heavenly vision of the Lord sitting on a throne in the temple is the nearest equivalent. When Ezekiel describes his visions in detail, his language is full of analogies. For example, 'As I looked, behold, a stormy wind came out of the north, and a great cloud, with brightness round about it, and fire flashing forth continually, and in the midst of the fire as it were gleaming bronze.' – 1:4: 'and the soles of their feet were like the sole of a calf's foot' – 1:7: 'In the midst of the living creatures there was something that looked like burning coals of fire, like torches moving to and fro' – 1:13. 'And above the firmament over their heads there was the likeness of a throne, in appearance like sapphire, and seated above the likeness of a throne there was the likeness as it were of a human form. And upward from what had the appearance of his loins I saw as it were gleaming bronze, like the appearance of fire enclosed round about: and downward from what had the appearance of his loins I saw as it were the appearance of fire, and there was brightness round about him. Like the appearance of the bow

that is in the cloud on the day of rain, so was the appearance of
the brightness round about. Such was the appearance of the
likeness of the glory of the Lord. And when I saw it, I fell upon
my face, and I heard the voice of one speaking.' – 1:26-28.
Block says, 'Things cannot be described for what they really
are, but only in relation to other familiar ideas and concepts.
The description climaxes in v. 28 by heaping up a series of
analogies.'[5] In Ch. 10, around thirteen months later, the abstract
has become concrete, and much of the analogical language
disappeared. The expression 'creatures' has been replaced by
the specific 'Cherubim.'[6]

Although Ezekiel speaks about his experience in v. 1, in v.
2-3, a third person report describes this in more detail. Namely,
that the word of the word Lord came to Ezekiel, and that the
hand of the Lord was upon him. The first three verses in Ch. 1,
contain the three central themes of the Book of Ezekiel – three
themes that will indelibly leave their mark on Ezekiel's entire
ministry. * Firstly, his visions of God. * Secondly, the word of
the Lord came to him. * Thirdly the hand of the Lord was upon
him. These three introductory verses are the prelude, and the
overture to the Book of Ezekiel.

A main feature of Ezekiel's oracles is in the formula, 'The
word of the Lord came to me saying' – and this occurs more
than 50 times, especially in 11:14 – 39:29. Apart from 1:3, this
formula always introduces divine speech, as an objective
reality that highlights the divine source of revelation. The
divine coercion formula, *watthei alay yhwh* – 'the hand of the
Lord came upon me,' occurs seven times – 1:3, 3:14, 3:22,
33:22, 8:1, 37:1, 40:1, exerts complete control over Ezekiel's
movements, and at times transports him to and fro to distant
places. 'This affirmation of God's direct action in Ezekiel's life
recalls the ministry of Elijah – 1 Kings 18:46 and Elisha – 2
Kings 3:15. As with those prophets of ancient days, the hand of
the Lord empowers Ezekiel.'[7] The hand of the Lord signifies
pressure or compulsion to do something and also the Lord's
sovereign action, will, and power in Ezekiel's life in his

prophetic ministry. It is an ecstatic supernatural manifestation
verifying the Lord is with him. 'More than any other prophet
Ezekiel is a man possessed.'[8] Here, in Babylon, Ezekiel sees
visions of God and, 'the appearance of the likeness of the glory
of the Lord' – 1:28. God has come to Babylon. The Lord
whose glory and presence dwelt in the holy of holies in the
temple in Jerusalem, has appeared to Ezekiel in an alien land.

THE FOUR LIVING CREATURES – 1:4-14

'As I looked, behold, a stormy wind came out of the north,
and a great cloud, with brightness round about it, and fire flashing forth continually, and in the midst of the fire as it were
gleaming bronze. And from the midst of it came the likeness of
four living creatures. And this was their appearance: they had
the form of men, but each had four faces, and each of them had
four wings. Their legs were straight, and the soles of their feet
were like the sole of a calf's foot: and they sparkled like burn-
ished bronze. Under their wings on their four sides, they had
human hands. And the four had their faces and their wing thus:
their wings touched one another, they went everyone straight
forward, without turning as they went. As for the likeness of
their faces, each had the face of a man in front. The four had
the face of a lion on the right side, the four had the face of an
ox on the left side, and the four had the face of an eagle at the
back. Such were their faces. And their wings were spread out
above, each creature had two wings, each of which touched
the wing of another, while two covered their bodies. And each
went straight forward: wherever the spirit would go, they went,
without turning as they went.In the midst of the living creatures
there was something that looked like burning coals of fire, like
torches moving to and fro among the living creatures: and the
fire was bright, and out of the fire went forth lightning. And the
living creatures darted to and fro, like a flash of lightning.'

The four living creatures with their four faces looking
simultaneously in all directions represent God's omnipresence
and omniscience. In the 21st century, in our digital and tech-

nological age, while Ezekiel's image of the four living creatures with four faces was bizarre, it may not seem so far fetched and certainly not beyond our imagination, as it can remind us of science fiction movies with their remarkable visual effects. Initially, Ezekiel's vision looks like a normal thunderstorm, but as it progresses, its strangeness is captured by his description that indicates, 'rare spellings, grammar, style and substance,' as he is at a loss for words that will adequately report the vision. Ezekiel's ecstatic visionary experience is couched in analogous terms, and when the vision returns around 13 months later in Ch. 10, in which Ezekiel describes the living creatures as Cherubim, most of the grammatical difficulties have been settled, and much of the analogous language has gone. 'In other words, the reason for the garbled and obscure shape of the account of the vision is to be found in the emotional state of the recipient, who by internal data is purported to have been the narrator of the experience as well.'[9]

The animals in the vision frequently appear on iconographic and glyptic art across the ancient world and for Israel they had symbolic significance. 'The lion was renowned for its courage, ferocity and strength and also served as a symbol of royalty. The eagle was the swiftest and most stately of birds. The ox was a symbol of fertility and divinity...In the absence of abstract philosophical tools, these images expressed the transcendent divine attributes of omnipotence and omniscience.'[10] Ezekiel's vision reflects a number of traditional Near Eastern elements, such as the image of the Lord riding on a storm, surrounded by fire and lighting, that was a common way of describing the coming of the divine warrior. The wheels of his vision also represent a chariot, a typical aspect of the divine warrior image. The windstorm that was coming out of the north points to the direction of Israel's enemy. 'The divine warrior is here approaching to wage war against his own people, not to deliver them.'[11] The repetition of the number 'four' – four living creatures, with four heads, and four wings, is almost likely to refer to the four corners of the earth, or the four winds.

'The vision is declaring that the deity so awesomely attended by this fourfold supporting cast is sovereign over all the earth, in all directions. His all seeing presence can be anywhere, almost literally in a flash.'[12] Ezekiel's vision is visually stunning. 'It glowed with a stunning brilliance, and a blinding radiance.'[13] There is a spectacular, vivid display of 'brightness' – 'fire flashing forth' – 'gleaming bronze' – and 'burning coals of fire, like torches.' Moreover, it is not a static but a thunderous vision as the creatures were in almost constant motion, with 'awesome movement and tumultuous sound,'[14] as the four living creatures 'darted to and fro, like a flash of lighting' – 1:14. The number four in Ezekiel is striking, because it occurs over fifty times in the book. There are not only four living creatures with four faces, four wings and four wheels, four plagues are in Ch. 14, and the winds come from four corners of the earth in Ch. 37. Ezekiel climaxes with the 'foursquare' eschatological temple in chs. 40-43. Symbolically, the number 4 seems to indicate a totality and completeness.[15]

THE GLEAMING WHEELS – 1:15-22

'Now as I looked at the living creatures, I saw a wheel upon the earth beside the living creatures, one for each of them. As for the appearance of the wheels and their construction, their appearance was like the gleaming of a chrysolite: and the four had the same likeness, their construction being as it were a wheel within a wheel. When they went, they went in any of their four directions without turning as they went. The four wheels had rims and they had spokes, and their rims were full of eyes round about. And when the living creatures went, the wheels went besides them: and when the living creatures rose from the earth, the wheels rose. Wherever the spirit would go, they went, and the wheels rose along with them: for the spirit of the living creatures was in the wheels. When those went, they went, and when those stood, they stood: and when those rose from the earth, the wheels rose along with them: for the spirit of the living creatures was in the wheels.'

In the next phase of Ezekiel's vision, the animated creatures who 'darted to and fro, like a flash of lightning' – 1:14, were mobile as each had an identical set of wheels, 'a wheel within a wheel' – 1:17. While there is an element of mystery about the wheels, this feature of their construction allowed the living creatures to move anywhere without any resistance, and while their movement was dependent on their wheels, they did not move independently of their own free will. Instead, 'Wherever the spirit would go they went, and the wheels rose with them, for the spirit of the living God was in the wheels' – 1:20. The wheels symbolise some form of four-wheeled chariot able to move in any direction, and they gleamed with the brilliance of chrysolite with their rims full of eyes that can be interpreted as the awesome splendour of the vehicle or the all-seeing, all-knowing character of God. 'The wheels moved with perfect synchronisation with those of the creatures and the harmony between them is attributed to the spirit of life (*ruach hahayya*) – denoting the life giving energising power of God. It was this animating spirit that also determined the direction and freedom of movement of the heavenly vehicle.'[16]

THE GLORY OF THE LORD – 1:22-28

'Over the heads of the living creatures there was the like-ness of a firmament, shining like crystal, spread out above their heads. And under the firmament their wings stretched out straight, one toward another: and each creature had two wings covering its body. And when they went I heard the sound of their wings like the sound of many waters, like the thunder of the Almighty, a sound of tumult like the sound of a host: when they stood still they let down their wings. And there came a voice from above the firmament over their heads: when they stood still they let down their wings.

And above the firmament over their heads there was the likeness of a throne, in appearance like sapphire – *lapis lazuli*: and seated above the likeness of a throne was a likeness as it were of a human form. And upward from what had the appearance of his loins I saw as it were gleaming bronze, like the appearance of fire enclosed round about: and downward from what had the appearance of his loins I saw as it were the appearance of fire, and there was brightness round about him. Like the appearance of the bow that is in the cloud on the day of rain, so was the appearance of the brightness round about him. Such was the appearance of the likeness of the glory of the Lord. And when I saw it, I fell upon my face, and I heard the voice of one speaking.'

Verses 22-28, are the climax of Ezekiel's vision. Like other OT theophanies in which the Lord or his Angel (the preincarnate Christ) appears as a man – Gen. 18:32, 24-30, this points to the incarnation of Jesus Christ (the divine man) as true man, (without sin) fully human and yet fully God.[17] In vs. 22-28, Ezekiel's eye-witness account of the appearance of the likeness of the glory of God, also finds its closest parallels in those of the glorified Christ and at his transfiguration, and in his revelation to the apostle John, especially John's vision of the throne room. The Hebrew translation 'Glory' in English, does not begin to do justice to the divine glory that is revealed to Ezekiel. The Glory of Yahweh is the same as that which is revealed between Jesus Christ and God the Father.[18]

'No theophany in the entire OT matches Ezekiel's inaugural vision,'[19] that has literally taken him out of this world as he has been transported to the throne room of heaven, a vast crystal firmament – expanse (dome NRSV) above the heads of the living creatures, which sparkled with an awesome white brightness. 'Being crystal, this great platform had a transparent quality so that Ezekiel could look through it to what was higher still – what looked like a throne.'[20] He records that the living creatures were moving – 1:24, but Ezekiel does not give a reason for this. As the living creatures move the motion of their wings was accompanied by a very loud noise, the sound of many waters – '*mayim rabbi,* the thunder of the voice of El Shadday, (an ancient title for God) and the tumult or commotion like an army camp.'[21] The thunder of the

Almighty, is like the crashing roar of the waves and the sound of loud rumbling similar to that heard after a flash of lightning. These sounds may be reminiscent of the Lord's appearance on Mount Sinai that was accompanied by peals of thunder.

No vision in the Old Testament matches the supernatural impact of the theophany of Ezekiel's vision, which now comes to a climax when above the firmament he sees the likeness of a throne in appearance like sapphire, and seated above the throne is a figure like that of a man. He has seen four sphinxlike winged creatures above whom is a dazzling crystal platform, on which stood a glittering throne of lapis lazuli – sapphire. And seated on the throne was Yahweh in human form. 'The climactic vision is of the deity himself in human form...his vision involves a fascinating reversal of the concept of 'image of God.' He uses the word 'likeness, similarity' – *d'mut,* which first occurs in Genesis 1:26-27, when God created human beings in his own image and likeness. Here in anthropomorphic reversal, God appears in the likeness of a human being, albeit in glowing, fiery splendour that anticipates the transfiguration of the incarnate Son of God himself, and certainly provides the imagery for John's great vision of the heavenly throne in Revelation 4.'[22]

Ezekiel's vision has profound theological significance for a number of reasons. Everything in his vision proclaims the transcendent glory of God – a supernatural glory beyond our imagination: and manifests upon Ezekiel's consciousness the immeasurable gulf between God and man. His vision also emanates with God's holiness and sovereignty symbolised through his elevation on his throne. Ezekiel's vision embraces God's immanence as he revealed his presence in the likeness of human form in the midst of his people in exile.[23] It is not surprising Ezekiel records that after the vision of the glory of the Lord and after the Lord spoke to him he was overwhelmed, as what has been revealed to him was truly breathtaking. Block perceives that Ezekiel has finally caught onto the significance of the vision: 'This is none other than the glory of Yahweh.

The doors of heaven have been flung wide open and he beholds Yahweh in all his splendour, enthroned above the living creatures. The term '*kabod*' derives from a root meaning 'to be heavy' but when applied to royalty and divinity it denotes the sheer weight of that person's majesty, that quality which evokes a response of awe in the observer. The prophet has witnessed the incredible far away from the Temple. Among the exiles in the pagan land of Babylon Yahweh has appeared to him. Ezekiel responds appropriately by falling down on his face in worship.'[24]

EZEKIEL THE PROPHET – 2:1-7

'And he said to me, "Son of man, stand upon your feet, and I will speak with you." And when he spoke to me, the Spirit entered into me and set me upon my feet, and I heard him speaking to me. And he said to me, 'Son of man, I send you to the people of Israel, to a nation of rebels, who have rebelled against me, they and their fathers have transgressed against me to this very day. The people are also impudent and stubborn: I send you to them, and you shall say to them, 'Thus says the Lord God.' And whether they hear or refuse to hear (for they are a rebellious house) they will know that a prophet has been among them. And you son of man, do not be afraid of them, nor be afraid of their words, though briers and thorns are with you and you sit upon scorpions: be not afraid of their words, nor be dismayed at their looks, for they are a rebellious house. And you shall speak my words to them, whether they hear or refuse to hear, for they are a rebellious house.

'But you, son of man, hear what I say to you, be not rebellious like that rebellious house, open your mouth and eat what I give you. And when I looked, behold, a hand was stretched out to me, and lo a written scroll was in it: and he spread it before me, and it had writing on the front and on the back: and there were written words of lamentation and mourning and woe.'

In Ch. 2, there are some striking features to be aware of. The narrative description is relatively small in comparison to the direct speech in Ch. 2 and 3, and Ezekiel is essentially a passive recipient as there is only one speaker. Ezekiel's vision in Ch. 1 culminated in the appearance of the glory of the Lord, and the Lord's speech is now the overwhelming focus of Ch. 2. 'These features have a significant bearing on the intention of the text: to describe Ezekiel's conscription into divine service. Yahweh is the divine king who calls and who determines the nature of the mission that his emissary is to fulfill. Its terms are not-negotiable.'[25] The literary style of the direct speech in chs. 2 and 3 is also striking. This is punctuated by the phrase *'wayyo'mer elay'* – 'And he said to me,' and *wayyo'mer* occurs 41 times in Ezekiel. On every occasion, Yahweh is the subject, but only 5 times is his name given (4:13, 9:4, 23:36, 44:2, 5). 'And he said to me' reflects the relationship between Yahweh and Ezekiel.

> It reflects the unidirectional nature of most of the communication that occurs between God and Ezekiel. The instances in which the prophet responds verbally are rare. For the most part the prophet remains a passive recipient.[26]

After seeing in the climax of his vision the appearance of the glory of the Lord in the firmament above a sapphire throne, Ezekiel fell on his face as he heard the voice of the Lord speaking to him. We may well imagine the remarkable things he has seen in his vision that culminated in the glory of the Lord, was so powerful in its intensity that he involuntarily fell on his face. The Lord addressed him as 'son of man' a title that in Hebrew simple means 'human being,' which occurs 94 times in Ezekiel and 8 times in chapters 1-3. The term 'son of man' alludes to Ezekiel's humanity and his mortality and the vast distance between him and Almighty God. Hummel posits that 'Son of Man' clearly has some connection with Daniel's crucial vision of the 'Son of Man' in Daniel 7, which must have occurred not too long after Ezekiel's call. 'Son of Man' appears as a simile in Daniel 7, and the reference is to a divine figure, the essential meaning is the same as 'the likeness of the appearance of a man' Ezekiel describes in 1:26, The 'Son of Man' from Daniel 7, became important to the Christian faith when Jesus made it his own favoured self-designation in the Gospels.[27] Having been overwhelmed by his vision of the glory of the Lord on his heavenly throne, Ezekiel is now instructed to stand on his feet: and as the Lord speaks to him, and his Spirit enters him, sets him on his feet and Ezekiel experiences the power of God's Spirit. If up to now, he had entertained the thought his visions had been hallucinatory, this confirmed to Ezekiel that all that had taken place was real.

Ezekiel is supremely a prophet whose ministry bears the distinctive hallmark of God's Spirit, and initially the role of the Spirit in his experience is described as, '*wattabo bi ruah,*' 'and the Spirit entered me' – 2:2, 3:24. Here the power of the Spirit is demonstrated by raising the prophet on his feet, '*he emid al-raglay.*' Moreover, in Ezekiel's experience, '*watthei alay yhwh*' – 'the hand of the Lord came upon me,' indicates the Spirit asserts complete control over him and at times transports him back and forth to distant places – 8:1, 37:1, 40:1. Equally, '*wattippol alay ruah yhwh,*' 'the Spirit of Yahweh fell upon me' – 11:5a, represents a spiritual variation.[28] Saul's experience in 1 Kings 10 sheds light on Ezekiel's encounter with the Spirit. In Ch. 10, Samuel prophecies, 'Then the Spirit of the Lord will come mightily upon you, and you shall prophecy with them (the prophets) and be turned into another man' – 10:6. This is fulfilled, 'When he turned his back to leave Samuel, God gave Saul another heart: and all these signs came to pass that day. When they came to Gibeah, behold, a band of prophets met him, and the Spirit of God came mightily upon him' – 10:9-10. 'The Spirit entered Ezekiel,' is none other than the Spirit of God coming powerfully upon him, and coupled with his visions of God compels him to be the Lord's servant.

Ezekiel's visions of God, the appearance of God's glory and his encounter with God's Spirit, come to a climax as the Lord speaks to him. If up to now Ezekiel has been left speechless by these remarkable events that have bombarded his senses, we should not underestimate their impact on him, especially as the Lord now informs him he is sending him as a prophet to Israel, although not until Ch. 6 will the Lord tell him to prophecy for the first time. Ezekiel's call and commission as a prophet is the ultimate purpose for his visions of God: a call that was totally unanticipated. 'The Hebrew word for sending is *salah* that is characteristic of the call and ministry of all the prophets, and which is emphasised in 2:3, 2:4, 3:5, 3:6.'[29] Prophets were essentially God's messengers and as we shall see in The Book of Ezekiel, the crucial question is whether a prophet was a false or a true messenger of God.[30] The Lord anticipates Ezekiel is understandably afraid and somewhat apprehensive at his call to be a prophet and to declare God's word to the nation. But he exhorts him not to be afraid of the hostility he will encounter, through the image of thorns, briers and scorpions – 2:6. The Lord also exhorts Ezekiel to be faithful in declaring God's word regardless of success or if the people listen – 2:7. Although the Lord strongly hints they are a rebellious and stubborn people, and implies they are unlikely to respond. Ezekiel's success is measured by his faithfulness as a prophet that is to be the defining hallmark of his ministry, even when the people are unresponsive.

The Lord's initial speech sets out before Ezekiel the nature of his mission and informs him of the spiritual condition of Israel, who are a nation of rebels and whose ancestors have a history of rebellion against the Lord. They are impudent and stubborn – 2:3-4, 6, 8. They have a 'hard forehead and a stubborn heart' – 3:7. 'The term *marad* that occurs twice in v. 3 (rebels who have rebelled) primarily denotes, 'to rise up in revolt against an overlord, to refuse allegiance to one's sovereign…In v. 5, rebell-ious household *bet meri* is literally 'house of insubordination/ defiance,' and describes Israel's recalcitrance toward Yahweh.'[31] The expression 'rebellious house of Israel' is unique to Ezekiel, and '*meri*' occurs only twenty three times in the Hebrew bible and sixteen of those are in Ezekiel.[32] The Lord also speaks to Ezekiel and confirms that when he sends him he will be endowed with his authority, as he will address the people with the words: 'Thus says the Lord.' This command unmistakably states Ezekiel is neither free to choose his message nor to tailor it to his audience. The Lord also instructs him not to be afraid or dismayed at the peoples' response to him. 'The messenger of God must be prepared to encounter hostility, contempt and actual bodily harm, all painful as the sting of a scorpion' – 2:6.[33] Although the Lord says to Ezekiel, 'I am sending you to the people of Israel, to a nation of rebels' – 2:3, we do well to remember the ten northern tribes of Israel had been swallowed up in the neo-Assyrian empire in the 8th century. And like the rest of the prophets, Ezekiel continues to use the designation Israel for those who are left in Judah.[34]

EZEKIEL EATS THE SCROLL – 2:8–3:1-11

"But you son of man, hear what I say to you, be not rebellious like that rebellious house: open you mouth and eat what I give you." And when I looked, behold, a hand was stretched out to me, and lo a written scroll was in it and he spread it before me: and it had writing on the front and on the back, and there were written on it words of lamentation and mourning and woe. And he said to me, "Son of man, eat what is offered to you: eat this scroll and go speak to the house of Israel." So I opened my mouth and he gave me the scroll to eat. And he said to me, "Son of man, eat this scroll that I give you and fill your stomach with it." Then I ate it: and it was in my mouth as sweet as honey.

And he said to me, "Son of man, go get you to the house of Israel, and speak my words to them. For you are not sent to a people of foreign speech and a hard language, but to the house of Israel – not to many peoples of foreign speech and a hard language, whose words you cannot understand. Surely if I sent you to such, they would listen to you. But the house of Israel will not listen to you, for they are not willing to listen to me: because all of the house of Israel are of a hard forehead and of a stubborn heart. Behold, I have made your face hard against their faces, and your forehead hard against their foreheads. Like adamant harder than flint have I made your forehead: do not be afraid of them, nor be dismayed at their looks for they are a rebellious house." Moreover, he said to me, "Son of man, all my words that I shall speak to you receive in your heart, and hear with your ears. And go get you to the exiles, to your people and say to them, 'Thus says the Lord God' – whether they hear or refuse to hear."

Then the Spirit lifted me up, and as the glory of the Lord arose from its place, I head behind me the sound of a great earthquake. It was the sound of the wings of the living creatures as they touched one another, and the sound of the wheels beside them, that sounded like a great earthquake. The Spirit lifted me up and took me in bitterness in the heat of my spirit, the hand of the Lord being strong upon me: and I came to the exiles by the river Chebar. And I sat among there overwhelmed among them seven days.'

Ezekiel has been exposed to dazzling and spectacular super-natural phenomenon in the heavenly places, prior to the Lord calling him to be a prophet to the rebellious house of Israel. Having informed him of the obdurate nature of his audience, he now sternly warns him not to be like the house of Israel and rebel against him. The exhortation to be submissive to the Lord as opposed to rebellious is followed by the command: 'be not rebellious like that rebellious house: open your mouth and eat what I give you' – 2:8. 'The Lord requires Ezekiel's uncond-itional surrender to the divine will and word.'[35] After this we read, 'And when I looked, behold, a hand was stretched out to me, and lo, a written scroll was in it, and he spread it before me' – 2:9. This is unusual for four reasons. Firstly, the Lord gave Ezekiel a *'rolled up scroll'* – *'megillat seper,'* which is the correct Hebrew translation, as opposed to a 'written scroll.' Secondly, it had writing on the front and on the back that indicates a specific message, whereas a scroll usually only had writing on one side. Thirdly, the Lord commanded Ezekiel to eat it. Fourthly, words of lamentation, mourning and woe were written on it, that indicate the Lord's message of judgment.

The Lord tests Ezekiel's obedience by his command to eat a scroll that comes from an outstretched hand that originates from the heavenly throne, indicating its contents come from the hand of God himself. The contents written on the scroll in Hebrew spell disaster. '*Qina,* refers to a lament or dirge whose form derives from the dirges wailed at funerals. *Hegeh,* which means literally rumbling, growling, is expressive of the moaning and groaning associated with grief. *Hi* is an expression echoing a cry of pain.'[36] These words describe the effects of the judgments that Ezekiel will announce which may have been inscribed on the scroll.[37] Eichrodt says, 'What is involved here is…an assurance that the message with which he is entrusted is independent of his own subjective judgments and is divine in origin.'[38]

Ezekiel is commanded by the Lord to eat the scroll on three occasions. The first is in Ch. 2:8-9, and on the second occasion the Lord says, 'eat what is offered to you: eat this scroll, and go speak to the house of Israel' – 3:1. The third command comes immediately after the second, 'Son of man, eat this scroll that I give you and fill your stomach' – 3:2. Ezekiel's commission as a prophet symbolically takes place as he obediently eats the scroll the Lord offers him, with God's word inscribed on it. 'Then I ate it, and it was in my mouth sweet as honey' – 3:3. Eating the scroll is reminiscent of Jeremiah's experience when he said, 'Thy words were found, and I ate them, and your words became to me a joy and the delight of my heart' – Jer. 15:15. However, the context in Ch. 15 actually finds Jeremiah protesting at his suffering because of his prophetic call.

Although the contents of the scroll were bitter judgment, by way of contrast as Ezekiel eats it, its taste is as sweet as honey in his mouth. 'The Word will give Ezekiel spiritual joy in his ministry despite the divine mandate to preach searing judgment.'[39] Any hesitation evoked in Ezekiel by the words of judgment written on the scroll is dispelled by the sweetness following his obedience to the Lord. 'Ezekiel is…a man filled, nourished, and empowered by the divine word. More than any other prophet, he will embody the message he proclaims, functioning as a sign of its reality and power. Herein lies the key to the prophet's authority: he carries in his own body the word of God.'[40] Eichrodt in effect perceives Ezekiel experienced an 'inner liberation' by his obedience in eating the scroll. In our experience, even strange and apparently unintelligible demands on the part of God when they are fulfilled by us bring an inner satisfaction that takes away all their bitterness.'[41] Eating the scroll represents the divine message that Ezekiel is to proclaim. The scroll is God's Word in an external, physical 'sacramental' form the prophet must consume, as it enables him to accept and internalise it.[42] The Collect for the 2nd Sunday in Advent is based on Ezekiel eating the scroll and reads, 'Blessed Lord, who has caused all holy Scriptures to be written for our learning: Grant that we may in such wise hear them, read, mark, learn, and inwardly digest them.'

During his ecstatic visions, Ezekiel's mind remains lucid, as he coherently reports his call and commission to be a prophet, that involved declaring God's word to His people. As he was commanded three times by the Lord to eat the scroll, this gave him an assurance confirming the Lord's will. Although Ezekiel is instructed on three occasions to go and speak to the house of Israel – 3:2, 3:4, 3:11, the Lord does not actually command him to do so until Ch. 6. Once Ezekiel has eaten the scroll, again the Lord commands him, 'go, get you to the house of Israel and speak my words to them' – 3:4. In effect, this is the Lord's second commissioning speech to Ezekiel, and Daniel Block thinks this reflects his continued hesitation to accept the Lord's prophetic charge.[43] Other biblical commentators also think Ezekiel may have been reluctant to take up the mantle of a prophet, as the Lord exhorts him not to be rebellious – 2:8. While this is speculative, this perception may have some substance, as he would have been aware of the opposition and suffering his contemporary Jeremiah encountered as a prophet.

When the Lord informs Ezekiel the people will not listen to him as they are not willing to listen to the Lord, we do well to be aware this has a parallel in 'the Christological principle of representation,' for those who are emissaries of Christ. For example, Jesus says, 'The one who listens to you listens to me, and the one who rejects you rejects me. But the one who rejects me rejects the one who sent me' – Luke 10:16.'[44] The Lord forewarns Ezekiel of two features that will characterise his ministry as a prophet. Firstly, because the house of Israel are rebellious, have a hard forehead and a stubborn heart, they will not listen to him – 3:7, as they will be unresponsive and are not willing to listen to the Lord. This highlights the stubbornness of Israel that exceeds the foreign nations in her ability to understand, and reflects a rock hard resistance to the Lord. Secondly, to counter the granite like unresponsiveness of the people, the Lord will equip Ezekiel emotionally and psychologically with an iron constitution – a 'divine toughening,'[45] likened to 'a hard face and a hard forehead' – so that he does not need to be dismayed by their resistance. 'A divine hardness will characterise Ezekiel and represent the thoroughgoing hardness of his message.'[46]

His forehead will be like adamant harder than flint against the peoples' forehead: adamant refers to a diamond that cuts through flint. So Ezekiel does not have to be afraid, dismayed, or intimated by their resistance no matter how great it is. 'The diamond-hard countenance given Ezekiel – 3:7-9 is apparently a deliberate play on Ezekiel's name. Three times in 3:8-9 the Hebrew adjective 'strong' applies to Ezekiel, and his name is compounded of that same root, 'God will strengthen. Ezekiel's whole life, as well as his name, is to be an action prophecy.'[47] Eichrodt adds, 'God's messenger need have no fear as he will be given a hardness like that of a diamond, so as to meet their closed hearts with ruthless unbreakable strength.'[48] Ezekiel's 'divine toughening' is reminiscent of Jeremiah when the Lord said to him, 'Do not be dismayed by them, lest I dismay you before them. And I, behold I make you this day a fortified city, an iron pillar, and bronze walls, against the whole land, against the kings of Judah and its princes, its priests, and the people of the land. They will fight against you, but they shall not prevail against you' – Jer. 1:18-19. We may perceive that Ezekiel in striking contrast to Jeremiah and his loud laments, conceals his feelings and his sensitivity beneath a tough armour (exterior), in which he seldom lets a single chink appear.[49]

After eating the scroll, Ezekiel is commissioned by the Lord to go to the house of Israel and speak His words to them – 3:1. This command is repeated again later with the divine prophetic formula, 'Thus says the Lord God' – 3:11. Just prior to this, the Lord instructs Ezekiel once again not to be rebellious, but this time he exhorts him, 'Son of man, all my words that I shall speak to you receive in your heart, and hear with your ears' – 3:10. This demands that he was to remain open and responsive to hear and receive God's word in the future. In the following chapters, we shall see that he repeatedly speaks of receiving God's word and being obedient.

EZEKIEL A WATCHMAN – 3: 12-21

'Then the Spirit lifted me up, and as the glory of the Lord arose from its place, I heard behind me the sound of a great earthquake. It was the sound of the wings of the living creatures as they touched one another, and the sound of the wheels beside them that sounded like a great earthquake. The Spirit lifted me up and took me away, and I went in bitterness in the heat of my spirit, the hand of the Lord being strong upon me: and I came to the exiles at Telabib, who dwelt by the river Chebar. And I sat there over-whelmed among them for seven days.

And at the end of seven days, the word of the Lord came to me: ''Son of man, I have made you a watchman for the house of Israel: whenever you hear a word from my mouth, you shall give them warning from me. If I say to the wicked, 'You shall surely die,' and you give him no warning, nor speak to warn the wicked from his wicked way, in order to save his life, that wicked man shall die in his iniquity: but his blood I shall require at your hand. But if you warn the wicked, and he does not turn from his wickedness, or from his wicked way, he shall die in his iniquity, but you will have saved your life. Again, if a righteous man turns from his righteousness and commits iniquity, and I lay a stumbling block before him, he shall die: because you have not warned him, he shall die for his sin, and his righteous deeds which he has done shall not be remembered: but his blood I will require at your hands. Nevertheless, if you warn the righteous man not to sin, and he does not sin, he shall surely live, because he took your warning: and you will have saved your life.''

Ezekiel's unique ecstatic visions of God came to a climax with the appearance of the glory of the Lord, and the Lord speaking to Ezekiel about his call and commission as a prophet to the rebellious house of Israel. When the Lord has finished speaking to him, his visionary experience ends with the thunderous roar of an earthquake made by the living creatures and their wheels that is consistent with his experience at the beginning of his visions. Simultaneously, the glory of the Lord arose-departed, as God's Spirit takes hold of him and transports him to the exiles at Telabib by the river Chebar. As Ezekiel was among the exiles at the river when he saw visions of God, biblical commentators acknowledge difficulty in reconciling that at the end of his visions he is transported back to the exiles at the river. 'The need for the return is understandable if 'by the Chebar canal' in the superscription is interpreted as a general designation for the area where the exiles resided.'[50] While it may not be exactly clear how to interpret Ezekiel's return, in his experience it is clear this is what has taken place.

Ezekiel's ecstatic visions of God in the heavenly firmament were a unique experience in the Old Testament. Only John in the Book of Revelation has visions that are comparable, but which supersede them and are also unique as they are the revelation of Christ. On a rare occasion, for the first time, Ezekiel who seldom will express his feelings describes how he felt. 'He offers a significant window into his mind and heart.' The impact of his experience has been so overpowering, the Lord has left him with a challenging call as a prophet to come to terms with. Ezekiel is bitter – *mar,* that may well be an abbreviation for *mar nepes* – 'bitterness of soul.' This acts as a contrasts with the pleasant experience when he ate the scroll, and he is deeply disturbed in his spirit as he returns to the river: *hamat ruhi,* is 'literally angry in my spirit.' Ezekiel is overwhelmed – *masmim,* that in the context means 'to be desolate, appalled,' by his entire experience as he sits a lonely figure by the river Chebar.[52] Ezekiel is stunned, and in a state of shock, as he silently reflects on the Lord's description of Israel as a nation of rebels, impudent and rebellious, who have a stubborn heart: and at his call to counter the granite like unresponsiveness of the people, in which the Lord will equip Ezekiel with an iron constitution. A 'divine toughening,' likened to 'a hard face and a hard forehead.' Horace Hummel is the only biblical commentator, who perceives Ezekiel's bitterness of spirit may well reflect his awareness of the thankless and dangerous task God has given him. Such a mood would reflect the lamentation, mourning and woe that had been written on the scroll he had eaten.[53] He is also aware of the hand of the Lord being heavy on him – 3:14. In Psalm 32 David says, 'For day and night your hand was heavy upon me' – v.4 While the context is different, David is aware of the Lord convicting him about his sin, which he describes as: 'your hand was heavy upon me.' For Ezekiel the Lord's hand being heavy on him, indicates an awareness of the Lord's relentless pressure to embrace his call as a prophet to the rebellious Israel, and the compulsion to preach the divine word he has received. He feels the power of a will superior to his own, in spite of   all his inward resistance.'[54]

What is striking in the narrative about Ezekiel's call and commission to be a prophet is the omission of any reference to Ezekiel having openly resisted the Lord's call. Moses resisted God's call by his insistence on his lack of eloquence as a speaker – Exodus 4:10-17, and Jeremiah objected to God's call because he was so young and 'didn't know how to speak' – Jer. 1:6. But, up to now, in the context of his visions and his call as a prophet, Ezekiel has not had an opportunity to object to God's call. Block perceives 'Ezekiel is infuriated by the divine imposition on his life and the implications of Yahweh's commission…The encounter with God, the digestion of the scroll, the charge to go and preach to an unresponsive audience, the hardening of his forehead, the sound of the throne-chariot, and the pressure of Yahweh's hand upon him, have left Ezekiel in a wretched state – socially ostracised, physically exhausted, and emotionally disturbed.'[55]

Similarly, Wright perceives, 'The total physical, spiritual and psychological trauma of the whole experience has left Ezekiel overwhelmed.'[56]

The Lord in his inscrutable sovereign will chose to reveal to Ezekiel in his visions, His glory and his call as a prophet to the rebellious house of Israel, and it is not at all surprising he felt overwhelmed. Understandably, he needed a period of time to assimilate all that had happened to him, and some breathing space to come to terms with the new orientation in his life that came unexpectedly, unanticipated, and reading in between the lines may well have been unwelcome, and to which he may have been resistant. He is now back to earth with a jolt, alongside the exiles at the river Chebar – concerned at the implications of his visions and his calling as a prophet. Ezekiel has now had a week to reflect on his experience and come to terms with 'the shock of his conscription into divine service,'[57] after which the Lord speaks to him again.

A question mark has been raised about Ch. 3:16-21 for a number of reasons. Eichrodt points out that this section is one of the most difficult in the Book of Ezekiel as these verses are verbally identical with Ch. 33:7-9.[58] Most scholars consider 16-21 to be a secondary insertion in which case the narrative in v. 22 can naturally follow v. 15. In terms of genre, the style of the oracle in vs. 16-21 is quite different from the divine speeches up to now. However, the differences between 3:16-21 and 33:1-9 are considerable. By way of contrast, 16-21 is a private oracle to Ezekiel about his role as a watchman, whereas the message about the watchman in Ch. 33 is to be declared to the people. Verses 16-21 concern God's judgment and death on those who do not respond, while Ch. 33 holds out the possibility of repentance. It is just as possible 33:1-9 expands and reapplies 3:16-21, as 3:16-21 has been taken from a later context and inserted here. Reinforcing the rightful place of 3:16-21 in its original setting is the force of the narrative about Ezekiel as a watchman – 'the divine determination to conscript a man resistant to the call of the prophetic office.'[59] The oracle from the Lord in 3:16-21 describes the burden and nature of Ezekiel's prophetic office and his personal responsibility and accountability to the Lord. Moreover, the serious nature of his calling is spelt out in detail as the Lord informs him that as a watchman he is to declare God's word whenever He speaks to him, whether it is to the wicked or to the righteous – as the Lord will hold him responsible if he does not warn them about God's message. Equally, when Ezekiel does declare God's word when He speaks to him, those who receive it will be held individually responsible for their response.

The noun *sopeh* – watchman, derives from the root meaning 'to look out, to spy, to watch.' In the ancient Near East the role of the watchman was as a sentry on duty strategically placed on lookout towers on the city walls, or the roof of gatehouses, or on towers outside the city. His role was to be alert and keep a lookout for the movements of the enemy and to blow his trumpet as a warning as they began to approach.[60] The image of watchman was not new to Israel and can also be found in Jeremiah, Hosea and Isaiah, divinely appointed watchmen whose warnings were not heeded. In Isaiah 56:10-11 we read, 'His watchmen are blind, they are all without knowledge…The shepherds also have no understanding, they have all turned to their own way.' This indicates they failed to warn the people. In Hosea we read, 'The prophet is the watchman of Ephraim, the people of my God, yet a fowler's snare is on all his ways, and hatred in the house of his God' – 9:8. And in Jeremiah the Lord says, 'I set watchmen over you saying, 'Give heed to the sound of the trumpet. But they said, 'We will not give heed' – 6:17. The metaphor of Ezekiel as a watchman, 'will be the defining model of his ministry, repeated later in the book in the context of the fall of Jerusalem, and the ongoing challenge the event would pose for the exiles.'[61] But the controversial aspect of Ezekiel's ministry as a watchman was that he was not warning God's people of imminent danger from a foreign enemy. Instead, he was to warn the people that the imminent danger was from God. Moreover, the Lord would be the one to sound the warning through Ezekiel. Whenever the Lord spoke to him, Ezekiel was to warn the people, and the alarming and shocking nature of his warning, was that the Lord was the source of the danger. 'Ezekiel is to sound the horn not only *when* God sends the signal but *as* God dictates…Yet the voice of the sentry symbolises the grace of God reaching out to those under the sentence of death.'[62]

EZEKIEL'S INITIATION – 3: 22-27

'And the hand of the Lord was there upon me, and he said to me, "Arise, go forth to the plain and there I will speak with you." So I arose, and went forth into the plain, and lo, the glory of the Lord stood there, like the glory which I had seen by the river Chebar and I fell on my face. But the Spirit entered into me, and set me upon my feet, and he spoke with me and said to me, "Go, shut yourself within your house. And you O son of man, behold, cords will be placed upon you, and you shall be bound with them, so that you cannot go out among the people: and I will make your tongue cleave to the roof of your mouth, so that you shall be dumb and unable to reprove them, for they are a rebellious house. But when I speak with you, I will open your mouth, and you shall say to them, for they are a rebellious house, 'Thus says the Lord God,' he that will hear, let him hear, and he that will refuse to hear, let him refuse, for they are a rebellious house."

Once the Lord has informed Ezekiel his role as a prophet is to be a watchman, he is now aware of the hand of the Lord being upon him again, with the Lord instructing him to go to the plain. This referred to the broad Mesopotamian plain in Babylonia away from the rivers and canals. This region was wasteland an appropriate place for a private encounter where the Lord spoke to him.[63] The plain is distinguished from the place of prayer where Ezekiel received his visions. On the three significant occasions of his call, the appearance of the glory of the Lord is manifest to him unequivocally confirming his call as a prophet. For the third time – 3:23, the glory of the Lord appears to him in what is regarded by biblical scholars as the most complex narrative initiation in all Scripture. It is quite possible verses 22-27 are not part of the original text and are the result of the final editing procedure,[64] because for Ezekiel to be struck dumb contradicts the Lord's repeated call to declare God's word. Yet while it is speculative, those involved in the final editing of Ezekiel, may have regarded his silencing as a recurrent sign of his preaching as it emphasised the decisive character of his message which accounts for 3:22-27, being placed near the beginning of the book.[65]

Up to this juncture, the Lord had clearly informed Ezekiel his task was to declare the word of God to the people, as and when the Lord revealed it to him. If he anticipated instructions to now go and declare God's word that the Lord was going to reveal to him, he was severely mistaken. Wright sums up the apparently contradictory instructions to Ezekiel to be shut up in his house and ironically and symbolically 'to shut up' – to be silent and not speak when he says: 'What happens next plumbs the depths of paradox almost to the point of farce. Ezekiel is told to be housebound and that he will be unable to speak.'[66] Block captures the unexpected nature of the Lord's command to Ezekiel when he says, 'The ways of the Lord are often strange and inscrutable. With cartoon-like caricature the drama enacted in Ezekiel's house portrays the complete mastery of God over his servant.'[67] The appearance of the glory of the Lord on a third occasion, alongside the experience of the God's Spirit on these three occasions, and the hand of the Lord resting upon him twice, unequivocally confirms to Ezekiel the authenticity of his visions and his calling and initiation as a prophet, 'which ironically stifles his freedom of expression rather than liberating it. Taken at face value, Ezekiel's speech-less state lasted more than seven years, from one week after his inaugural vision – 1:3, 3:16, to the day he received the news that Jerusalem has fallen – 33:21-22.'[68] But we know he delivered oracles during these years and he may have faced some hostility as we know that Jeremiah his older contemporary was beaten and put in stocks – Jer. 20:2, and Ezek. 2:6 indicates that he is forewarned by the Lord he will face hostility, as does 3:25 where the Lord informs him he will be bound with cords.

Ezekiel being bound and incapacitated and rendered dumb, clashes with his prophetic call to declare God's word and to be a watchman. This raises the dilemma of how to reconcile his freedom of movement that is required by his symbolic sign-acts in Ch. 4 and Ch. 5. This raises the issue of whether these restrictive issues were literal with Ezekiel actually being bound by cords by others in exile, or if they were metaphorical, and whether they were permanent or temporary. However, we do know, despite Ezekiel's restricted movement, the Lord bound his speech and he was commanded to remain silent, except when the Lord explicitly gave him an oracle to deliver – 3:27. The Lord's first command that preceded these restrictions was to shut himself up in his house and involved a divinely imposed silence. He is only to speak when he receives a message or oracle from the Lord. Ezekiel is to do and say nothing on his own initiative.

One reason for Ezekiel's binding and silencing is stated in v. 25-26, and indicates that his seclusion which stops him from socialising with the exiles is to prevent him from reproving them. A key task of a prophet was to intercede of behalf of the people, but Ezekiel is not allowed to do this because God's word that he will declare is that of inescapable judgment. The phrase, 'you will be unable to reprove-rebuke them' is better translated, 'you will be unable to act as a mediator on their behalf. 'The expression *is mokiah,* that literally means to be a man of litigation, and most commonly applies to one who rebukes or reproves.'[69] The Lord denies Ezekiel the freedom to warn the exiles of the fall of Jerusalem by appealing for a reprieve or calling people to repentance.[70]

The restrictions placed on Ezekiel may represent symbolic signs that precede the sign-acts he will perform which point to the siege and fall of Jerusalem. A straightforward metaphorical interpretation sees Ezekiel being confined to his house as the Lord instructs him to 'shut yourself within your house' – 3:24. This indicates his confinement was voluntary as opposed to being forced upon him by others, and it can be supported as there is no record of any hostility against Ezekiel recorded. In 8:1, 14:1-4 and 20:1, the elders come to Ezekiel's house for a message from the Lord, and when his audience request an explanation of his sign-acts –12:9, 21:12 and 24:9, they assume he has the powers of speech.[71] On the other hand, as the Lord forewarns him he will face hostility – 3:25, this may refer to hostility that he faced at some period after he began his prophetic ministry. The Lord's action in making Ezekiel's tongue cleave to the roof of his mouth so he cannot speak, is a further symbolic sign that he will only be able to speak when the Lord gives him an oracle to announce. When he speaks, it is because the Lord had something to say.

To grasp the significance of the two symbolic signs for the exiles the Lord imposed on Ezekiel it is helpful to be aware of how the exiles formed their communities. They lived in the region of Telabib by the river Chebar in their extended family groups – Ezra Ch. 8. The Levites, priests, and other former temple officials formed their own groups – Ezra Ch. 2. Alongside the priests and prophets, the elders had their own leadership roles – Jer. 29:1, Ezek. 7:1, 14:1, 20:1. We also know from the Book of Daniel that some of the royal family and nobility and leading young men who were well educated, found their way to the highest political offices,[72] as they were taught the Babylonian culture and language – Dan. 1:3-4. While Ezekiel was not an ordained priest, we can reasonably assume that he had responsibilities within the exilic community as a trained religious leader. For Ezekiel to suddenly shut himself up in his house and have no social contact with anyone would have attracted the attention of the exiles. Leading them to question what this may have symbolised and what the Lord may have been saying through Ezekiel.

CHAPTER THREE

JERUSALEM PROPHECIES – 4:1-7:27
THE BESIEGED BRICK – 4:1-3

"And you, O son of man, take a brick and lay it before you, and put siegeworks against it, and build a siege wall against it, and cast a mound against it: set camps also against it, and plant battering rams against it round about. And take an iron plate, and place it as an iron wall between you and the city: and set your face toward it, and let it be in a state of siege, and press the siege against it. This is a sign for the house of Israel."

Having been informed by the Lord Ezekiel was called and commissioned to be a prophet, and was repeatedly commanded by the Lord to declare his word exactly as He revealed it to him, his first instructions given by the Lord in Chapters 4-5 are bizarre symbolic sign-acts he is to carry out. Yet such is the overwhelming impact of the visions of God the Lord gave to Ezekiel, and the impact the revelation of the glory of the Lord had on him, that Ezekiel is obedient and faithfully carries them out despite the hardship and suffering they involve.

Chapters 4-7 are a series of judgment oracles about the siege and fall of Jerusalem and involve a series of symbolic sign-acts, while chs. 6-7 are about the desolation of the land of Israel depicted by two oracles. Hummel's preferred term for the sign-acts is 'action prophecy' A prophecy that is acted out rather than verbalised. Jeremiah uses ten action prophecies, while Ezekiel also has ten action prophecies and Isaiah only has one.[1] Ezekiel, 'By means of a series of disturbing but rhetorically powerful sign-acts is to address head-on the inevitable fate of Jerusalem.'[2] Block says:

> Ezekiel's messages of doom are evidently intended to dismantle official Jerusalemite theology by systematic-ally undermining the four pillars upon which Judah's (false) sense of security was built.[3]

'* The first pillar is the Lord's covenant with Israel. The people assumed they had divine protection against their enemies as they were in a covenant relationship with the Lord that could not be annulled. One of Ezekiel's tasks was to announce that by their persistent rebellion Israel had brought upon herself the consequences of their disobedience and rebellion (chs. 12-16, 18, 20, 22-24) that were the curses of the covenant as stated in Deuteronomy Ch. 28.

* The second pillar is the Lord's commitment to the land. Israel believed the land belonged to the Lord and he would defend it against foreign nations. Ezekiel announces the Lord is handing his land over to a foreign people – chs. 6, 21.

* The third pillar is the Lord's commitment to Jerusalem. This was the city the Lord had chosen for his dwelling place, in the temple in the holy of holies symbolised by the ark of the covenant. Israel's national, political, and religious security was based on their belief of the inviolability of Jerusalem. Ezekiel's oracles will announce the traumatic judgment of the Lord's abandonment of Jerusalem and the temple – chs. 4-5, 8-11.

* The fourth pillar is the Lord's unconditional covenant with David. The Lord promised David one of his descendents would always reign on the throne and the monarchy would be secure. But because Israel has been rebellious and is a nation in revolt against the Lord, Ezekiel will announce the covenant has been suspended – chs. 12, 17, 19.'[4]

The use of symbolic sign-acts is a characteristic feature of the prophetic literary tradition in Jewish society and prior to Ezekiel's use of them, Isaiah and Hosea had already utilised them. Ezekiel's contemporary Jeremiah, also often used symbolic sign-acts in his ministry. For example, wearing a soiled loincloth – Jer. 13:1-7, publicly smashing a jar of clay – Jer. 19, and wearing a wooden and then iron yoke on his neck – Jer. 27-28. Both Ezekiel's and Jeremiah's symbolic sign-acts were not merely illustrative or visual aids. 'Their purpose was to enhance the force of the spoken word, to make possible the more intense kind of identification which successful theatre can achieve.'[5] Equally, sign-acts can be interpreted as dramatic performances designed to visualise a message and enhance its persuasive force so observers' perceptions of a given situation might change and their beliefs modified.[6] Also, 'Ezekiel's tradition presents a unique pattern of symbolic sign-acts, as the prophet himself is told to function as 'a sign.'[7]

The use of the symbolic sign-acts in Ezekiel is reminiscent of earlier prophetic tradition. For example, in pre-classical prophecy both Hosea and Isaiah, the prophet's message has a visible form in his children and their names that convey messages – Hosea 1, Isaiah 7:3, 8:1-4. Zimmerli says, 'The purpose of the prophet's sign-actions is to set forth in a visible action, the event announced by Yahweh as something already begun…These symbolic sign-acts establish the character of the prophetic word as event. By this action, which is more than mere symbolism, the prophet prefigures as an event what he proclaims through his word. More precisely the event is brought into effect by the prophet and is commanded to happen. By accomplishing this action, the prophet guarantees the coming event.'[8]

The Lord forewarned Ezekiel that his audience the house of Israel were rebellious, impudent and stubborn – 2:3-4. These symbolic sign-acts were the equivalent of visual aids to get their attention about God's judgment concerning the fall of Jerusalem, to counter the exiles' false hopes of an imminent return to Jerusalem that made them resistant to his preaching, and their belief in the inviolability of Jerusalem and the temple. At times, Ezekiel uses evocative language that includes the sign-acts, in an attempt to penetrate the peoples' hardened hearts. In chapters 6, 16 and 23, his oracles are couched in potent sexual language, due the peoples' abhorrent apostasy and idolatry that is described as harlotry. 'His verbal proclamations and performed communication are often intentionally shocking, to wake the audience to the reality of their state.'[9]

Ezekiel's first symbolic sign-act is striking and is designed to capture the exiles' attention. He draws a plan of Jerusalem on the clay tablet, and erects five models against it, presumably clay models of siegeworks, a siege wall, a mound, camps, and battering rams, and the term *'against it'* is used for each model. A siege wall was a continuous mound or rampart or a series of them around the city, to keep an eye on it and prevent fresh supplies from reaching the city. A ramp was built from the ground at the foot of the city wall so that battering rams could be brought up along it breach the wall. Thousands of baskets of dirt, gravel and rock would be required to build such a ramp. The camps for the besieging army were strategically placed around the city walls, and the battering rams shaped like a spear had a metal rod at the tip to penetrate the city walls. All of these siegeworks are still clearly visible at the famous site of Masada on the western shore of the Dead Sea, where the dry desert air has preserved them phenomenally well for over two thousand years.[10] The clay brick was the usual building material that was always available in Babylonia. The brick was made of soft clay and was not yet fired so he could draw a map of Jerusalem on it. While this may sound unusual, drawing an outline of houses and temples on bricks and tablets is attested in Babylon from an early period.[11] Dugiud suggests perhaps the brick was the size of one or two sheets of A4 paper.[12]

The first sign-acts in 4:1–4:15 include nine actions: 4:1-2. 4:3, 4:4-6, 4:7, 4:8, 4:9-11, 4:12, 15, 5:1-2 and one in 5:3-4. These can be narrowed down to three sections: 4:1-4 relates to the siege of Jerusalem, 4:9-17 relates to the suffering of the exiles and the people in Jerusalem, and 5:1-4 relates to the final destruction of the city and its population. Wright says, 'Ezekiel produced a performance in which several central sections were repeated daily for over a year, interspersed, and then brought to a shattering climax, by shorter, more specific additional actions.'[13] After Ezekiel finishes his clay model of a siege, the RSV translation take an 'iron plate' and place it as an iron wall in v.3 is not correct. *Mahabat barzel* is an iron griddle (iron pan), a domestic utensil used to bake flat cakes over an open fire.[14] Using an iron instrument against the city represents an impenetrable barrier that denotes the Lord's rejection of his people, and as Ezekiel sets his face between the iron pan and the city wall he represents the Lord, as the Lord is the enemy laying siege to Jerusalem. While there may have been a question mark in the perception of the exiles as to which city the siege represented, the Lord makes it abundantly clear that the siege was a 'sign for the house of Israel' – 4:3.

Ezekiel performs the sign-acts in chapters 4-5 in silence and while the narrative does not record it, the silence of the text invites us to imagine the community of the exiles coming to witness his symbolic actions. Ezekiel is given an oracle by the Lord that explains his sign-acts to the exiles – 5:5-17. Block highlights that the shape of the text poses major logistical and conceptual problems. For example, how could Ezekiel lie on his side for 390 days? How could he have performed these actions when Yahweh had tied him up? He finds it difficult to see how his silence would have led the people to understand his action and visual aids would have led to confusion.[15] Yet the meaning of clay tablet depicting the siege of Jerusalem would have been evident, although the issue for the exiles is which city was it depicting, Babylon or Jerusalem? Although Zimmerli believes the action portrayed by Ezekiel is perfectly clear.[16]

SYMBOLIC PUNISHMENT – 4:4-8

"Then lie upon your left side, and I will lay the punishment of the house of Israel upon you, for the number of the days that you will lie upon it, you shall bear their punishment. For I assign to you a number of days, three hundred and ninety days, equal to the number of the years of their punishment: so long shall you bear the punishment of the house of Israel. And when you have completed these, you shall lie down a second time, but on your right side, and bear the punishment of the house of Judah: forty days I assign you, a day for each year. And you shall set your face toward the siege of Jerusalem, with your arm bared: and you shall prophecy against the city. And behold I will put cords upon you, so that you cannot turn from one side to the other, till you have completed the days of your siege."

In his portrayal of the siege of Jerusalem Ezekiel represented the Lord, now he represents the people in the role of the priest bearing the punishment for their sins. The Lord laying the punishment of Israel and Judah on Ezekiel – 4:1, 4:6, is similar to the language used in the scapegoat ritual on the Day of Atonement – Lev. 16:21-22, although it is representative and not expiatory. Block thinks that, 'As Ezekiel refers to Israel and Judah interchangeably elsewhere, *bet yisrael* – 'house of Israel' should be understood similarly here.'[17]

The 390 days the Lord instructs Ezekiel to lie on his left side with his face towards the city during which he lays on him the punishment of the house of Israel, refers approximately to the years between the building and dedication of the temple by Solomon to its final destruction in 587. This represents the national apostasy, rebellion, and sin of the entire covenant people and the house of Israel. The 40 days the Lord instructs Ezekiel to lie on his right side represents 40 years, being one generation, and refers to those in the exile from Judah. This is reminiscent of the 40 years the Israelites spent in the wilderness, one year for every day the spies spent exploring the land of Canaan until their entire generation had died.

Both Block and Hummel think it is unlikely Ezekiel lay on his side continuously for 390 days. The more realistic scenario is that in his prophetic action he lay on his side for several hours a day, during the busiest part of the day, when he would be exposed to the exilic community who would report his strange behaviour.[18] And during the rest of the day, and especially at night, he carried on with his normal activities in the privacy of his own home. Zimmerli in effect thinks Ezekiel lying bound is regarded as an event of substitutionary sin-bearing and publicly portrayed a meaningful sign of guilt. 'In the prophet's guilt-bearing there occurs at the same time an act of public identification as he brings together in his symbolic bondage the guilt of Israel as a burden in his own life.' He sees ideas that are set in motion to be more fully worked out in Isaiah 53, in the picture of the Servant of Yahweh who bears the guilt of many.[19] In some way this is a symbolic act of Ezekiel's identification with the peoples' guilt, and the idea of him bearing their guilt/punishment has a subtle nuance as he cannot absolve the people of their guilt. Block suggests '*awon* is to be interpreted as the peoples' iniquity not punishment, and the phrase *nasa awon* to suffer the consequences of one's sinful actions, arising out of Yahweh's hostile disposition.'[20] Because the exiles are in Babylon because of the Lord's judgment, and Jerusalem will also be destroyed as a sign of the Lord's punishment.

Not only did Ezekiel lie down with his face towards the city, as he did so he was instructed to bear his arm so it was outstretched. The Lord bearing his arm in Isaiah 52:10 demonstrates his great saving power, but here it represents a dangerous threat and symbolises the Lord's hostile intention against the city, as a raised outstretched arm is also a military gesture of preparing for battle.[21] Moreover, in this prostrate position, facing the city walls with his arm stretched out, Ezekiel is commanded by the Lord to prophecy against the city, to be certain the exiles understand his siege action. The combination of the siege works and lying on his side for over a year, and prophesying against the city left the exiles in no doubt about the meaning of his symbolic action. And to ensure the exact number of days are completed by Ezekiel the Lord informs him that He will bind him with cords. 'By being tied up Ezekiel affirms nonverbally the unalterable quality of his prophecy.'[22]

THE SIEGE FAMINE – 4:9-17

"And you take wheat and barley, beans and lentils, millet and spelt, and put them into a single vessel, and make bread of them. During the number of days that you lie upon your side, three hundred and ninety days you shall eat it. And the food that you shall eat shall be by weight, twenty shekels a day, once a day you shall eat it. And water you shall drink by measure, the sixth part of a hin, once a day you shall drink. And you shall eat it as a barely cake, baking it in their sight on human dung." And the Lord said, "Thus shall the people of Israel eat their bread unclean, among the nations where I will drive them." Then I said, "Ah Lord God!

Behold, I have never defiled myself. From my youth up till now I have never eaten what died of itself or was torn by beasts, nor has foul flesh come into my mouth.'' Then the Lord said to me, ''See, I will let you have cow's dung instead of human dung, on which you may prepare your bread.'' Moreover, he said to me, ''Son of man, behold, I will break the staff of bread in Jerusalem. They shall eat bread by weight and with fearfulness: and they shall drink water by measure with dismay. I will do this that they may lack bread and water and look at one another in dismay, and waste away under their punishment.''

In chs. 4-5, the prophetic sign-acts against Jerusalem symbolically enacted by Ezekiel for over a year build upon each other to reinforce the Lord's message of judgment, so that it will be unmistakably clear to the exiles in Babylon who had false hopes of a return to Jerusalem and a short period in exile. During the period of 390 days the Lord stipulates to Ezekiel that his food and water rations will also be a symbolic action to the exiles relating to the siege of Jerusalem. The size of the loaf of bread is equivalent to eight ounces and barely enough to sustain him, and the meager ration of water that is around two thirds of a quart could not prevent him from being dehydrated lying in the sun.[23] This indicates Ezekiel is only likely to perform his symbolic action lying down for a few hours a day. Verses 9-11 and 12 point to two different action prophesies. The former presents the diet of the residents during the siege of Jerusalem and symbolises a famine. While the latter represents what the diet of the people of Israel will be forced to eat in exile. Ezekiel is to combine the grains of wheat and barley along with the vegetables of beans and lentil to make dough and bake it as bread. This indicates that food will be so scarce these ingredients are to be used as there will not be enough of any one grain to make bread. This demonstrates that Jerusalem will be brought to the brink of starvation.

Ezekiel's second sign act in v.12 is to bake a barley cake in front of his fellow exiles and the Hebrew *uga* denotes a flat cake or disk of bread baked in a pan over hot stones.[24] In contrast to the bread in his first sign-act in v. 9, the issue the Lord mentions here is the actual composition of the barley cake because it is to be cooked over human dung. This demonstrates the people of Israel will eat their bread unclean, among the nations in exile. The Hebrew word *tame* – unclean, refers to ceremonial and ritual impurity, as lands outside Israel were considered contaminated because of the abominable practices, particularly idolatry.[25] It was not uncommon to use dung as fuel for baking where other forms of fuel were scarce, but in Deut. 23:12-14, toilet facilities are designated outside the camp by the Lord, as the camp is holy. Consequently, Ezekiel is shocked and disgusted at the Lord's command to bake the barley cake on dung because it renders it unclean and is repulsive to him. The Hebrew in 4:12 is intended to invoke abhorrence at the vulgarity of baking bread on human dung and would cause outrage.[26] This results in Ezekiel's only verbal protest to the Lord despite the bizarre symbolic acts he was often asked to perform, as he was acutely aware about matters of holiness and ceremonial purity in Deut 26:13-15, due to his training as a priest. This sign-act was to shock Ezekiel's audience into taking seriously the threat of Jerusalem's collapse along with the exile of its inhabitants. Moreover, as his audience was already in exile, this reinforced the shame of their situation.[27]

Ezekiel's outburst at eating a barley cake baked on dung is a protest at what he considers to be a revolting action as this compromises his conscience and sense of purity. However, the Lord makes an allowance and concedes to Ezekiel's personal sensibilities and allows him to bake the barley cake on cow's dung, while his symbolic act still makes the point that cooking food over a fire fuelled by dung renders the food unclean, so too preparing food in a foreign land results in the exiles food being defiled. The Lord's intention in this deliberate act that contravenes the traditional dietary laws of Deuteronomy would shock his audience into taking seriously the siege of Jerusalem and the deportation of its population.

Ezekiel's first symbolic sign-acts – his prophetic actions in Ch. 4, begin a series of severe judgments the Lord is bringing upon his people as he is about to cut off the food supply in Jerusalem, or as the RSV puts it, 'I will break the staff of bread in Jerusalem. They will eat bread by weight and with fearfulness, and they shall drink water by measure and in dismay. I will do this that they may lack bread and water, and look at one another in dismay, and waste under their punishment.' This is tantamount to the fulfillment of the curses appointed by the Lord in Deut. 28:15-18, 21:

> But if you will not obey the voice of the Lord your God, or be careful to do all his commandments and his statutes which I command you this day, then these curses shall come upon you and overtake you. Cursed shall you be in the city, and cursed shall you be in your field. Cursed shall be your basket and your kneading-trough...The Lord will make the pestilence cleave to you until he has consumed you off the land which you are entering to take possession of.

The words fearfulness-anxiety and dismay-devastated 'describe the emotional distress the scarcity of food in Jerusalem will bring on the besieged population.' In Hebrew, the statement the people will 'waste away' – 4:17, that refers to the people languishing in its figurative sense, *maqaq* refers to the decomposition of flesh.[28] This is a repulsive condition that will lead to self-loathing – Ezek. 6: 9, 'they will be loathsome in their own sight.' Loathsome also occurs in 20:43 and loath in 36:31. The Lord's calculated actions are a fulfillment of the covenant curses and the Lord's judgment has the explicit aim of destroying his people. One cannot help but reflect God's people, especially their leaders, their kings and also their priests, had forgotten to read the 'small print' of their covenant obligations and the devastating curses they were liable to bring upon themselves, if they failed to obey God's commandments and his statutes.

EZEKIEL'S SHAVED HEAD – 5: 1-4

''And you, O son of man, take a sharp sword, use it as a barber's razor and pass it over your head and beard, then take balances for weighing and divide the hair. A third part you shall burn in the fire in the midst of the city when the days of the siege are completed, and a third apart you shall take and strike with the sword round about the city, and a third part you shall scatter to the wind, and I will unsheathe the sword after them. And you shall take from these a small number, and bind them in the skirts of your robe. And of these again you shall take some, and cast them in the fire: from there a fire will come forth into all the house of Israel.''

Around fourteen months had passed. The end of Ezekiel's long siege is in sight and there is one final climatic act that will bring this astonishing drama to an unforgettable finale. He was to shave his head and beard after it had been left to grow during the long siege, that was likely to have been a physically very painful act using a sword.[29] This new bizarre sign-act comes at the beginning of Ch. 5 and follows the symbolic signs in Ch. 4. As we can assume Ezekiel's hair and beard had grown long when he cut them off as the Lord instructs him, this was a visible symbolic sign-act. Shaving one's head was associated with mourning – Ezek. 7:18, and may have initially been interpreted by the exiles a sign of grief or self-inflicted disgrace.[30] Also shaving one's head was totally forbidden to priests and for Ezekiel it was likely to have been humiliating and emotionally embarrassing. But this is not a random act, he is to carefully weigh his hair on a balance (scales) and divide the hair into three parts, and he is to dispose of the hair on the model of Jerusalem made of brick as the Lord instructs him. Carefully weighing his hair in the balance emphasises the significance of this symbolic act to the exiles that the Lord's judgment on Jerusalem, 'is not haphazard, but deliberate and carefully measured.'[31] This indicates the fate of the besieged city is sealed. Eichrodt interprets this symbolic sign-act of Ezekiel's hair as 'a cynically mocking process as no one would ever weigh their hair in scales.'[32]

This sign-act has two dramatic parts. Firstly, Ezekiel is to dispose of his hair. Secondly, he is to keep a remnant of it. What is striking is that he divides his hair into three parts. It is disposed of in three different ways, and the expression 'take for yourself' –

'laqah leka' occurs three times.[33] The first third of his hair is to be
set on fire in the centre of the city. Fire in the OT is a symbol of
destruction and represented the practice of razing a city to the
ground. Ezekiel burning his hair when the days of the siege have
ended symbolises the fate of Jerusalem and dashes any hope the
exiles may have had of returning. The second portion of hair that
is to be struck with the sword and scattered around the city,
represents the violent death of those who escape the destruction of
the city but suffer at the hands of Nebuchadnezzar. At the end of
v. 2, the Lord is the one who wields the sword and identifies
himself as the one who brings judgment on the city. The third part
of hair that Ezekiel scatters in the wind symbolises the dispersion
and disappearance of the remaining population. 'Like those who
fall to the fire and the sword, they will be lost forever to the
history of the people of God. The cumulative effect of these three
actions is to emphasis the totality of the impending judgment.'[34]
From his hair that Ezekiel was to scatter in the wind, the Lord
instructs him to save a small number of hairs and secure them in
the hem of his garment. These represent a small number in
Jerusalem who will escape the Lord's judgment.

INTERPRETATION OF SIGNS – 5: 5-17

"Thus says the Lord God: This is Jerusalem, I have set her in
the centre of the nations with countries round about her. And she
has wickedly rebelled against my ordinances more than the
nations, and against my statutes more than the countries round
about her, by rejecting my ordinances and not walking in my
statutes. Therefore, thus says the Lord God: Because you are more
turbulent than the nations that are round about you, and have not
walked in my statutes or kept my ordinances, but have acted
according to the ordinances of the nations that are round about
you, therefore thus says the Lord God: Behold, I even I, am
against you, and will execute judgment in the midst of the nations.
And because of all your abominations I will do with you what I
have never done, and the like of which I will never do again.
Therefore fathers shall eat their sons in the midst of you, and sons

shall eat their fathers, and I will execute judgment on you, and any of you who survive I will scatter to all the winds. Wherefore as I live says the Lord God, surely because you have defiled my sanctuary with all your detestable things and with all your abominations, therefore I will cut you down, my eye will not spare and I will have no pity. A third part of you shall die of pestilence and be consumed with famine in the midst of you, as third part shall fall by the sword round about you, and a third part I will scatter to the winds.

Thus shall my anger spend itself and I will vent my fury upon them and satisfy myself, and they shall know that I, the Lord, have spoken in my jealousy when I spend my fury upon them. Moreover, I will make you a desolation and an object of reproach among the nations round about you and in the sight of all that pass by. You shall be a reproach and a taunt, a warning and a horror, to the nations round about you when I execute judgments on you in anger and fury, and with furious chastisements – I the Lord, have spoken – when I loose against you my deadly arrows of famine, arrows for destruction which I will loose to destroy you, and when I bring more and more famine upon you, and break your staff of bread. I will send famine and wild beasts against you, and they will rob you of your children: pestilence and blood shall pass through you, and I will bring the sword upon you. I, the Lord, have spoken.''

Any possibility the siege enacted by Ezekiel represents a city other than Jerusalem is now completely ruled out. Daniel Block posits that vs. 5-17 consist of 'a remarkable collage of sayings, which, in its present literary form, is best classified as a complex prophetic judgment speech.'[35] Verses 5-17 divide into two sections: 5-10 and 11-17. Verses 5-10 consist of the indictment of Jerusalem that is followed by two accusations and two respective judgments. The structure and vocabulary of the prophetic speech in 5-17, 'display heavy influence from proceedings conducted in courts of law.'[36] In v. 5 when the Lord says 'This is Jerusalem' – he formally introduces the city, the accused as in a trial conducted in a court of law, accompanied by the charges-indictments that in turn are followed by the Lord's judgments. Jerusalem is charged with rebellion against the Lord's laws and the abominations erected in the temple. Moreover, her rebellion exceeds even that of the pagan nations. Chapters 8-11 expound that Jerusalem is no longer God's residence and her privileged status among the nations has been forfeited. 'According to Deut. 4:7-8, Israel's covenantal obligations to Yahweh were the envy of the nations: none of them had received such a just set of laws from its god. However, instead of treasuring the revealed will of Yahweh as a sign of divine grace, Israel adopted her neighbour's wicked patterns of behaviour.'[37]

Consequently, the Lord declares his judgment on Jerusalem, with the formal announcement, 'Therefore, thus has the Lord declared, because you are more turbulent than the nations that surround you, and have not walked in my statutes or kept my ordinances, but have acted according to the nations that are round about you, therefore thus says the Lord God: Behold, I, even I, am against you: and I will execute judgments in the midst of you in the sight of the nations' – v. 7-8. The announcement comes twice in v.7-8, 'Thus has the Lord declared' – *koh amar adonay yhwh, and* occurs in a variety of combinations over twenty four times in Ezekiel.'[38] This double emphasis reiterates the seriousness of the Lord's charges against Jerusalem. 'Turbulent' in the RSV – v. 7, in Hebrew is riotous uproar derived from the Hebrew *hmn* 'to rage, riot' that is closely related to *hama,* to roar, be boisterous, that refers to the roar of the waves, that describes Jerusalem's sin,[39] which is an affront to the law of God.[40] Especially, as in the Lord's eyes the city had the privileged position of her election being central among the nations. 'This involved a missiological as well as a theological responsibility for Israel to be a light to the nations.'[41] But Jerusalem's behaviour turned out to be worse than the pagan nations she should have been a witness to.

Therefore, Jerusalem elicits the full force of the Lord's covenant wrath as he declares, 'Behold, I, even I, am against you, and I will execute my judgments in the midst of you in the sight of the nations' – 5:8. Verses 9-17 provide a description of the horrific consequences of the abominable and detestable practices that had defiled his sanctuary and were taking place in the temple in Jerusalem. So abhorrent to the Lord is the sin of the city that in these verses the Lord announces his judgment on his people, as the city's unprecedented sin has resulted in the unprecedented judgment of cannibalism. This covenantal curse is found in Lev. 26:29, 'You shall eat the flesh of your sons, and the flesh of your daughters you will eat.' The word abominations occurs forty-three times in Ezekiel and far outweighs its occurrence in the other prophets.[42] Verses 9-17 give an insight into the Lord's unbridled wrath against his own people and the extreme judgment the Lord exacts on them may appear vindictive to us and offend our 21st century sensibilities and perception of a loving God. 'With our comfortable per-ceptions of deity, we may be so offended by the sheer terror of Yahweh's pronouncements and the violence of the divine disposition, that we dismiss it as irrelevant or sub-Christian. While these reactions may be natural, we must not let them detract from the profoundly theological nature of the message comm-unicated by Ezekiel's first dramatic performances.'[43]

Ezekiel along with Jeremiah reveal the Lord's response in his covenant relationship with Israel when they committed apostasy and idolatry, and in Ezekiel's day were involved in abominable practices in the temple. For example, in Jer. Ch. 2 the Lord reveals his deep love for his people and like a spurned lover he pours out his heart at the loss of his loved one Israel. The Lord declares his love for his people and calls them to repent and return to their first love for him. Tragically, this was unreciprocated. Consequently, we perceive a great sense of loss, as the Lord is heartbroken by his peoples' failure. Jer. Ch 2:4 sums up what happened to God's people: 'They went far from the Lord' – because they turned to idols and failed to worship him. There are four key words in Ch. 2 that describe God's people.

      4-8: they were FAITHLESS to the Lord.

      9-13: they had FORSAKEN the Lord.

      14-28: they were FEARLESS-had no fear of the Lord.

      29-32 the people had FORGOTTEN the Lord.

Faithless: forsaken: fearless: forgotten: these are four charges in
Jer. Ch. 2 the Lord brings against Israel as in a court case. As New
Testament Christians, what Ezekiel and Jeremiah both reveal to us
is an aspect of God's holy character that we may overlook. The
Lord made us in his image and this reflects he also has profound
feelings in his relationship with his people.

The first declaration of the Lord's judgment in Ezekiel 5:7-10,
is followed by the second in vs. 11-17, as the Lord makes an oath
in his own name about the horrific judgments he is   will execute
on his own people, because of their abominable sins committed in
the temple as they desecrated his sanctuary. 'Therefore, as I live
says the Lord God' – v. 11, declares that the Lord swears by his
own self/life, and asserts there is no higher authority than himself
that guarantees the irrevocable nature of his judgments. In vs. 11-
17 the Lord also reveals his response to his peoples' sins. In his
judgment, he expresses his divine jealousy as he shall 'spend his
anger on' and 'vent his fury' and 'his furious chastisements of
famine, pestilence and destruction' – 5:13-16 upon them. God's
people brought upon themselves the covenant curses that resulted
from Israel's disobedience to God's commandments and statutes
recorded in Lev. Ch. 26 and Deut. Ch. 28. The Lord declared he
was going to show no mercy and no pity to his own people –
v. 11. As Ezekiel's audience grasped the significance of his
symbolic actions in chs. 4-5, they are likely to have been shocked
as they would have expected God's enemies to be on the receiving
end of his judgments. But the Lord's intention was not just to
punish his people for their disobedience, it was to remind them of
his character as the sovereign God in his covenant relationship
with them. 'Like Yahweh's mighty acts of deliverance centuries
earlier, his acts of judgment on a rebellious people are intentionally designed to bring them to an acknowledgement of his
presence, character, and claims on their lives.'[42] Block captures
the significance of God's judgment in Ch. 5 when he says,
'The final statement in v. 13 is the key to the chapter, if not to
Ezekiel's prophetic ministry as a whole. Yahweh's announcement
of the impending destruction of Jerusalem and the decimation of

its population has been *driven* by his passion. The word *qin'a* occurs frequently in Ezekiel's preaching. Rather than interpreting this term as *'jealousy'* which is often associated with envy, one should understand *qin'a* to represent the fire of divine passion, Yahweh's enthusiasm for his covenant relationship with Israel. He had not entered into this relationship lightly, and he cannot stand by idly while it is threatened. The intensity of his wrath at the defilement of his sanctuary and the repudiation of his will arises out of the profundity of his covenant love. Because he loves so deeply, he must respond vigorously. His relationship with his people has been violated."[45]

JUDGMENT ON HIGH PLACES – 6: 1-14

'The word of the Lord came to me, "Son of man, set your face toward the mountains of Israel and prophesy against them, and say, You mountains of Israel hear the word of the Lord God. Thus says the Lord God to the mountains and the hills, to the ravines and the valleys: Behold, I, even I, will bring a sword upon you and I will destroy your high places. Your altars shall become desolate and your incense altars shall be broken: and I will cast down your slain before your idols. And I will lay the dead bodies of the people of Israel before their idols, and I will scatter your bones round about your altars. Wherever you dwell your cities shall be waste and your high places ruined, so that your altars will be waste and ruined, your idols broken and destroyed, your incense altars cut down and your works wiped out. And the slain shall fall in the midst of you and you shall know that I am the Lord.

Yet I will leave some of you alive. When you have among the nations some who escape the sword and when you are scattered through the countries, then those of you who escape will remember me among the nations where they are carried captive. When I have broken their wanton heart which has departed from me, and their blinded eyes which turn wantonly after their idols: and they will be loathsome in their own sight for the evils which they have committed, for all their abominations. And they shall know that I am the Lord. I have not said in vain that I would do this evil to them.''

Thus says the Lord God, ''Clap your hands and stamp your foot and say, Alas! Because of all the evil abominations of the house of Israel – for they shall fall by the sword, by famine and pestilence. He that is far off shall die of pestilence and he that is near shall fall by the sword, and he that is left and is preserved shall die of famine. Thus I will spend my fury upon them. And you shall know that I am the Lord when their slain lie among the idols, round about their altars, upon every high hill, on all the mountain tops, under every green tree, and under every leafy oak, wherever they offered pleasing odor to all their idols. And I will stretch out my hand against them and make the land desolate and waste, throughout all their habitations, from the wilderness to Riblah. Then they will know they I am the Lord.''

Chapter six begins with a new revelation and a hostile decl-aration from the Lord directed at the 'mountains of Israel' that occurs seventeen times in Ezekiel but nowhere else in the OT. In Hebrew, 'Stylistically the passage is marked by a uniform repetitiveness, involving alliteration rhyme, parallelism and synonyms...and the passage is a rich blend of motifs.'[46] 'Mountains of Israel' alludes to the landscape of Palestine dominated by a ridge of mountains running the entire length of the country from north to south where Jerusalem was located. Ezekiel's reference to the mountains and hills, ravines and valleys, embraces his vision of the entire landscape of Israel. The Lord's declaration to the 'mountains of Israel' refers to the widespread idolatrous shrines built on every high hill and mountaintop. From the beginning, high places had an important connection in Israel's life early history (1 Sam. 9:11-25, 10:5, 1 Kings. 3:4). 'When Israel came into the Promised Land, the existing 'high places' of the inhabitants become initial sites also of her worship. Thus the Lord was worshipped on the hilltops well before there was a temple in Jerusalem, an attachment to them was deep in the heart of the people.'[47] Hilltops often served as sites for cultic rituals. In valleys and within city walls high places were artificially constructed, where the central feature was a raised platform on which rituals were performed. Canaanite rituals with animal and human sacrifices, ritual copulations and orgiastic meals were perform-ed on many of the high places. Hezekiah (2 Kings 18:4 and Josiah 2 Kings 23:4-20) attempted to eradicate these evils practices, but without success. The hostile oracle from the Lord now announces the time has come for him to rid the land of its pagan worship.[48] The Lord was going to destroy their altars, their chapels, and their high places and their idols. Violent language describes the Lord's hostile action, as their altars will be broken and desolate, and their chapels smashed, which housed the pagan deities in which their rituals were performed that would be eradicated. The Lord would eliminate and wipe out 'every vestige of idolatry.'[49] The Hebrew for idols is *gillulim* and this occurs three times in Ch. 6, and 39 out of 48 uses are found in Ezekiel. Modern sensitivities prevented translators from interpreting *gillulim* as Ezekiel intended it, as he would have used a four letter word for excrement. However, Daniel Bodi captures his intended sense with his translation – *'shitgods.'*[50] Hummel translates *gillulim* as 'fecal deities' although he views this as a santisied version![51]

However, the Lord does not only target the idolatrous inst-allations with his wrath, his people too are victims of his wrath. This is alluded to by a horrific image of corpses-dead bodies with their bones scattered around their altars. A shocking image as they are denied a proper burial and final resting place with their bodies left to the mercy of scavengers and vultures. Their corpses defile and pollute the local sanctuaries designating them obsolete and their idols impotent. This horror evokes the threat of ignominy the ancient world attached to the lack of a decent burial.[52] The consequence of the Lord's divine judgment results in complete annihilation as the peoples' bones are scattered and their works-memory wiped out. The result of the Lord's divine judgment is that his people would know that 'I am the Lord' – 6:7. 'You shall know that I am Yahweh,' is found around 60 times in Ezekiel.[53]

The Lord's devastating judgment is not the last word as his next oracle – 8-10, offers a remnant of the survivors in exile a glimmer of hope they will remember the Lord in a foreign land. Remembering involves recollecting the past and God's saving acts on behalf of Israel and is not just a rational act. It involves repentance as an act of faith in response to the Lord leading to a renewal of their relationship with the Lord. Ezekiel's older contemporary Jeremiah prophesied about the survival of a remnant – Jer. 31, and Ezekiel's symbolic sign-act of preserving a few of his hairs in the folds of his garment also points to the survival of a remnant. The peoples' repentance and spiritual renewal will only take place after they realise the Lord was *'heartbroken'* by their wanton heart – 6:9, which is a more accurate translation of the Hebrew than the RSV's, 'when I have broken their wanton heart. This refers to the Lord's relationship with Israel that is likened to a marriage covenant. In Hebrew the RSV's 'wanton heart' is more accurately, *'whoring or promiscuous heart.'* Their repentance will lead to a self-loathing for all the abominable evils they committed. They will loathe themselves when they see how unfaithful they were and how depraved they have become. As a result of the Lord's judgment the survival of a remnant who remember and repent of their evil abominations will know the Lord – 6:10.

The oracle Ezekiel is instructed by the Lord to announce in 11-17 is essentially a repetition of the first part of Ch. 11. But it is accompanied by an action prophesy from Ezekiel who the Lord instructs, 'Clap your hands, and stamp your foot, and say, Alas! Because of all the evil abominations of the house of Israel, for they shall fall by the sword, by famine and by pestilence' – 6:11. Ezekiel represents the Lord in this action that symbolises his anger at their abominations and his action expresses intense emotion that indicates how strongly the Lord feels about their idolatry and sins. The clapping of hands could express celebratory joy, anger or derision, but in this context of the Lord's wrath, it stands for his anger. Also, the outward gestures of clapping hands and stamping feet were to give a dramatic emphasis to the indignation and sorrow of the Lord. In 22:13 the Lord says, 'Behold, therefore, I strike my hands together at the dishonest gain you have made and at the blood which has been in the midst of you,' and this also expresses his anger. As Ezekiel stamps his feet this is a sign of the Lord's wrath. This action can also refer to trampling one's enemies and points to the Lord's judgment in a vivid visual aid. And in the latter part of Ch. 6, the Lord declares he will stretch out his hand against his people to reinforce his judgment so they will know he is the Lord.

THE DAY OF THE LORD – 7: 1-13

'The word of the Lord came to me: "And you son of man, thus says the Lord God to the land of Israel: An end! The end has come upon the four corners of the land. Now the end is upon you and I will let loose my anger upon you, and I will judge you according to your ways, and I will punish you for all your abominations. And my eye will not spare you, nor will I have pity on you, but I will punish you for your ways, while your abominations are in your midst. Then you will know that I am the Lord."

"Thus says the Lord God: Disaster upon disaster! Behold, it comes. And end has come, the end has come: it has awakened against you. Behold it comes. Your doom has come to you, O inhabitants of the land. The time has come. The day is near. A day of tumult, and not of joyful shouting upon the mountains. Now I will soon pour out my wrath upon you and spend my anger against you, and judge you according to your ways, and I will punish you for all your abominations. And my eye will not spare, nor will I have pity. I will punish you according to your ways, while your abominations are in your midst. Then you will know that I am the Lord who smite."

"Behold, the day! Behold, it comes! Your doom has come, injustice has blossomed, pride has budded. Violence has grown up into a rod of wickedness. None of them shall remain, nor their abundance, not their wealth: neither shall there be preeminence among them. The time has come. The day draws near. Let not the buyer rejoice, nor the seller mourn for wrath is upon all their multitude. For the seller shall not return to what he sold while they live. For wrath is upon all their multitude. It shall not turn back, and because of his iniquity, none can maintain his life."

Chapter 7, in a poetic like staccato style, abruptly announces an alarming new oracle from the Lord, couched in distinctly apocalyptic and eschatological language. Linguistically, vs. 2-9 are noticeably full of repetition and the entire chapter is marked by a heightened emotional intensity, and 'presents at least as many problems as the inaugural vision in Ch. 1.'[54] 'Disaster upon disaster is more accurately translated, 'Disaster! An exceptional disaster.'[55] Moshe Greenberg eloquently says, 'Language and ideas characteristic of Ezekiel are combined in our chapter with an unusually rich array of poetic elements echoing passages from elsewhere in the Bible. Abrupt changes in perspective, obscurity, even incoherence (v. 11b) bespeak a passion and excitement that could not be contained in the prophet's usual prosaic framework, and that sought release in language and figure drawn from a reservoir of Hebrew poetry evidently known to him. As in the few other instances in which he demonstrated his poetic range (e.g. chs. 21, 28:11-19) the modern interpreter encounters insuperable difficulties in following him.'[56]

Ch. 7. in Hebrew begins abruptly with one word that has no definite article – 'end' and occurs five times in the first seven verses. Its brevity and suddenness accentuate the impending disaster. The Lord instructs Ezekiel to announce the 'end' three times in succession – vs. 2-3. In Hebrew, the first occasion is a one word sentence, 'An end.' Then comes a two word sentence, 'Comes – 'the end.' Then follows a three word sentence, 'Now – the end – upon you.'[57] The initial staccato like utterances of the oracle in Ch. 7, are like the opening movement (sonata) of a symphony that builds into a crescendo of heavy hammer strokes of destruction. In v. 2, the 'end' first announced to the land of Israel concerning the 'four corners of the land,' refers to an apocalyptic and eschatological judgment. The allusion to the land represents health and economic wellbeing: addressed to the exiles it has a special poignancy, as opposed to dwelling and belonging in one's land, being in exile hints at a life of 'perpetual vagrancy and wandering.'[58]

'The end has come' – v. 2, is the opening note, an alarming sound from Ezekiel as a watchman that conveys an urgency at the horror to be played out. When he repeats, 'Now the end is upon you' – v. 3, this heralds the ominous note of judgment that will arrive. This prophetic formula 'the end has come,' conveyed to Ezekiel's audience an image of sheer terror, especially as the Lord's oracles proceed to describe in detail the impending doom. But God's judgment is not vague, his oracles unambiguously declare that his punishment is because of their abominable sins. The first oracle reveals the Lord's wrath: 'I will let loose my anger upon you according to your ways, and I will punish you for all your abominations' – v. 2. 'And my eye will not spare you, nor will I have pity: but I will punish you for your ways, while your abominations are in your midst' – v. 4. The first oracle concludes with the words, 'Then you will know that I am the Lord' – v. 4, and is a refrain that is repeated at the end of the second oracle in v. 9, and also at the end of the third oracle in v. 27. Although up to now, Ezekiel has already declared God's judgment in horrific terms in chs. 5 and 6, what will become apparent in Ch. 7, is that the Lord's judgment will be linked to the 'Day of the Lord' which Israel believed represented the Lord's judgment on the nations, but is now ironically destined for them instead.

In our modern sensibilities, one may view God in Ezekiel as vindictive as this negates his steadfast love and mercy, and he may appear ruthless in his judgments. Daniel Block says, 'While some marginalise this deity by speaking of him as a creation of Ezekiel's mind, others find the God of Ezekiel to be a narcisstic, self-absorbed, ruthless and graceless deity.'[59] David Halperin sees Ezekiel's God as, 'a monster of cruelty and hypocrisy' whose restoration of Israel is driven by 'his thirst for self-aggrandisement,' his obsessive fear that no one is going to know who he is.'[60] Biblical scholars acknowledge the Lord's wrath and judgment in His oracles to Ezekiel, result from the consequence of Israel's disobedience and abominable sins, clearly spelt out by the Lord in the covenant he made with Israel. God's character revealed in the covenant resulted in the Lord upholding the curse

of the covenant Israel inflicted on herself. The Lord also chose
Israel to be a witness to Him and be light to the nations, but she
failed miserably. To redeem Israel's failure and uphold the honour
of his name, the Lord carries out the curses as his judgment and
punishment on Israel's disobedience and sin. But the Lord saves a
remnant, to acknowledge his peoples' spiritual renewal can only
come by a work of his grace. 'A new heart I will give you, and a
new spirit I will put within you: and I will take out of your flesh
the heart of stone and give you a heart of flesh' – Ezek. 36:26. An
integral aspect of the Lord's judgment was for his people to come
to a realisation of their sins and feel a sense of shame and remorse,
that is captured by the phrase 'they will be loathsome in their
sight' – 6:9. Jacqueline Lapsley captures the transformative outcome of the people coming to loath themselves in 36:31 when she
says:

> In sum, for Ezekiel sin is not an inherent part of
> human identity, a 'given' of the human condition, but
> something bestowed by an external source. But the
> inversion of conventional thinking about shame goes
> even further: the very capacity to experience shame
> constitutes a salvific act by Yahweh – it is a gift from
> God. The disgrace-shame is a gift from God because it
> strips the peoples' delusions about themselves, their
> old self disintegrates, paving the way for the peoples'
> identity to be shaped by a new self-knowledge that
> results from the experience of shame. And this new
> identity, in which people see themselves as 'they really
> are' as Yahweh sees them, will ultimately lead to a
> restoration of their relationship with Yahweh.[61]

The second oracle in vs. 5-9, reiterates the day of the Lord's
judgment has arrived, and this is emphatically stressed by the
words, 'disaster,' 'the end,' 'doom,' and 'tumult.' The Lord's
condemnation of his peoples' abominable sins in vs. 5-9 repeats
the same indictments from vs. 2-4 and this second oracle of doom
also has 'many parallels' with verses 2-4.[62] The staccato rhythm of

the oracle hammers home a message of judgment, 'Disaster after disaster. Behold, it comes. An end has come: the end has come' – v. 5. This also includes a sixfold repetition of 'comes/has come' in vs. 5-9. The Lord's judgment was aimed at the land in vs. 2-4 and now its target is the inhabitants of the land – v. 7. The motif of the 'day' – a day of tumult, and not of joyful shouting' – v.7, is echoed in the third oracle in v. 10 – 'Behold, the day,' and also in v. 19, 'the day of the wrath of the Lord.' The allusion to 'the day' was a well established concept that Amos and Isaiah refers to (Isa. Ch. 2), along with Hosea. The motif of 'the Day of the Lord' signified the Lord meeting with his people, and his intervention in human history determined by the Lord on Israel's behalf.[63] It signalled God overcoming his peoples' enemies, and the victories the Lord won for his people over their enemies as they entered the Promised Land, gave rise to a tradition that the Lord intervened on behalf of his people in history to subdue other nations. But there was also a new and all-but-unbelievable element in the message of Amos and his prophetic contemporaries: the people of the covenant are to be the objects of the destructive action of the Lord. We see this when Amos refers to the day of the Lord as, 'Woe to you who desire the day of the Lord. Why would you have the day of the Lord? It is darkness and not light' – Amos 5:16. The climax of the day of the Lord will result in the people acknowledging it is the Lord who acted in judgment against them, 'Then they will know that I am the Lord, who smite' – Ezek. 7:9, which is virtually a repetition of 7:4.

The third and longest oracle warning of impending disaster in v. 10 continues to the end of Ch. 7:27, and the brevity of the Hebrew indicates heightened alarm or grief.[64] But here the peoples' injustice, pride, violence and wickedness, are identified by the Lord as the cause for their destruction. These vices deemed to have 'blossomed,' was an allusion to the budding of Aaron's staff that was a sign of his election. Ezekiel's use of this metaphor is turned on its head, 'into an emblematic cudgel of oppression and wickedness.'[65] The use of 'blossomed' indicates growth, but in keeping with the botanical allusion, the vices referred to and the people who practiced them shall be cut down. Their 'doom' has been announced – 7:10. 'None of them shall remain: nor their abundance: nor their wealth: neither shall their be preeminence among them' – 7:11. 'Man's destruction is the 'flowering' of his activity.'[66] Verses 11-13, outline the devastating collapse of all business and commercial life that results in financial ruin, as the day of the Lord's wrath draws near and affects everyone – the multitude. Everyone will be helpless to save themselves from the coming onslaught on the day of the Lord's wrath – 7:13.

AN ALARMING HUMBLING – 7:14-27

"They have blown the trumpet and made all ready, but none goes to battle for my wrath is upon all their multitude. The sword is without, pestilence and famine are within: he that is in the field dies by the sword, and he that is in the city famine and pestilence devour. And if any survivors escape they will be on the mountains, like doves of the valleys, all of them moaning, every one over his iniquity. All hands are feeble, and all knees weak as water. They gird themselves with sackcloth and horror covers them: shame is upon all their faces and baldness on all their heads. They cast their silver into the streets and their gold is like an unclean thing: their silver and gold are not able to deliver them in the day of the Lord's wrath: they cannot satisfy their hunger or fill their stomachs with it. For it was the stumbling block of their iniquity. Their beautiful ornament they used for vainglory, and they made their abominable images and their detestable things of it, therefore I will make it an unclean thing to them. And I will give it into the hands of foreigners for a prey, and to the wicked of the earth for a spoil: and they shall profane it, and make a desolation."

"Because the land is full of bloody crimes and the city is full of violence, I will bring the worst of the nations to take possession of their houses: I will put an end to their proud might, and their holy places shall be profaned. When anguish comes they will seek peace, but there shall be none. Disaster comes upon disaster, rumour follows rumour. They seek a vision from the prophet, but the law perishes from the priest, and the counsel from the elders. The king mourns, the prince is wrapped in despair, and the hands of the people of the land are palsied by terror. According to their way I will do to them, and according to their own judgments I will judge them, and they shall know that I am the Lord.''

Although the word humbled does not appear in the passage, a dreadful and terrifying humbling of God's people occurs. Eichrodt's headings for Ch: 7 are, 'judgment on all pomp' – 'judgment upon accumulated riches' – 'judgment upon the temple.'[67] This judgment involves an alarming and sustained humbling as the Lord announced his peoples' way of life was coming to an end, because the day of the Lord's wrath had been unleashed on them – 7:19. The irreversible fate of the people had been sealed. There was no escape.

Verses 11-13, speak of the devastating collapse of business and commerce that will result in financial ruin, because of the day of the Lord's wrath. 'The collapse of the economy will be total, rendering all business transactions futile.'[68] After the economic and emotional affects of the disaster there follows the physiological impact, as everyone's strength and courage will fail them – 'every hand will hang limp' – 7:17. Also, in 7:17, 'All knees will flow with water,' from the Greek is literally translated, 'and all their knees will run with urine.' The loss of bladder control occurs when the people are fleeing from their enemies in a moment of extreme crisis.[69] As a result, 'They gird themselves with sackcloth, and horror covers them: shame is upon all their faces, and baldness upon all their heads' – 7:18. These events express forms of grief, and the Hebrew in this verse describes shuddering like a garment to cover ones self, along with the shame that accompanies it.[70] After the physiological impact, follows the psychological effect of the day of the Lord's wrath, when the people are emotionally paralysed, 'horror covers them,' overtakes them – 7:18. In the midst of the Lord's terrifying judgment there will be a remnant that remains, 'And if any survivors escape, they will be on the mountains, like doves of the valleys, all of them moaning, every one over his iniquity' – 7:16. The simile of moaning like doves indicates the people will lament the disaster that has happened to them. Moaning may also point to doves cooing, and people sobbing relentlessly at the dawning awareness that their sins have been the cause of their plight.

The day of the Lord's wrath will also affect the value of their gold and silver as it will not buy them food, and it cannot provide them security. They have in effect become bankrupt. Moreover, their accumulated wealth led to their becoming proud (vainglory). In turn, their hubris resulted in them making idols of gold and silver into abominable images, but their gold and silver cannot save them from the Lord's wrath – 19-20. The peoples' wealth became the 'stumbling block of their iniquity' – v. 19 as they misused it to make idols. We shall see in Ch. 8, that they also misused the temple treasure, desecrating it by making disgusting pagan images from the temple gold and silver in God's sanctuary. Block says 'For the moment, Ezekiel simply alludes to the utilisation of the temple treasures for the fashioning of images as the height of arrogance. Instead of patterning their own lives after the will of Yahweh, and sanctifying his house with true worship, the Israelites have fashioned gods, rivals to their covenant Lord, after their own imagination. They should not be surprised then at the fury of Yahweh's passion, or at his determination to destroy them. This reaction is in precise keeping with his character, which was also reflected in his earlier warnings (Deut. 4:25-28).'[71]

As a result, of the misuse of the peoples' wealth they have aroused the Lord's wrath, consequently the Lord declares his judgment – v. 20. The Lord will make their precious objects of gold and silver tarnished, worthless. More emphatically, so repulsive is their idolatrous behaviour, the Lord will deliver their precious wealth into the hands of foreigners. A ruthless enemy described as the 'wicked of the earth' – v. 21, who will carry off the temple treasures. In hindsight, we know this refers to Nebuchadnezzar and the Babylonians ransacking Jerusalem and destroying the temple. So reprehensible and shocking has the peoples' idolatrous behaviour been over a sustained period of years, the Lord distances himself from them. So grievous and offensive is the peoples' sin that involves violent crimes committed by the leaders against the ordinary people, including the blood of innocent victims, the Lord is left with no choice but to turn his face away from his holy sanctuary in the temple: and 'robbers shall enter and profane it, and make it a desolation. Because the land is full of bloody crimes, and the city is full of violence, I will bring the worst of the nations to take possessions of their houses: I will put an end to their proud might, and their holy places shall be profaned' – v. 22-24. The Lord has turned his back on his chosen place that symbolised his glory and presence – the temple in Jerusalem, God's city.

Just as the sins of the people have multiplied, so too the fury of the Lord's wrath has escalated and climaxes in a tidal wave of judgment that will overwhelm them. Once again, a staccato refrain sounds the alarming nature of what lies ahead. Anguish will come: there will be no peace: disaster comes upon disaster: prophets have no vision: the law perishes from the priest: the king mourns: the prince despairs and the people are paralysed with fear – 25-27. This results in comprehensive and sustained judgment that envelops the king, the prophet, the priest, the prince, and the people. No strata of society is exempt as the entire nation's economic, political, religious and social structures disintegrate. Just as at the end of the first oracle in v. 4, and at the end of the second oracle in v. 9, so too now at the end of the third oracle in v. 27, the Lord's intention is that his people acknowledge and recognise that He is the one who has executed his judgment upon them. Hummel concludes his comments on Ch. 7, when he says, 'The antepenultimate and penultimate clauses of the chapter are chilling – 'According to their way I will do to them, and according to their own judgments I will judge them: and they shall know that I am the Lord' – v. 27.'[72]

Between chapters 4-7, the Lord's anger, his fury, his judgment, and the Day of the Lord's wrath, was announced and executed against his people, for their abominable apostasy and idolatry in the land and in the temple. As we progress further into the Book of Ezekiel, we will encounter God's justice and indignation at his peoples' offences against him. We can barely imagine how devastating it was to experience them first hand. Ezekiel challenges us to pause and reflect on God's holy character and the aspect of his nature that cannot but judge sin. Christ himself referred to the 'Day of Judgment' in his ministry: for example in Math. 10:14-15, 11:20-24, 12:38-42 and 25:31-46. As we declare the Gospel of Salvation in and through Christ alone, are we more concerned to make it 'accessible' or do we have the courage and integrity to speak about God's righteous character and his judgment as an integral aspect of the Gospel? In our day, do we nullify the 'Day of Judgment' by omitting it, as we declare the Gospel of Christ?

CHAPTER FOUR

ORACLES AGAINST ISRAEL
8: 11: 12: 16: 17: 19: 20: 22: 24
ABOMINATIONS IN THE TEMPLE – 8:1-18

'In the sixth year, in the sixth month, on the fifth day of the month, as I sat in my house with the elders of Judah before me, the hand of the Lord God fell there upon me. Then I beheld, and lo, a form that had the appearance of a man, below what appeared to be his loins it was fire, and above his loins it was like the appearance of brightness, gleaming bronze. He put forth the form of a hand, and took me by a lock of my head, and the Spirit lifted me up between earth and heaven, and brought me in visions of God to Jerusalem, to the entrance of the gateway of the inner court that faces north, where was the seat of the image of jealousy. And behold, the glory of the God of Israel was there, like the vision that I saw in the plain.

Then he said to me, ''Son of man, lift up your eyes now in the direction of the north.'' So I lifted up my eyes towards the north, and behold, north of the altar gate, in the entrance was this image of jealousy. And he said to me, ''Son of man, do you see what they are doing, the great abominations that the house of Israel are committing here, to drive me far from my sanctuary? But you will see still greater abominations.''

And he brought me to the door of the court and when I looked, behold, there was a hole in the wall. Then he said to me, ''Son of man, dig in the wall'' and when I dug in the wall, lo, there was a door. And he said to me, ''Go in and see the vile abominations that they are committing here.'' So I went in and saw, and there portrayed upon the wall round about were all kinds of creeping things, and loathsome beasts, and all the idols of the house of Israel. And before them stood seventy men of the elders of the house of Israel, with Jaazaniah the son of Shaphan standing among them. Each had his censer in his hand and the smoke of the cloud of incense went up. Then he said to me, 'Son of man, have you seen what the elders of the house of Israel are doing in the dark, every man in his room of pictures? For they say, 'The Lord does not see us, the Lord has forsaken the land.' He also said to me "You will see still greater abominations which they commit."

Then he brought me to the entrance of the north gate of the house of the Lord and behold, there sat women weeping for Tammuz. Then he said to me, "Have you seen this, O son of man? You will see still greater abominations than these."

And he brought me into the inner court of the house of the Lord, and behold, at the door of the temple of the Lord, between the porch and the altar were about twenty-five men, with their backs to the temple of the Lord, and their faces toward the east, worshipping the sun toward the east. Then he said to me, "Have you seen this, O Son of man? Is it too slight a thing for the house of Judah to commit the abominations which they commit here, that they should fill the land with violence, and provoke me further to anger? Lo, they put the branch to their nose. Therefore, I will deal in wrath: my eye will not spare, now will I have pity: and though they cry in my ears with a loud voice, I will not hear them."

Biblical scholars acknowledge there is a problem with the flow of the narrative in chs. 8-11, that is the result of editorial redaction. This is readily apparent as Ch. 10 diverges from Ch. 9 where the glory of the Lord leaves the temple and God's judgment is carried out. Also, Ch. 11:14 is deemed to have been an independent unit integrated into the account of the temple. Despite this, chs. 8-11 presents itself as single visionary experience.[1]

The main theme in this unique, pivotal visionary narrative in Ezekiel 8-11, is the departure of the glory of the Lord from the temple in Jerusalem, along with the ensuing judgment because of the disgusting abominable idolatrous practices of the elders in the temple. Ch. 8 begins with a chronological date that records Ezekiel sitting in his house with the elders of Judah, around fourteen months after his inaugural vision that confirms his confinement in his home. Keeping a record of the significant dates in his memoirs after the fall of Jerusalem would validate the claims of the oracles he announced prior to this happening. (Biblical commentators calculate the date was September 18th 592 BC).'This is explicit in 24:2 (and 33:33) when Ezekiel is given prophetic information about the beginning of the siege of Jerusalem, news of which would not, of course, reach the exiles in Babylon for several months (it was almost 1000 miles from Jerusalem).'[2] Although the text is silent about why the elders visited Ezekiel, it is likely they had come to consult him about his symbolic sign-acts and their meaning, or to seek an oracle from the Lord about the future of the exiles and Jerusalem. (The elders will also visit Ezekiel in 14:1 and 20:1 when they come to enquire of the Lord). The Lord did indeed have an oracle for them, but it was one of judgment. As Ezekiel's ecstatic visionary trance takes place, the elders are present. (The elders represented the form of self-government of the exiles in Babylon, that Jeremiah sent a letter to – Jer. 29:1).

The narrative in Ch. 8 records Ezekiel's encounter with the Lord when once again the hand of the Lord fell upon him – v. 1. This indicates the sudden and overwhelming nature of the Lord's intervention on his consciousness.[3] Hummel points out, 'the *hand* of the Lord Yahweh *fell* upon me' is unique, and is more dramatic than, 'the hand of Yahweh being strong on me' in 3:14, which indicates its overpowering nature.'[4] As on the third time the Lord reveals himself to Ezekiel similar to his first visions, Hummel believes he sees the same human, yet supernatural form of Yahweh's glory and this is an appearance of the pre-incarnate Christ.[5]

Ezekiel's ecstatic out of body experience is unique among Israel's classical prophets as he is transported in his visions by God's Spirit to the temple in Jerusalem – 1:3. The timing is significant because the abominations the Lord shows him taking place in the temple, confirm to Ezekiel the disgusting idolatrous practices of the elders in Jerusalem, and his visions justify the necessity of the Lord's judgment. Wright sees their significance saying, 'Firstly, it helps us to understand the ferocity of the way he describes the sin of Israel. Ezekiel is unsurpassed in the range

of vocabulary and imagery he uses to portray the sheer repug-
nance of Israel's active rejection of Yahweh and their wallowing
in every kind of religious paganism and social corruption...
Secondly, it accounts for the strong emphasis on 'theodicy' in the
preaching of Ezekiel. Theodicy means 'providing justification for
the actions of God.'[6] Of course another important reason for the
Lord giving Ezekiel visions of the temple, was to confirm to the
elders in Babylon that what was taking place in Jerusalem justified
God's judgment, as he shared the contents of his visions with
them when they had ended – 11:25. The report of these visions
would in the future validate and authenticate the oracles he
received from the Lord.

In Ezekiel's visions, the Lord takes him to the entrance of the
temple in Jerusalem on the north side where he sees 'the glory of
the God of Israel,' that he saw in his inaugural vision in Ch. 1.
There the Lord takes him on a journey through the precincts of the
temple, and in fours stages he is gradually taken closer to the Holy
of Holies, the holiest part of the temple, during which he is shown
four abominations, each of which progressively is more wicked.
In his visions, he arrives at the entrance of the gateway of the
inner court on the north side of the temple that led to the courtyard
surrounding it. Since the palace was on the north side of the
temple it is likely the king used this entrance when he went to
worship and this marked its importance.

At the entrance, Ezekiel's first sighting is of 'the statue of
jealousy,' the first of the abominations that he will be shown. We
read in 2 Chron. 33:7, that Manasseh erected an idol which he
placed in the temple. The parallel text in 2 Kings 21:7, describes
his idol as, 'the carved image of an Asherah.' And although after
his death Josiah removed and burnt it, it was reinstated by
Jeoiakim after Josiah's death. It is likely that this is the statue
Ezekiel sees which was seated (the seat of jealousy-8:3), a flagrant
challenge to the Lord enthroned above the cherubim in the Holy
of Holies. Wright perceives this idol of a god challenged the
Lord's sovereignty and invaded his sacred space and confronted
worshippers as they entered the temple.[7] The presence of this

monolithic idol may have diverted the worship of God's people, implying that syncretism in worship was acceptable. Block says, 'The image is further described *as the outrageous statue of jealousy* – '*haqqin'a hammaqneh,*' 'the jealousy that provokes jealousy' an emphatic reference to the passion that the object ignites in Yahweh's heart…from the emotion the sculpture evokes in Yahweh it is clear that this image is not simply an ornament or a symbolic temple guard. It is overtly idolatrous posing a direct challenge to Yahweh, who is enthroned above the cherubim inside the temple.'[8] If the idol was a statue of Asherah it represented the degraded sexuality of the fertility cult that was associated with the worship of Baal and Asherah.[9] Odell suggests that the statue was a monument symbolising human devotion that provoked Yahweh's jealousy because of the prohibitions against worshipping other gods and idols the Lord decreed in Exodus 20:4-6, Deut. 5:8-10.[10] In his vision of the temple, as Ezekiel is shown the four areas desecrated by the abominations we may wonder how these came to be established. Although we know a statue was at the entrance to the gate on the north side, Blenkinsopp points out, inscriptions discovered at Kuntilelt on the northern border of Sinai, dated to the 9th or 8th century BC, associate Yahweh with 'his Asherah' and confirm the impression gained from certain passages in the Hebrew Bible that in the popular religion she was understood to be Yahweh's consort. It was perhaps in this capacity that her cult was established in the temple alongside that of Yahweh.[11]

Between vs. 8-18, four scenes reveal four abominations in the temple, and as the scenes move progressively closer to the Holy of Holies, the shocking pagan abominations escalate in their offensiveness to the Lord. As the Lord takes Ezekiel to the four scenes, he reveals Israel's betrayal and infidelity along with their abominations that they so blatantly and unashamedly perpetrated. The four scenes are located in 8:5-6, 7-13, 14-15 and 16-18, and 'form one of the most tightly knit literary units in the entire book.'[12] Each scene follows a similar pattern that begins with the location and abomination, after which the Lord asks Ezekiel a question, 'Son of man do you see what they are doing? This ends with a statement, 'You will see still greater abominations,' apart from the fourth scene which is the last. Hummel notes three different expressions that describe the temple. In 8:6, the Lord refers to the 'sanctuary.' In 8:14 and 8:16, the Lord refers to 'the house of the Lord, and twice in 8:16, the Lord refers to 'the temple of Yahweh.' 'The three terms represent increasing degrees of sanctity as one moves from the entire compound inward toward the heart of the temple.'[13] In v. 6, 'my sanctuary' refers to the sacred nature of the entire temple compound that belongs to the Lord. But tragically this sacred place is desecrated by the abominable practices of the elders. In 8:14, 16, 'the house of Yahweh' reflects the temple is the Lord's dwelling where his presence is in the Holy of Holies, but pagan idols and abominable images have invaded and trespassed the Lord's holy ground. The most outrageous abomination is seen in the fourth scene where the Lord says, 'Look at them, they put the branch to their nose' – 8:17. While biblical commentators agree the exact meaning of this saying is unclear, it describes some supremely obscene and insulting physical gesture, and reveals the countless ways that the Lord's people demonstrated their contempt for him. Hummel points out, this gesture appears to have been part of the sun worship described in 8:16-17 and the rabbis regarded this as blasphemous.[14]

In the first brief temple scene, the Lord draws Ezekiel's attention to the 'statue of jealousy' he has already seen at the beginning of his visions. When the Lord says to him, 'Son of man, do you see what they are doing, the great abominations that the house of Israel are committing here, to drive me far from my sanctuary? But you will see still greater abominations' – 8:6, this initial statement introduces Ezekiel to the principal issue of the abominable practices the Lord will show him, that result in driving him out of the temple consecrated to the Lord. In the second temple scene in 7-13, which is the most detailed, Ezekiel is brought to the door of the inner court. Eichrodt points out, 'This was the entrance to a whole complex of buildings with two wings containing rooms of various sizes, that were likely to be used for storage, maintenance or the preparation of services (like the vestry in a church).'[10] At the door of the inner court, Ezekiel sees a hole in the wall and the Lord instructs him to dig a hole that leads to an entrance to a private chamber, where he sees the subversive worship of the elders held in secret. In his vision, two things stand out. Firstly, he sees images of all kinds of creeping things and loathsome beasts portrayed on the walls, along with the idols of the house of Israel. Secondly, he sees 70 elders of the house of Israel, with Jaazaniah (*that means the Lord listens*), the son of Shapan standing amongst them in dark recessed chapels, 'every man in his room' – 8:12. 'The Hebrew term *heder* refers fundamentally to an interior area that is screened from exterior view, esp-ecially the inner chamber of a building. The present context envisage separate cubicles in which every man performed his rituals'[16] and each elder also had a censer in his hand, with smoke rising from them – 8:10-12. Incense played a prominent role in the divine services Yahweh prescribed for worship – Exodus 30, and its abuse incurred God's wrath that resulted in death – Lev. 10:1-2.[17] That Ezekiel recognised Jaazaniah indicates he knew him prior to his exile in 597, and that he was almost certainly an influential figure in Jerusalem. During the reign of Josiah, Jaazaniah's father, Shapan, was the scribe-state secretary. Shapan's other sons were Ahikam who helped save Jeremiah's life – Jer. 26:24. Elasah the messenger who delivered Jeremiah's letter to the exiles in Babylon – Jer. 29:3, and Gemariah, who tried to prevent Jehoiakim the king burning Jeremiah's prophetic scroll – Jer. 36:25. Although Jaazaniah's family had been faithful to the Lord, and despite the symbolic meaning of his name, he rebelled against the Lord.

The Hebrew for elders – *zeqenim,* refers to the important leaders in the government of the community who had risen to prominence in the city, after the deportation to Babylon.[18] Blenkinsopp suggests that these ceremonies conducted by the official representatives of Judean society were probably aimed at enlisting the support of Egyptian deities.[19] Tragically, these elders thought the Lord didn't see what they were doing in the dark in secret, as they thought the Lord had forsaken them – 8:12, because of the exile of the people by the Babylonians. They had forsaken the Lord and put their faith in the pagan gods evidenced through their subversive worship. Sadly and tragically, we can see a contrast between the 70 elders in their secret worship, and the 70 elders who assisted Moses in governing Israel, who were filled with God's Spirit – Num. 11:26. The 70 elders clandestine worship of the pagan idols of their gods lends itself to the sardonic irony that the claim the Lord has forsaken the land would soon come true. If Ezekiel was horrified at the 70 elders blasphemous worship, worse was to follow as the Lord said to him, 'You will see still greater abominations which they commit' – 8:13.

The third temple scene the shortest of the four, moves closer to the Holy of holies, as the Lord brings Ezekiel to the entrance of the north gate that gave him full view of the temple forecourt, where he sees the women publicly in broad daylight weeping for Tammuz – 8:14. Hummel points out the usual translation, 'mourning for Tammuz' is not quite correct, they were 'bewailing the Tammuz.' The Hebrew construction has a particular nuance, such as intensive or prolonged mourning, or the performance of a special type of lament or liturgy bewailing the god. One might compare our idiom 'chant the Te Deum.'[20] In Sumerian times a complex mythology developed around Tammuz and the literature especially focuses on his death and departure to the underworld.[21] His cult was connected to the end of spring and the cessation of the rains, which was counteracted by weeping and mourning, and several forms of lament over him were widely practiced as women's rites for centuries.[22] The women's cultic weeping was believed to counteract the loss of power of new life and to hasten the return of fertility.[23] Their weeping for Tammuz was offensive to the Lord because they turned their backs on him as the one who was the giver of life, the harvest and who controlled nature. The harvest festivals honoured the Lord as the covenant God who blessed the land and its produce, but weeping for Tammuz dishonoured the Lord, and failed to acknowledge his provision and was tantamount to apostasy, as were the previous abominations that Ezekiel was shown. 'That this ritual was being carried out in the temple precincts suggests that it too was a part of an officially sponsored syncretism involving the monarchy, the ruling class, and the priesthood.'[24] But instead of worshipping the living God, the women by their mourning were perpetuating the memory of a dead pagan god in the temple. This was a brazen act of idolatry.

In the fourth scene, Ezekiel is brought to the inner court, at the entrance in front of the temple. In the previous three scenes, the Lord said he would witness greater abominations, now he will see the worst because of its location between the vestibule and the altar, which is closest to the Holy of Holies. (We learn from Joel 2:17, the priests stand in this place on a fast day, with their faces towards the temple door that led through the holy place to the Holy of Holies beyond it, to offer up intercessory prayer). The twenty-five men are not the elders and Eichrodt suggests they may be representatives of Zedekiah's proletarian government, showing their loyalty to Babylon by engaging in her cult-state worship of Marduk.[25] The twenty-five men have their backs to the temple with their faces towards the east, worshipping the sun toward the east – 8:16. Literally and metaphorically, they have turned their backs on the covenant God as they bow down to worship the sun. Wright says, 'The insult is blatant and breathtaking…And what a picture of utter political and spiritual anarchy in the house of the Lord.'[26] As they prostrate themselves to worship the sun, their backsides are toward the temple and to the Lord, as they have rejected the Lord in favour of the sun god. These cultic gestures in the fourth and climatic abomination are considered the supreme and ultimate contempt for the Lord.[27]

In this last scene, the Lord says to Ezekiel, 'Have you seen this, O son of Man? Is it too slight a thing for the house of Judah to commit the abominations which they commit here, that they should fill the land with violence, and provoke me further?' – 8:17. By saying, 'Is it too slight a thing?' the Lord identifies the disrespectful and unbelievable nature of his peoples' behaviour. As if these were not shameful enough, not only have they committed the abominations in the temple in their rejection of the Lord, they also perpetrated ethical and social sins of violence that provoked the Lord's anger. As has been mentioned earlier, the peoples' disregard for the Lord reaches a climax when the Lord says, 'Look at them, they put the branch to their nose' – 8:17. While the exact meaning of this saying is unclear it describes some supremely obscene and insulting physical gesture, and reveals the countless ways the Lord's people demonstrated their contempt for him. Hummel points out, this gesture appears to have been part of the sun worship described in 8:16-17 and the rabbis regarded this as blasphemous.[28] The modern equivalent would be to hold up one's index finger at someone, or to two stick two fingers up. Both are rude and insulting gestures. Because of the peoples' outrageous idolatrous abominations, and their social sins, they provoked the Lord's anger and his wrath that would result in judgment. Judgment that will not spare: judgment that will not have pity: judgment that will not hear their cry – 8:18.

God's anger and wrath was not directed against the foreign nations and their pagan worship, it was against his own people, whose apostasy and idolatry led them to indulge in abominable worship practices. As we look to discern what idols may inadvertently infiltrate our Christian worship, it is helpful to identify what influenced God's people to contaminate their worship. The first thing they did was to disobey God's commands concerning their worship of the Lord. In Exodus 20:3- 4 and Deut. 5:7-8, the Lord specifically states:

> You shall have no other gods before me. You shall not make for yourself a graven image, or any likeness that is in heaven above, or in the earth beneath, or that is in the water under the earth: you shall not bow down to them or serve them.

God's people surrounded by pagan nations succumbed to their insidious influence traced back to Manasseh who was 12 years old when he became king. He reigned for 55 years – 2 Kings 21:1. In 2 Chronicles 33:1-9 we read, 'Manasseh was twelve years old when he became king, and he reigned in Jerusalem fifty-five years. He did evil in the eyes of the Lord, following the detestable practices of the nations the Lord had driven out before the Israelites. He rebuilt the high places his father Hezekiah had demolished: he also erected altars to the Baals and made Asherah poles. He bowed down to all the starry hosts and worshiped them. He built altars in the temple of the Lord, of which the Lord had said, "My Name will remain in Jerusalem forever." In both courts of the temple of the Lord, he built altars to all the starry hosts. He sacrificed his children in the fire in the Valley of Ben Hinnom, practiced divination and witchcraft, sought omens, and consulted mediums and spiritists. He did much evil in the eyes of the Lord, arousing his anger. He took the image he had made and put it in God's temple, of which God had said to David and to his son Solomon, "In this temple and in Jerusalem, which I have chosen out of all the tribes of Israel, I will put my Name forever. I will not again make the feet of the Israelites leave the land I assigned to your ancestors, if only they will be careful to do everything I commanded them concerning all the laws, decrees and regulations given through Moses." But Manasseh led Judah and the Jerusalemites astray, so they did more evil than the nations the Lord had destroyed before the Israelites.'

As Christians in the 21st century, we may think the example of the king leading God's people into such idolatrous worship practices is obsolete and hardly likely to influence us. While we are unlikely to incorporate physical idols into our corporate Christian worship, we should take care to discern what other more insidious idols we may have embraced. In this respect, there are three areas ministers and their congregations may have introduced in their worship that inadvertently are idols of our own making. These involve our approach, content and style of our worship that reflects the tendency for these criteria to be – 'accessible,' 'informal,' and 'selective.'

One definition of accessible is, 'Simplified so as to be intellectually undemanding.' Another definition of accessible includes the following: 'Easy going: informal: friendly: easy to understand: agreeable.' The intention of worship so that it is accessible for the congregation is to simply the content so it is deemed contemporary in its format, language and style, making it easy to participate, so the second definition would apply. But the first definition can also be deemed to be applicable as well, as there is an considerable degree of dumbing down that takes place in contemporary worship. It is particularly interesting to note, The Cambridge English Dictionary definition of dumbing down is: *'The act of making something simpler and easier for people to understand, especially in order to make it more popular.'* Bearing this in mind, the profound issue at stake is: to what extent is accessible, informal, and selective, appropriate theological concepts to determine what constitutes acceptable, glorifying, pleasing and profound worship to the Lord – and which results in deep, enriching and profound worship for the congregation? So we do well to consider who our corporate Christian worship is primarily for – is it the Lord or is it for church members? The following questions can enable us to reflect on the theological foundations of our corporate worship.

1) On what authority is the content and format of our corporate worship in our main Services derived from? 2) To what extent is it based on the authorised services of the Church of England in the Anglican Common Worship Prayer Book 2000? 3) To what extent it based on the class or cultural background of the church? 4) To what extent is it based is our worship based on the subjective preference of the clergy? 5) To what extent is it based on our denominational allegiance? 6) To what extent is our worship based on the authority of Scripture?

Another important aspect of our corporate worship is the role of liturgy that is an essential component of the content, order and style of our worship, because the concept of our worship being accessible, informal and selective, reflects our own preference. Liturgical worship sounds old-fashioned and it is often linked with traditional worship, but it is crucial to understand its meaning. 'Liturgy comes from the Greek word leitourgia, and is made up of words for work (ergon) and people (laos). In ancient Greece, a liturgy was public work performed for the benefit of the city or state. Similarly, liturgy in worship is a work performed by the people for the benefit of others…To call a service liturgical is to indicate that it was conceived so that all worshippers take an active part in offering their worship together. The word liturgy is used in the specific sense of the Eucharist, but Western Christians use liturgical to apply to all forms of public worship of a part-icipatory nature.'[29] In the report 'Transforming Worship' The Liturgical Commission of the Church of England, reminds us, 'Liturgy is also the work of God. God addresses us through the readings of Scripture, and in our prayers of invocation, we ask the Lord to be present and active among. There is a two-fold aspect of liturgy. It is both human construction and divine gift.[30]

I believe that Christians are ignorant of the important role liturgy has to play in or worship. Christopher Cocksworth, the Bishop of Coventry says, 'The shape and words of the liturgy have the capacity to be used by God to bring about encounter and engagement with his real presence.'[31] We have sacred texts rooted in history and inspired by the Holy Spirit to mediate God's presence and truth to us. This is a constant reminder that, 'The story the liturgy tells and enacts is the story of God's dealings with the world from creation to consummation.'[32] From this perspective we can readily see that liturgy is evangelistic as it declares the saving activity of God, when we celebrate the major festivals in the Church's calendar. 'Underlying the liturgical reordering of time in events of worship is the yearly rehearsal of the story of salvation in the liturgical year. God's history is impressed on the months and seasons of the year.'[33]

One of the weaknesses of contemporary worship is the selective omission of 'liturgical texts.' Liturgical texts are integral to worship because they enable the congregation to encounter the Lord. Worship involves participation by God's people and includes liturgical texts. For example, the Lord's Prayer and Scripture readings are liturgical texts. In Anglican worship, the Creed and the Gloria in Communion Services are liturgical texts, as is the prayer of thanksgiving. Christopher Cocksworth, in a lecture on 'The Liturgy and the Spirit,' given at a conference in Norway early in 2007 refers to 2 Chronicles Ch. 5 and 7. He raises questions about liturgy that can shape our encounter with God in worship. 'Did God by his Spirit interrupt the carefully planned liturgy and elaborate ceremonial worship of the Temple consecration with his wild, untamable, unpredictable presence? Or did the Temple liturgy provide the structure within which, and the platform within which, God moved and worked? Did the sovereign God somehow manage to find his way around the 'liturgical police officers?' Or had the sovereign God inspired drafters and leaders of the liturgy to be architects of spiritual encounter to which God faithfully and graciously responded?

> The liturgy of the Church and the liberty of the Spirit are not two opposites that have to be chosen between. They are gifts that are to be woven together in the rich ecology of God's grace. But this is a view which runs counter to many contemporary charismatic evangelical instincts.'[34]

JUDGMENT ON THE WICKED – 11:1-13

'Then the Spirit of the Lord lifted me up, and brought me to the east gate of the house of the Lord, which faces east. And behold, at the door of the gateway there were twenty-five men: and I saw among them Jaazaniah the son of Azzur, and Pelatiah the son of Benaiah, princes of the people. And he said to me, "Son of man, these are the men who devise iniquity and who give wicked counsel in the city: who say, 'The time is not near to build houses, this city is the cauldron, and we are the flesh.' Therefore prophesy against them, prophesy, O son of man."

And the Spirit of the Lord fell upon me, and he said to me, "Say, Thus says the Lord: So you think, O house of Israel: for I know the things that come into your mind. You have multiplied your slain in this city, and have filled its streets with the slain. Therefore thus says the Lord God: Your slain whom you have laid in the midst of it, they are the flesh, and this city is the cauldron:

but you shall be brought forth out of the midst of it. You have feared the sword, and I will bring the sword upon you, says the Lord God. And I will bring you out of the midst of it, and give you into the hands of foreigners, and execute judgments upon you. You shall fall by the sword: I will judge you at the border of Israel, and you shall know that I am the Lord. This city shall not be your cauldron, nor shall you be the flesh in the midst of it: I will judge you at the border of Israel, and you shall know that I am the Lord. For you have not walked in my statutes, nor executed my ordinances, but have acted according to the ordinances of the nations that are around you.''

And it came to pass, while I was prophesying, that Pelatiah the son of Benaiah died. Then I fell down upon my face and cried with a loud voice, and said, ''Ah Lord God, will you make a full end of the remnant of Israel?''

The last time God's Spirit was on the scene was in 8:3, now under the influence of the Spirit Ezekiel is taken in a vision to the east gate of the house of the Lord. Here he sees twenty-five men, two of whom he recognises, princes-leaders of the people. The Lord informs him of the intention of their hearts as he has seen they plot evil and offer wicked advice to the people in Jerusalem, giving them false hope about the inviolability of the city. The Lord reveals their thoughts that it is not the right time to build houses, as they quote a metaphor about the city being a cauldron with themselves as the flesh – 11:3-4. While their thoughts can be ambiguously interpreted, the cauldron-pot is a reference to Jerusalem providing them with security in contrast to those taken into exile. But their arrogant smug confidence about their status provokes the Lord's anger as he instructs Ezekiel to prophesy his judgment against them. The prophesy he receives expands on the social wickedness mentioned in 9:9, and is described in v. 6: 'You have multiplied your slain in this city, and have filled its streets with the slain.' They exploited their status, and the Hebrew term for the slain-victims *halalim,* which has military overtones, also denotes victims of judicial murder who have been sentenced to death by corrupt courts.[35] They perpetrated injustice, oppressed the poor, shed innocent blood, reconstructed parts of the city after the exile, and with the leading citizens of the population taken into exile, seized their land and houses they left behind. 'These powerful few, and the class they represent, were taking full advantage of the national distress to line their own pockets, a well know phenomenon in wartime.'[36]

Having provoked the Lord by their wicked behaviour he declares his judgment upon the ruling class of the elders and leaders. While they lived under the allusion they were secure in Jerusalem as the leading ruling class, identifying themselves as the flesh in the cauldron, the prime choice of the population so to speak, the Lord declares their worst fears will take place. They will be given over into the hands of their enemies, be put to their sword and cast out of the city of Jerusalem: and when this takes place, they will recognise this was the Lord's judgment against them – 11:7-12. As the elders hear Ezekiel announce the Lord's judgment, he also ends his prophecy by declaring they brought this upon themselves because they did not walk in the Lord's statutes, and because they did not carry out his ordinances-laws, and also because they lived according to the laws of the nations that were around them – 11:12. While Ezekiel was prophesying, he saw in his vision that Pelatiah the son of Benaiah died. In one of his rare emotional outbursts, he is shocked at his death and loudly cries out with an astonished exclamation, concerned the Lord was going to wipe out all the remnant of his people left in Jerusalem. 'The cry of the prophet reveals the deep menace of this severe threat of judgment by God.'[37] The irony would not have been lost on Ezekiel as Pelatiah's name means 'Yahweh has delivered-rescued.' His death is significant because when it takes place it will confirm Ezekiel's status as a prophet.

THE GOSPEL IN EZEKIEL – 11:14-25

'And the word of the Lord came to me, "Son of man, your brethren, even your brethren, your fellow exiles, the whole house of Israel, all of them are those of whom the inhabitants of Jerusalem have said, 'They have gone far from the Lord: to us this land is given as a possession.' Therefore, say, 'Thus says the Lord God: Though I removed them far off among the nations, and though I scattered them among the countries, yet I have been a sanctuary to them for a while in the countries where they have gone.' Therefore say, 'Thus says the Lord God: I will gather you from the peoples, and assemble you out of the countries where you have been scattered, and I will give you the land of Israel.' And when they come there, they will remove from it all its detestable things and all its abominations. And I will give them one heart, and put a new spirit within them. I will take the stony heart out of their flesh and give them a heart of flesh, that they may walk in my statutes and keep my ordinances and obey them: and they shall be my people and I will be their God. But as for those whose heart goes after their detestable things, I will requite their deeds upon their own heads says the Lord God."

Then the cherubim lifted up their wings, with their wheels beside them: and the glory of the God of Israel was over them. And the glory of the Lord went up from the midst of the city, and stood upon the mountain which is on the east side of the city. And the Spirit lifted me up and brought me in the vision by the Spirit of God into the Chaldea, to the exiles. Then the vision that I had seen went up from me. And I told the exiles all the things that the Lord had showed me."

Daniel Block eloquently describes vs. 14-25 as 'The Gospel according to Ezekiel.'[38] It is with a sigh of relief that we now encounter the first sign of hope of the restoration of Israel that will be expanded in 'glorious detail, especially in chapters 34, 36 and 37.'[39] As the Lord informs Ezekiel what they were saying in Jerusalem, their rejection of the exiles was like to be initially demoralising. However, the Lord contradicts the Jerusalemites claims they are secure, as he has in fact rejected them, and not those in exile who will compromise the remnant that survives. In his oracle to Ezekiel, the Lord identifies him as belonging with the exiles in three ways. He is associated with his entire nuclear family, his fellow exiles, and the whole house of Israel. This Trinitarian reference to Israel shows the Lord's sympathy.

In verses 14-25, the Lord answers Ezekiel's outcry as he foresaw the annihilation of Israel, as earlier in 9:8-11 the Lord confirmed his intention to judge Jerusalem. But here the Lord's response is emphatically Gospel with the promise of hope and restoration for the exiles. This counteracts the disconcerting news for the exiles, that those in Jerusalem had claimed the inheritance to the land they had lost and that they had gone far from the Lord in Babylon, claiming 'to us this land is given for a possession' – 11:15. The Lord also refutes the claim of those in Jerusalem that the exiles' expulsion from the land alienates them from the Lord. Contrary to what the Jerusalemites thought, despite the deportation of the exiles, the Lord had not abandoned them and they were not alienated from Him in Babylon. This revolutionary theology was without parallel in the OT, as they believed the Lord's presence dwelt in the sanctuary in the Holy of Holies in the temple in Jerusalem. Block sublimely captures the importance of this extraordinary theological truth:

> Here Yahweh promises to be for the exiles what the temple up until now has been for them in Jerusalem. On the other hand, he changes the locus of worship, promising to be with the exiles on foreign soil, the unclean land to which they have been banished. Both the content of this statement and the channel through which it reaches Israel are remarkable. Ezekiel himself was heir to the tradition in which the notion of the sanctuary, sacred space/place, was at the heart of Israel's spiritual self-consciousness. The temple served as a visible sign of Yahweh's presence among them, and as a symbol of their status as the people of Yahweh. Now this prophet, whose clan's interests are vested in defending the centrality of the temple, announces the possibility of a relationship with Yahweh apart from the temple![40]

Bearing in mind that at the end of his vision in Ch. 11, Ezekiel would see the glory of the Lord depart from the temple, which he will report to the exiles, the Lord graciously promises his presence will be with them while they are in Babylon and there he will be a sanctuary to them. After Ezekiel received this vision, he told the elders what the Lord had said. The Lord also revealed his glory to Ezekiel in his visions in Babylon. Moreover, the elders knew the Lord's presence was with him, as on the occasions they came to his house to enquire of the Lord, in 8:11, 'the hand of the Lord fell upon Ezekiel,' and in 14:1, 'the word of the Lord came to Ezekiel,' and in 20:1, 'the word of the Lord came to Ezekiel.'

Verses 17-20 announce the Lord's deliverance for the exiles from foreign lands as he will gather and assemble them out of the countries where he scattered them – 11:17. The Lord's salvation also involves the restoration of the land of Israel to his people. Equally, their restoration involves spiritual renewal as the land is purged of idols and abominable cultic practices, and the Lord will give them a single heart and a new spirit. He will also remove their stony heart (as they were formerly 'hard-hearted' – 2:4, and 'stubborn-hearted' – 3:7 towards the Lord), and give them a heart of flesh: that they may be obedient to the Lord and keep his commandments. As a result, they will be his people and the Lord will be their God – 19-20. These verses mark the climax of a formal announcement of the Lord's covenant renewal. As a result, spiritual renewal is achieved by God's transforming work. The transformation of their heart leads to covenant renewal in the Lord's relationship with his people as He gives them responsive and sensitive hearts toward the Lord. As a result, they will be empowered to be faithful and wholeheartedly obedient to the Lord. This is the Gospel in Ezekiel that is virtually repeated word for word in Ch. 36: 22-32.

Jeremiah Ezekiel's older contemporary, also prophesied the Lord would gather his people from the lands to which he drove them in his anger, and bring them back to the land of Israel: and they would be his people and he would be their God. Moreover, the Lord would give them one heart and one way that they may fear him for ever, for their good and the good of their children after them. And the Lord will make with them an everlasting covenant – Jer. 32:37-40. In vs. 16-20, 'This oracle serves as a powerful witness to Yahweh's covenant faithfulness.His promises to restore the nation of Israel to her land and to renew his covenant are based on the irrevocability of the promises he made to the fathers and the marriage entered into at Sinai.'[41] Hummel says, 'The 'Gospel according to Ezekiel reaches its climax with what is commonly known as the covenant formula: 'They will be my people and I will be their God.'[42] Robert Jenson also captures the remarkable theology of vs. 17-20. He views this as 'the spectacular eschatological promises in our passage.' Israel who collectively has a heart of stone will return from the exile with a heart of flesh. Heart is a key term of Israelite anthropology and is closely related to 'soul' which denotes the person with an individual stamp.[43] While 11:21 may seem out of place after the hope and promise of spiritual renewal and the return to the land of Israel for the exiles, the Lord's announcement that if they did not repent they too would perish, was a sober reminder not to assume they would automatically be part of the remnant that returned to Israel.

Jeremiah prophesied that after 70 years of exile in Babylon the Lord would bring his people back to the land of Israel – Jer. 29: 10-14. And when the Lord informed Ezekiel the house of Israel were impudent, stubborn and rebellious – 2:4-6, after the fall of Jerusalem – 33:30-35, the census reveals when the Lord stirred up Cyrus to build him a house in Jerusalem – Ezra 1:1 and he gave permission to the Jews to return to their homeland to rebuild the house of the Lord in 538, just over 40,000 returned – Ezra 2:64. This was like a second exodus during Cyrus' reign and although with the encouragement of the prophets Haggai and Zechariah the second temple was rebuilt, there was no physical manifestation of the glory of the Lord's presence in the temple to match the dedication of Solomon's first temple in 1 Kings 8.

After the Lord's oracle to Ezekiel ends, he sees the glory of the Lord depart from Jerusalem and rest on the Mount of Olives on the east side of the city – 11:22. The closing scene of his vision represents the fulfillment of all the predictions of the impending doom upon the city.[44] The glory of the Lord would not appear again in the temple until Ezekiel's vision twenty years later – 43:1-5. As his vision ends, he finds himself back in his house with the elders and he tells them everything the Lord showed him, but he does not record their response.

As we reflect on the Lord's character He reveals to Ezekiel, it is salutary to reflect on the content of the Gospel we proclaim as New Testament believers. I cannot remember the preaching of the Gospel that included the Day of Judgment as an integral aspect of salvation in the Gospel. Have we lost the sharp cutting edge of the heart of Christ's salvation by the omission to proclaim this Gospel to the nation, as by default we preach an accessible Gospel?

EZEKIEL PREPARES FOR EXILE – 12: 1-16

"The word of the Lord came to me, "Son of man, you dwell in the midst of a rebellious house, who have eyes to see, but see not, who have ears to hear, but hear not, for they are a rebellious house. Therefore, son of man, prepare for yourself an exile's baggage, and go into exile by day in their sight: you shall go like an exile from your place to another place in their sight. Perhaps they will understand, though they are a rebellious house. You shall bring out your baggage by day in their sight, as baggage for exile: and you shall go forth yourself at evening in their sight, as men do who must go into exile. Dig through the wall in their sight, and go out through it. In their sight you shall lift the baggage on your shoulder, and carry it out in the dark: you shall cover your face, that you may not see the land, for I have made you a sign for the house of Israel."

And I did what I was commanded. I brought out my baggage by day, as baggage for exile, and in the evening, I dug through the wall with my own hands: I went out in the dark, carrying my outfit upon my shoulder in their sight. In the morning, the word of the Lord came to me: "Son of man, has not the house of Israel, the rebellious house said to you, 'What are you doing?' Say to them, 'Thus says the Lord God: This oracle concerns the prince in Jerusalem and all the house of Israel who are in it. Say, 'I am a sign for you: as I have done, so shall it be done to them: they shall go into exile, into captivity. And the prince who is among them shall lift his baggage upon his shoulder in the dark, and shall go forth: he shall dig through the wall and go out through it, he shall cover his face, so that he may not see the land with his eyes. And I will spread my net over him, and he shall be taken in my snare, and I will bring him to Babylon in the land of the Chaldeans, yet he shall not see it and he shall die there. And I will scatter toward every wind all who are round about him, his helpers and all his troops: and I will unsheathe the sword after them. And they shall know that I am the Lord, when I disperse them among the nations and scatter them through the countries. But I will let a few of them escape from the sword, from famine and pestilence, that they may confess all their abominations among the nations where they go, and may know that I am the Lord.''

Chapters 12:1-16 pose noticeable textual problems. Initially, apart from the confused state of 10b and 12b considered to be errors in transmission, tensions are reflected in the different versions of the MT – *(the authoritative Hebrew and Aramaic text used as the basis for translations of the OT)*. It has been argued these reflect the distance between Ezekiel's performance and being committed to writing. More recently, scholars argue the tensions that are literary, reflect the stages in the evolution of the text.[45]

The Lord had already commanded Ezekiel to carry out a number of symbolic sign-acts in chs. 4 and 5 and informed him the people were rebellious. And despite the message of hope contained in Ch. 11, this latest symbolic sign-act in which Ezekiel himself is the sign by preparing to go into exile, this clearly indicates the people have not grasped the message his sign-acts were intended to convey, because after he performs his sign the people ask him what he is doing.

The language in the action prophecy which focuses on the frequent use of 'in their sight' in 12:3, 12:4, 12:5, 12:6, 12:7, has an element of hope the exiles would perceive its meaning. Perhaps the Lord intended the exiles to identify with this sign-act from their own experience of going into exile, but clearly, it did not cross their mind. Also in vs. 2a, 2b, 3, 9, the exiles are described as a 'house of rebellion.' During the day, Ezekiel is to dig a hole in the wall of his house and go through it. For the first, time he records that he carried out the Lord's instructions in a symbolic sign-act preparing to go into exile, in their sight – 12:7. When the Lord says, 'perhaps they will understand, although they are a rebellious house'– 12:3, this appears somewhat inauspicious as they failed to understand the former signs in chs. 3-4. Eichrodt perceives the exiles have lost the faculty to perceive what God is saying and doing.[46] It is likely their idolatrous lifestyles in Jerusalem left them spiritually blind in Babylon, as they fail to understand how the Lord is speaking to them through Ezekiel. The Lord instructs him to perform his symbolic sign during the day and evening of the first day, he then interprets it in the morning.

Before the Lord commands Ezekiel to prepare his baggage for exile, he reminds him that he lives amongst a rebellious people 'who have eyes but do not see and ears but do not hear' – 12:1-2. Ezekiel's prophecy is about the residents of Jerusalem, while his audience are the exiles in Babylon, and it appears to have been recorded before the fall of Jerusalem to confirm his authentic status as a prophet. Ch. 12 consists of a collection of two action prophesies, and the first prophecy – 1-16 consists of two parts, the prophetic sign-act and an oracle explaining its symbolic meaning. Ezekiel is instructed by the Lord to prepare his baggage for exile outside his house in the daylight for the exiles to see. This would have been wrapped up in a bundle, probably including the barest essentials, some bedding, water, a little food, and cooking utensils.[47] In vs. 3-4, Ezekiel represents those in Jerusalem who would be exiled, and in v. 5 he represents the Babylonians who deport them. While he digs a hole in the wall he represents the Babylonians besieging Jerusalem, and once inside his house he portrays the people going into exile. While biblical commentators offer various reasons for Ezekiel leaving in the dark at twilight to go into exile, for example, darkness may be symbolic of a time of judgment, anguish or mourning, while Medieval interpreters perceive it as public disgrace, the shame of deportation, as they leave their homeland because he covers his face as leaves – 12:6. 'The public character of the event, open to every eye, is once again strongly emphasised.'[48]

Ezekiel's bizarre action in vs. 3-7 has captured the exiles' curiosity and in vs. 8-9, the Lord reminds him they asked him to explain it, and as they did not understand the meaning of Ezekiel's sign-act the Lord gives him an oracle to announce. The Lord informs the exiles that the oracle is about the prince in Jerusalem – Zedekiah and all the house of Israel – people in Jerusalem – 12:8. The reference to the king and the people symbolises the captivity of the nation. But Ezekiel is also to announce that he himself is a sign to the exiles as what he enacted will also be done to the Jerusalemites. They shall go into exile, and share the same fate as the exiles in Babylon, which negates any hope of the exiles' restoration to the land of Israel. Ezekiel then prophesies that Zedekiah will prepare his own baggage, cover his face, and to try escape under cover of darkness, but like a hunter the Lord will spread his net over the king and he shall be taken to Babylon – 12-13: he will not see the land as his eyes will be gouged out. 2 Kings 25:1-7 records this happened to Zedekiah. Ezekiel's oracle from the Lord was to ensure the exiles understood it was the Lord's judgment on Zedekiah and the Jerusalemites, and when Nebuchadnezzar was the Lord's instrument to execute his judgment. Eichrodt says:

> When we recall how symbolic action by a prophet, was regarded as being not merely an illustration of his word, but an irresistible power operating to bring about the fulfillment of that word, we can appreciate the full force of this attack on the hardened stubbornness of the exiles.[49]

While Ezekiel's oracle declares the Lord's judgment as he will – 'unsheathe the sword' – his twofold purpose will be to save a remnant, who will confess all their abominations in exile, as they acknowledge the Lord is responsible for what happened to them – 12:14-16.

SIGNS OF FEAR & TREMBLING – 12:17-20

'Moreover, the word of the Lord came to me, ''Son of man, eat your bread with quaking, and drink your water with trembling and fearfulness: and say of the people of the land, Thus says the Lord God concerning the inhabitants of Jerusalem in the land of Israel: They shall eat their bread with fearfulness and drink water in dismay, because their land will be stripped of all it contains, on account of the violence of all those who dwell in it. And the inhabited cities shall be laid waste, and the land shall become a desolation: and you shall know that I am the Lord.''

Presumably, Ezekiel had to use facial expressions as he ate and drank, to portray the fear and trembling the Lord required that was probably similar to a game of charades, which must have seemed very bizarre to the exiles who observed him. This action prophecy has only two parallel lines, 'you shall eat' and 'you shall drink. But, 'The brevity of this prophecy does not detract from its rhetorical force nor minimise its significance.'[50] As the Lord speaks to Ezekiel instructing him to carry out another symbolic sign-act, he is to eat bread with quaking and drink water with trembling and fearfulness – 12:17. This is reminiscent of what the inhabitants of Jerusalem will do in 4:16, 'they shall eat bread by weight and with fearfulness, and they shall drink water by measures and in dismay.' If in vs. 12-16, the Lord's judgment is ominous, the emotional and psychological horror of the prospect of exile intensifies through Ezekiel's prophecy of eating bread and drinking water, with trembling and fearfulness. The Hebrew word that describes the trembling – *raas,* is usually associated with the earth quaking.[51] Ezekiel's prophetic sign-act depicts the people in Jerusalem carrying out the basic activities of life with excessive fear, and trembling uncontrollably as they eat and drink. The devastating picture of the Jerusalemites being taken into exile by the Babylonians is spelt out by Ezekiel as he interprets his prophetic action of eating and drinking to the exiles, and also announces the land will become a desolation – 12:19-20. The devastation of the land can be traced back to the covenant curses in Lev. 26:14-46. We can but conclude that as the Lord's judgment on his people was so comprehensively devastating, this reflects how serious were the sins of God's people to provoke the Lord to such wrath.

VISIONS FULFILLED –12: 21-28

"And the word of he Lord came to me: "Son of man, what is this proverb that you have about the land of Israel saying, 'The days grow long, and every vision comes to nought?' Tell them therefore, 'Thus says the Lord God: I will put an end to this proverb, and they will use it no more as a proverb in Israel. But say to them, The days are at hand, and the fulfillment of every vision. For there shall be no more any false vision or flattering divination within the house of Israel. But I the Lord will speak the word which I will speak, and it will be performed. It will no longer be delayed, but in your days, O rebellious house, I will speak the word and perform it, says the Lord God."

Again the word of the Lord came to me: "Son of man, behold they of the house of Israel say, 'The vision that he sees is for many days hence, and he prophesies of times far off.' Therefore say to them, Thus says the Lord God: None of my words will be delayed any longer, but the word which I speak will be performed, says the Lord God."

In Ch. 12:21-28 the word vision occurs five times, and there is an emphasis on, 'the word the Lord will speak' – twice in 12:25, and also on, 'the Lord's 'words' – twice in 12:28. The exiles are spiritually blind and have been deceived because of their idolatry and apostasy when they lived in Jerusalem, and so they fail to discern between false and true prophecy. Also, they cynically dismiss Ezekiel's prophecies and fail to take them seriously saying, 'every vision comes to nothing' – 12:22, and, 'he prophesies of times far off' – 12:27. The exiles were skeptical and derisive about prophesies that led to the proverb, 'The days grow long and every vision comes to nought'–12:22. These sayings reflect the conflict between the exiles and their response to Ezekiel as they have rejected his prophesies.[52] (This proverb may also have been a reaction to Jeremiah's prediction of the nation's collapse and judgment). Eichrodt says, 'Here, as often, the remarkable word *masal,* which covers wisdom-sayings, legal precepts, formulas of cursing or blessing, oracles or lyrics, because it probably meant at first a powerful and therefore effective word, designates a pungent piece of mocking wit. It was put into circulation about the land of Israel, and everyone was discussing the fate that pursued the exiles at every turn...This mocking phrase asserts the general uncertainty of all prophetic words, and uses that as an excuse to avoid having to decide in face of a particular prophet.'[53]

However, the Lord has heard the two proverbial sayings of the exiles and he refutes and counters each one in turn. Firstly, in an oracle that begins, 'Thus says the Lord,' he declares the visions that were prophesied will take place during their lifetime, because he will not only speak the word, but carry it out – 12:25. Secondly, again in an oracle that begins, 'Thus says the Lord,' the words he declared will not be delayed any longer, but he will carry out what he has said – 12:28.

JERUSALEM'S ELECTION –16: 1-14

'Again the word of the Lord came to me: ''Son of Man, make known to Jerusalem all her abominations, and say, Thus says the Lord God to Jerusalem: Your origin and your birth are of the land of the Canaanites, your father was an Amorite and your mother a Hittite. And as for your birth, on the day you were born your navel string was not cut, nor were you washed with water to cleanse you, nor rubbed with salt, nor swathed with bands. No eye pitied you, to do any of these things to you out of compassion for you: but you were cast out on the open field, for you were abhorred, on the day that you were born.

And when I passed by you, and saw you weltering in your blood, I said to you in your blood, 'Live and grow up like a plant of the field.' And you grew and became tall and arrived at full maidenhood: your beasts were formed, and your hair had grown, yet you were naked and bare.

When I passed by you again and looked upon you, behold you were at the age of love: and I spread my skirt over you, and covered your nakedness, yes, I plighted my troth to you and entered into a covenant with you, says the Lord God, and you became mine. Then I bathed you with water and washed off your blood from you, and anointed you with oil. I clothed you also with embroidered cloth and shod you with leather, I enveloped you in fine linen and covered you in silk. And I decked you with ornaments, and put bracelets on your arms, and a chain on your neck. And I put a ring on your nose, and earrings in your ears, and a beautiful crown upon your head. Thus you were decked with gold and silver, and your rainment was of fine linen, and silk and embroidered cloth: you ate fine flour and honey and oil. You grew exceedingly beautiful and came to regal estate. And your renown went forth among the nations because of your beauty, for it was perfect through the splendour which I had bestowed upon you says the Lord God."

The oracle in Ch. 16 can raise conflicting issues about God's character in the Book of Ezekiel. For example, as Israel is referred to as the female in the covenant relationship with the Lord, one may see a striking contrast between symbolically casting the female in a negative light, in comparison to the positive image of the male. Also Ezekiel can be seen to portray female sexuality as the object of male possession and control, that incites violence as a means of restoration. God also can be seen to be vengeful, his retribution violently excessive. Or the female violation of the marital bed can be treated more seriously than male infidelity.[54]

Up to this juncture, studying Ezekiel has been hard going as God's judgment, punishment and wrath on his people is so strident, and expressed so passionately because of their idolatry and apostasy, that it is difficult to relate to their abominable sins that are likely to be outside of our experience. However, in the lengthy narrative of Ch. 16:1-63, their idolatry and apostasy is nakedly described and enables us to comprehend the Lord's judgment against his people that led to their exile and eventually to the destruction of the temple and Jerusalem.

In Ezekiel Ch. 16 the Lord describes Israel's apostasy in terms of 'whoring after other gods.' A metaphor used by Hosea to portray the Lord's marriage relationship with Israel – Hosea 2:2-25. Through Jeremiah the Lord also spoke about his relationship with Israel when he said, 'You have played the harlot with many lovers, and would you return to me? Lift up your eyes to the bare heights, and see. Where have you not been lain with? By the wayside you have sat awaiting lovers like an Arab in the wilderness. You have polluted the land with your vile harlotry' – Jer. 3:1-2. In his oracle to Ezekiel the Lord speaks of his relationship with Israel metaphorically about her marital infidelity and promiscuousness. 'The Lord takes this metaphor and expands it into a narrative, that assaults his listeners with a rapid succession of garish scenes, offensive language and sickening violence, that is unbearable to listen to.'[55] Ch. 16 is full of shocking imagery, especially sexually explicit graphic language. Block says, 'The repeated use of the Hebrew root *znh* and its other derivates – 'to commit harlotry, to practice illegal sex,' occurs twenty-one times in Ch. 6, that describes Jerusalem's unrestrained nymphomaniacal adventures with her lovers.'[56] The allusion to Israel's adultery is not an isolated incident and this refers to 'prolonged, addictively repeated, insatiable promiscuity with multiple partners.'[57] Block mentions the Lord's explicit sexual references spoken in an unrestrained manner: '*tepasseqi' et-regalim* – speaks of a woman opening her legs wide to passers by v. 25 – (RSV – offering yourself to any passer by): the Egyptians with their enlarged penis – *gidle basar* v. 26: (RSV – your neighbours with the huge organs): the female genital fluid produced at sexual arousal – *nehuset* v. 26.'[58]

At the beginning of his oracle instead of tracing Israel's roots to Abraham, Isaac and Jacob, the Lord describes Jerusalem's ancestors with an insulting, unflattering allusion to her pagan roots couched in abusive satire. The Lord alludes to the ethnic origins of

Jerusalem (the city stands for the entire nation), a mixture of Hittites and Amorites, before David captured the city and made it his capital. Abraham purchased the region around the cave of Machpelah near Hebron from Hittites – Gen. 23, and Esau married Hittite women – Gen. 26:34. Also, in Deut 26:5, when the Lord speaks about the land he is going to give the Hebrews, he says, 'And you shall make response before the Lord your God, 'A wandering Aramean was my father.' The reference to Israel's birth and origin being the land of Canaan, 'is probably almost sarcastic, virtual shorthand for moral decadence representative of everything antithetical to Yahwism and to Israel as God intended her to be.'[59]

Ch. 16 is an allegory of Jerusalem as an abandoned and rejected young girl rescued because of the Lord's compassion and grace who grows into a beautiful woman. The Lord speaks intimately and lovingly to her when he says, 'behold you were at the age of love, and I spread my skirt over you and covered your nakedness, and I plighted my troth to you and entered into a covenant with you, and you became mine' – 16:8. The gesture of spreading a garment over someone was an ancient Near Eastern custom that signified 'the establishment of a new relationship and the symbolic declaration of the husband to provide for the sustenance of his future wife.'[60] Moreover, the Lord clothed her with fine linen and ornaments, and she became regal and beautiful. Her beauty was renowned among the nations because of the splendour the Lord bestowed upon her – 16:10-14. The clothes and the ornaments the Lord adorns her with represent her magnificent beauty and the status of a queen, signified by placing a crown on her head – 16:12. That her beauty was acknowledged by other nations probably refers to the reign of David and Solomon. This transformation from rags to riches was a gift of the Lord's grace – 16:14. The fine linen – *ses*, and embroidered cloth – *rigma*, the Lord provides were specially used to provide the curtains and priestly vestments for the tabernacle. The leather her sandals were made of *tahas,* is also used only in the context of the tabernacle. And her special food, *solet* and *semen*, fine flour and oil, were used in sacred offerings in the tabernacle. Symbolically, Jerusalem the Lord's bride is clothed with the garments that clothe the sanctuary and eats the food of its offerings.[61] Wright says:

> The personified Jerusalem is clothed and fed with the furnishings and food of the temple, signifying the most precious thing about this whole picture is the presence of Yahweh himself, dwelling with and among his people. Temple and priesthood combine in the imaging of the people as a whole. This points to the role of Israel not just to be famous among the nations for its own sake, but to be Yahweh's priesthood among the nations – the means by which the nations would come to acknowledge Yahweh.[62]

JERUSALEM AN ADULTEROUS WIFE – 16: 15-34

'But you trusted in your beauty and played the harlot be-cause of your renown, and lavished your harlotries on any passer-by. You took some of your garments and made for your-self gaily decked shrines and on them played the harlot: the like has never been, nor ever shall be. You also took your fair jewels of my gold and of my silver which I had given you and made for yourself images of men, and with them played the harlot: and you took your embroidered garments to cover them, and set my oil and my incense before them. Also my bread which I gave you – I fed you with fine flour and oil and honey – you set before them for a pleasing odour, says the Lord God. And you took your sons and your daughters whom you bore to me and these you sacrificed to them to be devoured. Were your harlotries so small a matter that you slaughtered my children and delivered them up as an offering to them? And in all your abominations and your harlotries you did not remember the days of your youth, when you were naked and bare, weltering in your blood.

And after all your wickedness (woe, woe to you says the Lord God), you built yourself a vaulted chamber, and made yourself a lofty place in every square: at the head of every street you built your lofted place and prostituted your beauty, offering yourself to any passer by and multiplying your harlotry. You also played the harlot with the Egyptians, your lustful neighbours, multiplying your harlotry to provoke me to anger. Behold, therefore, I stretched out my hand against you, and diminished your allotted portion and delivered you to the greed of your enemies, the daughter of the Philistines who were ashamed because of your lewd behaviour. You played the harlot also with the Assyrians, because you were insatiable: yes, you played the harlot with them, and still you were not satisfied. You multiplied your harlotry also with the trading land of Chaldea, and even with this you were not satisfied.

How lovesick is your heart says the Lord God, seeing you did all these things, the deeds of a brazen harlot: building your vaulted chamber at the head of every street, and making your lofty place in every square. Yet you were not like a harlot because you scorned hire. Adulterous wife who receives strangers instead of her husband. Men give gifts to all harlots, but you gave your gifts to all your lovers, bribing them to come to you from every side for your harlotries. So you were different from other women in your harlotries: none solicited you to play the harlot, and you gave hire, while no hire was given to you: therefore you were different.''

Chapter 16:15-34 can be viewed with one major point of comparison: Israel's gross unfaithfulness in contrast to the Lord's gracious love.[63] In these verses, explicit, shocking sexual language, describes Jerusalem's scandalous sins. Tragically, Israel turned her back on the Lord, abused her gifts, failed to trust him, and instead in her hubris – her excessive pride and arrogance, falsely put her confidence and trust in her own beauty and her reputation – 'lavished her harlotries on any passer by' – 16:15. Israel repaid the Lord with her 'flagrant depravity and pathological infidelity.'[64] She played the harlot – prostitute, and indiscriminately worshipped other gods and idols and abused the gifts the Lord gave her. She established her own idolatrous cult, made idols, built shrines for them, and cared for them and fed them. Block says, 'For Jerusalem the newly found beauty and fame were intoxicating…the temporal and ephemeral replaced the eternal: the gifts displaced the giver.'[65] This describes the rebelliousness of God's people. In verses 16, 17, 18, and 20, Israel's harlotry is that she 'took' the Lord's gifts and abused them. Her ultimate betrayal was sacrificing her children to these idols – 16-22. God's people failed to grasp that their children were also the Lord's offspring in his covenant relationship with Israel. By sacrificing her children, Jerusalem confirmed her Canaanite ancestry beyond doubt. This is the Lord's first indictment against Israel, that ends with the Lord charging his people with forgetting and not remembering the 'days of your youth' – 16:22, when Israel was alone, naked and vulnerable.

The Lord's second indictment against Israel is she played the harlot in her alliances with other nations, the Egyptians v. 26, the Assyrians v. 28 and Chaldeans v. 29. The former indictment was primarily religious prostitution, while the latter was political.[66] Sacrificing children particularly took place during the reign of Manasseh. 'Manasseh rebuilt the high places his father Hezekiah had broken down, and erected altars to the Baals, and made Asherahs, and worshipped all the host of heaven, and served them. And he built altars in the house of the Lord, of which the Lord had said, ''In Jerusalem shall my name be for ever.'' And he built altars for all the host of heaven in the two courts of the house of the Lord. And he burned his sons as an offering in the valley of the son of Hinnom and practiced soothsaying and augury, and sorcery, and dealt with mediums and with wizards' – 2 Chron. 33:3-6. Ahaz the king of Judah also burned his son as an offering – 2 Kings 16:3. The people of Israel too burned their sons and daughters as offerings, and used divination and sorcery, and sold themselves to do evil in the sight of the Lord – 2 Kings 17:17.

At the beginning of the second indictment, so serious is this in the eyes of the Lord that he exclaims, 'Woe, woe to you' – 16:23, a negative congratulatory term that hints at disastrous consequences of Jerusalem's alliances with other nations. 'Every nation fostered worship of its god(s) for protection and prosperity. Political alliances inevitably involved recognition and veneration of the deities of the partner nations.'[67] 'Woe, woe,' also expresses the Lord's passionate response to her religious harlotry that provoked him to anger – 16:26. The central concept of the covenant the Lord had made with Israel was that in their relationship they were not to enter into treaties with any foreign nations. In Deut. 34:11-16 these alliances were prohibited by the Lord because of the threat of religious compromise. Instead of trusting the Lord Jerusalem took the initiative to enter into alliances with other nations and hired them by luring them with gifts and by erecting shrines to worship foreign idols, gifts that the Lord had given to her. She erected brothels in busy commercial places. These installations are described as *geb* and *rama* – shrines, high places, which may have resembled the Canaanite style rooftop shrines strategically located to capture travellers' attention.[68] As a result she had reversed the roles of prostitute and clients – 16:33-34. The Lord describes this action as openly 'brazen' – 16:30, and implies she has no sense of shame as she publicly flaunted her immoral behaviour he describes as 'an adulterous wife' – 16:32.

JERUSALEM A HARLOT'S DISGRACE –16: 35-43

'Therefore, O harlot, here the word of the Lord. Thus says the Lord God, Because your shame was laid bare and your nakedness uncovered in your harlotries with your lovers, and because of all your idols and because of all the blood of your children that you gave to them, therefore, behold, I will gather all your lovers with whom you took pleasure, and all those you loved and all those you loathed: I will gather them against you from every side and will uncover your nakedness to them, that they may see all your nakedness. And I will judge you as women who break wedlock and shed blood are judged, and bring upon you the blood of wrath and jealousy. And I will give you into the hand of your lovers and they shall throw down your vaulted chamber and break down your lofty places. They shall strip you of your clothes and take your fair jewels and leave you naked and bare. They shall bring up a host against you, and they shall stone you and cut you to pieces with their swords. And they shall burn your houses and execute judgments upon you in the sight of many women. I will make you stop playing the harlot, and you shall also give hire no more. So I will satisfy my fury upon you and my jealousy shall depart from you: I will be calm and will no more be angry. Because you have not remembered the days of your youth but have enraged me with all these things, therefore, behold, I will requite your deeds upon your head, says the Lord God.'

In vs. 35-43, the Lord addresses Jerusalem as a harlot, a whore, and then proceeds to announce a quadruple indictment against her, followed by four stages of his judgment. After declaring the reasons for these accusations the Lord brings against her, he announces 'the statutory penalty in Israel for adultery and murder, judicial execution.'[69] The first two charges against Jerusalem appear in 16:36, the third comes in 16:38, and the fourth comes in 39-41. In v. 37 the Lord says, 'I will gather all your lovers…I will gather them against you from every side.' In v. 38 the Lord says, 'I will judge you as women who break wedlock and shed blood.' And in v. 39, the Lord says, 'And I will give you into the hand of your lovers.' The nations that Jerusalem committed political adultery with will be the people the Lord uses to judge her. Jerusalem's blood will be poured out – v. 38. She will become a bloody victim at the hands of her former lovers. Just as when the Lord found her at her birth she was flailing about in blood, now at the time of her execution the Lord's sentence also cloaks her in blood. In v. 39, the second act of the Lord's sentence these nations will carry out the Lord's judgment, as they strip her of her clothes and her jewels and leave her naked. This public stripping of Jerusalem is an intentional shaming that also leaves her destitute.[70] Her former lovers carry out her execution in three stages. They will firstly destroy the shrines and idols she built, and strip her of the clothes and Jewels the Lord gave to her. Secondly, they will put the inhabitants of Jerusalem to death with the sword and execute the Lord's death sentence. Lastly, they will destroy their homes that prophetically anticipates the destruction of the temple and Jerusalem. Hummel says, 'In this way the Lord destroys the unholy liaisons Jerusalem sought to establish by her whorings. Her paramours turned executioners carry out her execution.'[71] Wright sees a kind of poetic justice about the portrayal of Israel's judgment.[72] Despite the years of prophetic warnings from Isaiah, Hosea, Jeremiah and now Ezekiel, the Lord finally removes his covenantal protection, and abandons Jerusalem to the consequences of her abominations that she insatiably pursued with shameless abandon. The Lord ends his four accusations against Jerusalem by reminding her that she had forgotten the days of her youth and what the Lord had done for her, and instead had enraged and provoked the Lord's anger and fury with her abominations, and is now answerable for all her deeds.

JERUSALEM'S EXCESSIVE SINS –16:44-52

'Have you not committed lewdness in addition to all your abominations? Behold, every one who uses proverbs will use this proverb about you, 'Like mother, like daughter.' You are the daughter of your mother, who loathed her husband and her children: and you are the sister of your sisters, who loathed their husbands and their children. Your mother was a Hittite and your father an Amorite. And your elder sister is Samaria, who lived with her daughters to the north of you: and your younger sister who lived to the south of you is Sodom and her daughters. Yet you were not content to walk in their ways, or to do according to their abominations: within a little time you were more corrupt than they in all your ways. As I live, says the Lord God, your sister Sodom and her daughters have not done as you and your daughters have done. Behold, this was the guilt of your sister Sodom, she and her daughters had pride, surfeit of food, and prosperous ease but did not aid the poor and needy. They were haughty and did abominable things before me. Therefore, I removed them when I saw it. Samaria has not committed half your sins: you have committed more abominations than they, and have made your sisters appear righteous by all the abominations which you have committed. Bear your disgrace, you also, for you have made judgment favourable to your sisters: because of your sins in which you have acted more abominably than they, they are more in the right than you. So be ashamed, you also, and bear your disgrace, for you have made your sisters appear righteous.'

The description of Sodom is audacious and cuts Jerusalem down to size as they look down on her with superior contempt.[73] The Lord reiterates Jerusalem's damning indictment as he declares her depravity exceeds the wickedness of Samaria and Sodom, whom he speaks of as her two sisters. The proverb 'Like mother, like daughter' – 16:45, also traces her family line once again to the ancestry of her mother as a Hittite and her father as an Amorite, he first mentions in 16:3. The provocative comparison with Samaria and Sodom who were notorious for their sinful behaviour is to shock Jerusalem into facing the reality of her degeneracy. In excelling the depravity of these two nations, ironically she made them appear less culpable and morally superior. 'Jerusalem has unintentionally intervened on her sisters' behalf by diverting attention to herself with her abominable behaviour.'[74] The Lord declares that Jerusalem should bear her disgrace and be ashamed as she has made her sisters appear more righteous because of all her abominations.

JERUSALEM'S SHAMEFUL RENEWAL –16: 53-63

'I will restore their fortunes, both the fortunes of Sodom and her daughters, and the fortunes of Samaria and I will restore your own fortunes in the midst of them, that you may bear your disgrace and be ashamed of all that you have done, becoming a consolation for them. As for your sisters, Sodom and her daughters shall return to their former estate, and you and your daughters shall return to your former estate. Was not your sister Sodom a byword in your mouth in the day of your pride, before your wickedness was uncovered? Now you have become like her an object of reproach for the daughters of the Philistines those round about who despise you. You bear the penalty of your lewdness and your abominations, says the Lord.

''Yes, thus says the Lord God: I will deal with you as you have done, who have despised the oath in breaking the covenant, yet I will remember my covenant with you in the days of your youth, and I will establish with you an everlasting covenant. Then you will remember your ways, and be ashamed when I take your sisters, both your elder and your younger, and give them to you as daughters, but not on account of the covenant with you. I will establish my covenant with you and you shall know that I am the Lord, that you may remember and be confounded, and never open your mouth again because of your shame, when I forgive you all that you have done, says the Lord God.''

After the condemnation of Jerusalem and the devastating sentence passed on her it comes somewhat as a surprise she is on the receiving end of an oracle of restoration. As we read about the Lord executing his fierce judgment on Jerusalem, such was the depravity of her abominable sins the only thing that saved his people from complete annihilation was the covenant he made with Israel. The Lord's covenant embraced both his wrath and mercy. Hummel draws our attention to the fact that restoration in the fullest biblical sense is not just restoration to the previous state but to something much better.[75] The Lord alludes to Samaria and Sodom and emphasises how much more abominable Jerusalem's sins are, so that she may be ashamed and feel the disgrace because of her depravity – 16:54. Previously, Jerusalem in her pride looked down upon Samaria as a byword, but now she too has become an object of reproach – 16:56-57. While the restoration of Samaria and Sodom is mentioned, as Sodom has been raised to the ground this may allude to the Canaanite element within the Israelite population.[76]

'Thus says the Lord' – 16:59, emphasises the long oracle Ezekiel delivered is from the Lord himself. The Lord reiterates that Jerusalem's judgment was brought upon herself because of her contempt for the covenant with its inbuilt blessings and curses. As she despised the oath in breaking the covenant – 16:59, the covenant curses have been evoked resulting in judgment. Yet despite this, the Lord's faithfulness, his steadfast love and mercy, lead to his covenant promise of restoration. Here we find a striking contrast between the Lord's faithfulness and the peoples' failure to abide by the oath of the covenant. Yet the Lord promises to remember his covenant with Israel in the days of her youth, and he will establish an everlasting covenant with his people – 16:60, the covenant in Lev. 26:40-45. Block captures the importance of a renewed covenant when he says:

> Ezekiel herewith envisions not the establishment of a new covenant to meet the needs of a new historical situation, but the reinstitution, the fulfillment, of the eternal covenant made long ago. Jerusalem's infidelity had caused him to suspend its benefits and to enforce its curses, but this response was neither permanent nor irrevocable. Ezekiel's present message of hope is based …on the irrevocable word of God. Jerusalem may treat his covenant with contempt, but he will not. If his punishment of his people follows the line of his ancient warnings, their restoration is assured by his ancient promises. After all, he is Yahweh: he has spoken, and he will make good his word.[77]

Due to their abominable sins the Lord's renewed covenant will astonish his people and his forgiveness will invoke an intense sense of shame as they remember their past conduct. The exiles felt let down by the Lord, as they believed he would always provide them with covenant protection, but the Lord has gone to great lengths to dispel their complaint against him. No longer would they have reason to open their mouth to complain because of the shame of being exiled – 16:63. As this lengthy chapter concludes the Lord announces the recognition formula, 'you will know that I am the Lord,' that plays such a prominent part in Ezekiel's prophesies – 16:62.

ALLEGORY OF THE EAGLE & VINE –17: 1-24

'The word of the Lord came to me: "Son of man, propound a riddle and speak an allegory to the house of Israel, say, 'Thus says the Lord God: A great eagle with great wings and long pinions rich in plumage of many colours, came to Lebanon and took the top of the cedar. He broke off the topmost of its young twigs and carried it to a land of trade, and set it in a city of merchants. Then he took of the seed of the land and planted it in fertile soil, he placed it beside abundant waters. He set it like a willow twig and it sprouted and became a low spreading vine and its branches turned toward him, and its roots remained where it stood. So it became a vine and brought forth branches and put forth foliage.

But there was another great eagle with great wings and much plumage, and behold this vine bent its roots toward him, and shot forth its branches toward him that he might water it. From the bed where it was planted he transplanted it to good soil by abundant waters, that it might bring forth branches and bear fruit, and become a noble vine. Say, Thus says the Lord God: Will it thrive? Will he not pull up its roots and cut off its branches so that all its fresh sprouting leaves wither? It will not take a strong arm or many people to pull it from its roots. Behold, when it is transplanted will it thrive? Will it not utterly wither when the east wind strikes it – wither away on the bed where it grew?''

Then the word of the Lord came to me: ''Say now to the rebellious house, Do you not know what these things mean? Tell them, behold, the king of Babylon came to Jerusalem and took her king and her princes and brought them to Babylon. And he took one of the seed royal and made a covenant with him, putting him under oath. (The chief men of the land he had taken away that the kingdom might be humble and not lift itself up, and that by keeping his covenant it might stand). But he rebelled against him by sending ambassadors to Egypt that they might give him horses and a large army. Will he succeed? Can a man escape who does such things? Can he break the covenant and yet escape? As I live says the Lord God, surely in the place where the king dwells who made him king, whose oath he despised, and whose covenant with him he broke, in Babylon he shall die. Pharaoh with his mighty army and great company will not help him in war when mounds are cast up and siege walls built to cut off many lives. Because he despised the oath and broke the covenant, because he gave his hand and yet did all these things, he shall not escape. Therefore, thus says the Lord God: As I live, surely my oath which he despised and my covenant which he broke, I will requite upon his head. I will spread my net over him, and he shall be taken in my snare, and I will bring him to Babylon and enter into judgment with him there for the treason he has committed against me. And all the pick of his troops shall fall by the sword and the survivors shall be scattered to every wind: and you shall know that I, the Lord, have spoken."

Thus says the Lord God, "I myself will take a sprig from the lofty top of the cedar and will set it out: I will bring of from the topmost of its young twigs a tender one, and I myself will plant it upon a high and lofty mountain. On the mountain height of Israel I will plant it, that it may bring forth boughs and bear fruit, and become a noble cedar: and under it will dwell all kinds of beasts. In the shade of its branches birds of every sort will nest. And all the trees of the field shall know that I the Lord bring low the high tree, and make high the low tree, dry up the green tree, and make the dry tree to flourish. I the Lord have spoken, and I will do it."

In Ch. 17, Ezekiel receives a prophetic oracle from the Lord for the house of Israel. Hummel points out, '12:1-16 and 17:1-24 have a similarity, although 12:1-16 is an action prophecy, while 17:1-24 is an allegorical drama.'[78] The literary composition of Ch. 17 has a duality that permeates the entire prophecy. There is a riddle and a fable, a fable and an interpretation. Two eagles, two plants, two judgments. Earthly and divine agents, and a message of doom and hope.[79] The riddle is in the form of a fable. The first part tells a story – 3-8, and the second part invites an interpretation – 9-10. In 11-21, the Lord gives Ezekiel the historical and theological interpretations to announce to the rebellious house of Israel. Ch. 17 divides into four parts. The allegory of the two eagles – 1-10: the historical interpretation – 11-18: the theological interpretation – 19-21, and a new allegory – 22-24.[80]

Up to Ch. 17, the Lord has described the abominations of his people, their political alliances and the broken covenant. Now he uses the allegory of two eagles, the first eagle represents Nebuchadnezzar and the tree is Jerusalem. The top of the cedar he breaks off refers to King Jehoiachin taken to Babylon with his family and leading nobility of Jerusalem who enjoyed the benevolence of the king. After the first exile to Babylon Nebuchadnezzar appointment Zedekiah as a puppet king, but he made an alliance with Egypt against Babylon. Because of this Nebuchadnezzar comes to besiege Jerusalem, however the Egyptians will not help Zedekiah against the Babylonians, who capture Zedekiah, kill his sons before him and gouge out his eyes, destroy the temple and Jerusalem. Zedekiah's political alliance with Egypt betrayed his alliance with Babylon, not only was he treacherous to them he also broke and despised the covenant with the Lord. So the Lord's judgment will be carried out by Nebuchadnezzar. The destruction of the temple and Jerusalem is not solely because of Zedekiah's alliances with foreign nations, it is because of the Lord's divine retribution through the Babylonians. The Lord's judgment is likened to a hunter en-snaring his pray with a net and deporting his captives to a foreign land, as Zedekiah despised the oath and broke the covenant and committed treason against the Lord – 17:18-20. When their defeat and deportation takes place, the exiles will acknowledge it is the hand of the Lord that accomplished this.

The Lord has already alluded to the survival of a remnant of his people that he will save, and now this theme is taken up again at the end of his oracle of judgment. Now the Lord likens himself to an eagle as he takes a sprig from the loft top of the cedar. A tender sprig is broken off from the highest of its young sprigs and planted on a lofty mountain of Israel –17:22-23. This sprig is a very special one and the Hebrew word used for 'tender, soft' is unparalleled and belongs to other horticultural expressions that have messianic overtones beginning with 'shoot' and 'branch' that refer to the line of David culminating in Christ.[81] Zedekiah's exile will not mark the end of the Davidic line of kings, as this tree will flourish, spread its branches and be fruitful and provide protection. In the Garden of Eden, there is the allusion to the tree of life, here the allusion is to the Hebrew mythological motif know as 'the cosmic tree.' This tree that is planted on the high mountain of is an allusion to Mount Zion, that is significant in later oracles, and which will have a widespread impact,[82] a reference to the universal salvation in Christ.

PARABLE OF THE LIONESS –19: 1-9

'And you, take up a lamentation for the princes of Israel, and say: What a lioness was your mother among lions. She couched in the midst of young lions rearing her cubs. And she brought up one of her cubs who became a young lion and he learned to catch prey to devour men. The nations sounded an alarm against him, he was taken in their pit: and they brought him with hooks to the land of Egypt. When she saw that she was baffled, that her hope was lost, she took another of her cubs and made him a young lion. He prowled among the lions, he became a young lion, and he learned to catch prey, he devoured men. And he ravaged their strongholds, and laid waste their cities and the land was appalled and all who were in it, at the sound of his roaring. Then the nations set against him snares on every side, they spread their net over him: he was taken into their pit. With hooks they put him into a cage, and brought him to the king of Babylon: they brought him into custody, that his voice should no more be heard upon the mountains of Israel.'

Ezekiel's previous oracles were about the kings of Judah. Ch. 12 was about Zedekiah, while Ch. 17 was about Jehoiachin and Zedekiah. Now in Ch. 19, the Lord commands Ezekiel to make a lament in the form of an allegory about the fate of the Davidic dynasty, using features of a dirge that creates a solemn atmosphere. Some biblical commentators think Ch. 19 originally came after Ch. 17. Eichrodt in effect says, Ezekiel transforms the lament for the princes of Judah into a declaration of judgment upon the Davidic dynasty who are prey to the powers of death, not only in the past but as a threat to still come.[83] 'Ten of the eighteen uses of lament in the OT occur in Ezekiel, usually in connection with prophecies of judgment and death…Usually a lament mourns a death that has already taken place, but Ezekiel turns the genre into an oracle impending judgment that represents future doom having already taken place.'[84] In this the Lord parodies the kings of Judah and announces the imminent judgment of the last king of the royal line, but he also counters the false hopes of the exiles, who believed that as long as a descendent of David was on the throne in Jerusalem they were under the Lord's covenant protection.[85] The title princes instead of kings is used so as not to dignify them but to mock them, because they no longer were deserving of the title.

Ch. 17:1-9 sub divides into two – 2-4 and 5-9, the lioness and her first cub, and the lioness and her second cub. In the first allegory, the dominant theme the metaphor of the lion is a common symbol of royalty in the ancient Near East. In Israel's history, the lion metaphor had special significance, and the nation of Judah is compared to a lion in Num. 23:24 and 24:9. Jesus himself is also the 'Lion of the tribe of Judah' – in Rev. 5:5. Most scholars identify the first lion Jehoahaz (who reigned only 3 months) and the only one of Judah's last kings taken to Egypt. While there is no consensus about who the second king is, many identify him as Jehoiachin (who also only reigned 3 months), although some think it may be Zedekiah as he was brought to the king of Babylon. And the mother lioness is deemed to represent the nation of Israel/Judah or Jerusalem, the Davidic dynasty.[86]

PARABLE OF THE VINE – 19: 10-14

'Your mother was like a vine in a vineyard transplanted by the water, fruitful and full of branches by reason of abundant water. Its strongest stem became a ruler's scepter. It towered aloft among thick boughs, it was seen in its height with the mass of its branches. But the vine was plucked up in fury. Cast down to the ground. The east wind dried it up, its fruit was stripped off its strong stem withered: the fire consumed it. Now it is transplanted in the wilderness, in a dry and thirsty land. And fire has gone out from its stem, has consumed its branches and fruit, so that there remains in it no strong stem, no scepter for a ruler. This is a lamentation and has become a lamentation.'

The allusion to your mother a lioness as a metaphor changes to your mother as a vine as a simile. The vine and her branches parallel the lioness and her cubs, although the mother is now the dominant theme – the nation of Judah and the Davidic dynasty. This is the third time the vine and the vineyard are symbolically used, having previously have been mentioned in Ch. 15 and Ch. 17. The vine is planted by the water and flourishes, spreads its boughs, grows tall and is fruitful. (The symbol of the vineyard is also found in the OT in Isaiah 5:1-7 and in the NT in John's Gospel 15:1-8). The description of the luxurious, magnificent vine with its strongest branches symbolises the succession of its royal rulers. But the lament mourns the termination of 400 years of Davidic rule as the vine is destroyed and uprooted because of the Lord's anger and wrath. But, more than that, it has been transplanted to a harsh environment in Babylon. The lamentation couched in terms of a riddle, prophetically alluded to the destruction of the temple and Jerusalem in 587.

THE LORD'S AVENGING SWORD – 21: 1-17

'The word of the Lord came to me, "Son of man, set your face toward Jerusalem and preach against the sanctuaries, prophesy against the land of Israel and say to he land of Israel: Thus says the Lord, Behold I am against you, and will draw forth my sword out of its sheath, and will cut you off from both righteous and wicked. Because I will cut you off from both righteous and wicked, therefore my sword shall go out of its sheath against all flesh from south to north, and all flesh shall know that I the Lord have drawn my sword out of its sheath: it shall not be sheathed again. Sigh therefore son of man: sigh with breaking heart and bitter grief before their eyes. And when they say to you, 'Why do you sigh?' you shall say, 'Because of the tidings. When it comes, every heart will melt and all hands will be feeble, every spirit will faint and all knees will be as weak as water. Behold, it comes and it will be fulfilled.'

And the word of the Lord came to me: "Son of man, prophesy and say, Thus says the Lord, say:

A sword, a sword is sharpened and also polished,
    sharpened for slaughter, polished to flash like lighting.
Or do we make mirth? You have despised the rod, my son, with
everything of wood. So the sword is given to be polished that is
may be handled: it is sharpened and polished to be given into the
hand of the slayer. Cry and wail, son of man, for it is against my
people: it is against all the princes of Israel, they are delivered
over to the sword with my people. Smite therefore upon your
thigh. For it will not be a testing – what could it do if you despise
the rod?'' says the Lord God.'

The Lord's relentless theme of judgment continues in Ch. 21,
with a series of four oracles whose common theme is the 'sword,'
and all four are closely linked to historical circumstances The
'sword' is one of the Lord's themes that permeates his oracles to
the exiles, occurring ninety times in the book and fifteen times in
Ch. 21. Although none of the oracles in this chapter are dated,
Ezekiel's call came in 593 and Ch. 24 is dated by him five years
later to 588. Ch. 21 can be subdivided into four sections.

* The riddle of the sword – 1-7.
* The song of the sword   – 8-17.
* The agent of the sword – 18-27.
* The return of the sword – 28-32.

The first three sections begin, 'the word of the Lord came to
me' and the fourth begins, 'Thus says the Lord God. 'A clear
progression in the sword's involvement is also evident. In the first
oracle, the Lord himself wields the sword. In the second, the
sword seems to act independently. In the third, the Lord gives the
sword to his agent to act for him. In the final oracle, the sword is
returned to its sheath after doing its job.'[88]

There are a number of textual difficulties in Ch. 21, and some
verses 'defy translation – or perhaps translation at all, due to
its semi-poetic nature, or an actual poem or song may underlie
it. There are many linguistic problems in Ch. 21, 'repetitions,
exclamations, choppy staccato constructions, incomplete and

garbled sentences, unusual forms, absence of rhythm, and puzzling motifs.'[9] Accompanying the riddle, the Lord instructs Ezekiel to perform three symbolic signs. To sigh with breaking heart and bitter grief – v. 6. To cry and wail – v. 12 and to clap your hands – v. 14.

The first half of the first oracle is in the form of a riddle, and the second half interprets it. In the first sword oracle, the Lord instructs Ezekiel to set his face toward Jerusalem and preach against the sanctuaries and prophesy against the land of Israel, although he is addressing the exiles – v. 2. This indicates the riddle is directed at the city and the Lord himself is against Jerusalem. The disturbing image portrayed is that of the Lord as a warrior wielding his sword against an enemy, against his own people, the inhabitants of Jerusalem. Wielding the sword represents an act of war as the agent of death and everyone will recognise the ruthless destruction is from the Lord.

'Because of these tidings. When it comes every heart will melt and all hands will be feeble, every spirit will faint, and all knees will be weak as water' – v. 7 describes the debilitating effect on the people as their courage fails and their strength deserts them. Verse 7 can be a warning about the Babylonian siege of Jerusalem, or the impact on the inhabitants when it is destroyed by Nebuchadnezzar, or a report that precedes the message of judgment on Jerusalem.[90] The Lord instructs Ezekiel, 'to sigh with breaking heart and bitter grief' – v. 6, as his oracles failed to convince the exiles. In this symbolic sign-act, he is to express the heartache and trauma of the Lord's judgment on Jerusalem, by groaning and expressing the deepest grief and emotional pain. At the end of the first oracle, the Lord declares, 'Behold, it comes and it will be fulfilled' – v. 7. This was to counter the false hope of the exiles that the Lord would rescue Jerusalem because of his covenant with his people.

The Lord informs Ezekiel that the people will ask him the meaning of his actions at which he is to interpret the riddle. 'The prophet enters into a very deep experience of fellowship with his people by sharing their suffering…The disturbance caused by the prophet's human cry becomes a symbol.'[91] And Block says, 'The first and third statements describe internal emotional and mental trauma. The second and fourth refer to the psychosomatic effects of the report,'[92] that are reminiscent of their response to the Day of the Lord in 7:17.

In verses 8-17, once again, the sword dominates the second oracle from the Lord as he instructs Ezekiel to prophesy. Poetically he says:

> A sword, a sword is sharpened and also polished,
> sharpened for slaughter, polished to flash like lighting.

Here the avenging sword in ominous tones takes on a life of its own with its own destructive power. And although it is not named it is the sword of the Lord, sharpened for slaughter, and a polished weapon ready to cause utter chaos. This poetic image of the sword, menacing and terrifying, 'Is a song full of ecstatic passion and uninhibited savagery…the description grows so intense as to be perceptible to the senses. The sword seems to have a power of its own as it darts and thrusts or swings to and fro to do its bloodthirsty and hideous task.'[93] 'Or do we make mirth' – v. 10, indicates the people do not take Ezekiel seriously and are somewhat derisive. Moreover, they have despised the Lord's discipline – v. 10, refusing to listen when the Lord rebuked them through Hosea, Isaiah and Ezekiel. The foreboding doom that accompanies the riddle of the sword sharpened for action is accentuated when it is handed over into the hand of 'the slayer' – v. 11, the agent of the sword. Once the sword is handed over the Lord instructs Ezekiel to cry and wail, and loudly beat his thigh – v. 12, to enact a dramatic sign of intense mourning: because the victims are the princes and the people of Israel. This sign also points to an overwhelming experience of pain and suffering at the judgment the sword meets out. Zimmerli says, 'In the prophet's groaning we hear that, in what is to happen, a truly catastrophic event, even in God's estimate, will be accomplished upon his own people.'[94]

THE DANCE OF THE SWORD –21: 14-17

'Prophesy therefore, son of man: clap your hands and let the sword come down twice, yes three times, the sword for those to be slain. It is the sword for the great slaughter, which encompasses them, that their hearts may melt, and many fall at all their gates. I have given the glittering sword: ah! it is made like lightning, it is polished for slaughter. Cut sharply to the right and left where your edge is directed. I also clap my hands and I will satisfy my fury: I the lord have spoken.''

In Ch. 17:1-13 the image of the sword wrecks havoc and destruction, but the devastating annihilation of the sword in 21:14-17 poetically depicts the Lord's sword as being even more catastrophic and deadly as it is described as – 'glittering' and 'like lightening' and 'polished for slaughter' – v. 15. When Ezekiel is instructed by the Lord to prophesy he is to 'clap his hands and let the sword come down, twice, yes thrice, the sword for those to be slain' – v. 14. The action of clapping his hands portrays his anger because the Lord was provoked by his people. As the sword swishes back and forth (does Ezekiel wield the sword also as a sign-act?) the image is one of carnage with dead bodies scattered everywhere. Ezekiel prophesies the dance of the sword or he enacts it, whatever the interpretation is, the sword represents in a concrete way the judgment of God that will take place. The extensive allegory of the sword in Ch. 17 and the frenzied activity in all directions of the slashing sword dance – 'cut sharply to the right and left' – v. 17, indicates to the exiles the reality of the drama it symbolises. When the Lord says, 'I myself will clap my hands,' this declares in the strongest way possible, his personal action and his judgment that is enacted by the sword and which will satisfy his fury – his wrath will be appeased. This shocking oracle depicts the sword as the Lord's instrument of judgment against his own people. Hummel says, 'That Yahweh himself will satisfy his own wrath by executing judgment is a prototype of God's climactic, vicarious satisfaction on Calvary.'[95]

BABYLON THE SWORD BEARER – 21: 18-27

'The word of the Lord came to me again: "Son of man, mark two ways for the sword of the king of Babylon to come, both of them shall come forth from the same land. And make a signpost, make it at the head of the way to a city: mark a way for the sword to come to Rabbah of the Ammonites and to Judah and to Jerusalem the fortified. For the king of Babylon stands at the parting of the way at the head of the two ways to use divination: he shakes the arrows, he consults the teraphim, he looks at the liver. Into his right hand comes the lot for Jerusalem to open the mouth with a cry, to lift up the voice with shouting, to set battering rams against the gates, to cast up mounds, to build siege towers. But to them it will seem like a false divination: they have sworn solemn oaths, but he brings their guilt to remembrance that they may be captured.

Therefore, thus says the Lord God: Because you have made your guilt to be remembered, in that your transgressions are uncovered, so that in all your doings your sins appear, because you have come to remembrance you shall be taken in them. And you O unhallowed wicked one, prince of Israel, whose day has come, the time of your final punishment, thus says the Lord God: Remove the turban and take off the crown, things shall not remain as they are: exalt that which is low and abase that which is high. A ruin, ruin, ruin I will make it: there shall not be even a trace of it until he comes whose right it is, and to him I will give it."'

This new oracle from the Lord to Ezekiel for the exiles is linked to the previous two sections by the prominent theme of the 'sword' – v. 19. The king of Babylon, Nebuchadnezzar, is identified as the bearer who wields the sword, and this oracle can almost definitely be dated to 588 (2 Kings 25:1, Jer. 39:1), or very early 587 BC, after Zedekiah, king of Judah, rebelled against Babylon his overlord, as did the nation of Ammon.[96] The Lord instructs Ezekiel to draw a map presumably in the sand where two roadways meet and to mark a signpost and place it at the fork in the road for the king of Babylon to come – v. 18. Nebuchadnezzar faces the decision about which two nations to attack first and Damascus is often identified as the major crossroad where the choice was made. The Lord's oracle dramatically prophesies he will make the fateful decision to attack Jerusalem, yet behind this choice is God's providential hand. Jeremiah, Ezekiel's older contemporary was informed by the Lord, 'Out of the north evil shall break forth upon all the inhabitants of the land. For, lo, I am calling all the tribes of the kingdom of the north, says the Lord: and they shall come and every one shall set his throne at the entrance of the gates of Jerusalem, against all its walls round about, and against all the cities of Judah. And I will utter my judgments against them for all their wickedness in forsaking me: they have burned incense to other gods, and worshipped the works of their own hands' – Jer. 1:13-16. The Lord's oracle also predicts the Babylonians will besiege Jerusalem with battering rams against the gates, and make mounds to build ramps to build siege towers – v. 22.

The Hebrew construction for Jerusalem being fortified, 'highlights the impregnability of the city that throws into sharper relief the devastating power of the sword.'[97] At the time Ezekiel received the oracle Nebuchadnezzar had still to arrive at the Damascus crossroad, and as Ezekiel sketched out a map probably on a clay brick this was a prophetically symbolic action. The mention of Nebuchadnezzar who uses divination to decide which city to attack is dismissed as fraudulent by those in Jerusalem, and the oath Zedekiah had with Nebuchadnezzar is also treated with contempt by them, as they think the Lord will protect Jerusalem – v. 21-23. But Zedekiah had also made an alliance with Egypt and had therefore broken the covenant with the Lord and forfeited his protection.

Following the anticipation of Nebuchadnezzar's siege of Jerusalem the Lord unequivocally announces his judgment on Jerusalem in phrases that progressively increase and intensify her guilt. This is indicated by the synonymous expressions for their offences: *'awon* – 'iniquity, perversion, guilt' – *pesaim* – 'rebellious actions' – *hatttot* – 'sins, the failure to meet the covenantal standards' – and *kol alilot* – 'all your vile deeds.'[98]

Simultaneously, three different verbs also highlight their crimes: '*hizkir* – 'to bring to remembrance, into account' – *higleh* – 'to reveal, disclose' – *nir'eh* – 'to be seen, brought to light.'[99] The Lord's condemnation of Jerusalem reaches its climax with a damning fury as he unleashes his wrath against Zedekiah whom he labels the 'unhallowed and wicked one' – v. 5. A denunciation unparalleled in other prophetic books. As the Lord announces his judgment on Jerusalem and specifically on Zedekiah he declares the day of punishment has arrived. The Lord's judgment will humiliate Zedekiah who, 'will be stripped of the insignia of royalty, the turban and the crown' – v. 26.[100] 'A ruin, ruin, ruin I will make it: there shall not even be a trace of it' – v. 27, emphatically indicates nothing that exists will ever be the same again, 'Yahweh himself will bring events that can almost be described as apocalyptic.'[101] Such is horrific prospect of the finality of the Lord's judgment. The destruction of the temple and Jerusalem in 587 by Nebuchadnezzar and deportation of its remaining inhabitants to Babylon was a fulfillment of the Lord's judgment – v. 27.

GOD'S WRATH ON JERUSALEM – 22: 1-16

'Moreover the word of the Lord came to me saying, "And you son of man, will you judge, will you judge the bloody city? Then declare to her all her abominable deeds. You shall say, Thus says the Lord God: A city that sheds blood in the midst of her that her time may come, and that makes idols to defile herself. You have become guilty by the blood which you have shed and defiled by the idols which you have made: and you have brought your day near, the appointed time of your years has come. Therefore, I have made you a reproach to the nations and a mocking to all the countries. Those who are near and those who are far from you will mock you, you infamous one full of tumult."

"Behold, the princes of Israel in you, every one according to his power, have been bent on shedding blood. Father and mother are treated with contempt in you: the sojourner suffers extortion in your midst, the fatherless and the widow are wronged in you. You have despised my holy things and profaned my Sabbaths. There are men in you who slander to shed blood, and men in you who eat upon the mountains: men commit lewdness in your midst. In you men uncover their father's nakedness: in you they humble women who are unclean in their impurity. One commits abominations with his neighbour's wife: another lewdly defiles his daughter-in-law: another in you defiles his sister, his father's daughter. In you men take bribes to shed blood: you take interest and increase and make gain of your neighbours by extortion, and have forgotten me, says the Lord God.''

'Behold, therefore, I strike my hands together at the dishonest gain which you have made, and at the blood which has been in the midst of you. Can your courage endure, or can your hands be strong, in the days that I shall deal with you? I the Lord have spoken and I will do it. I will scatter you among the nations and disperse you through the countries, and I will consume your filthiness out of you. And I shall be profaned through you in the sight of the nations: and you shall know that I am the Lord.''

Ch. 22 contains three separate oracles 1-16, 17-22, and 23-31. 'The word of the Lord came to me,' introduces each oracle, and the recognition formula 'you will know that I am the Lord,' concludes the first oracle, and a variation concludes the second. The first oracle is addressed to 'the bloody city,' the second to 'the house of Israel' and the third to 'the unclean land.'[102] 'The themes of the three are similar, but with different approaches or metaphors. 1) A general indictment of Jerusalem for a great variety of ceremonial and moral violations. 2) The use of metallurgical imagery to describe the house of Israel. 3) The offences of all classes of Israelite society.'[103] The Lord instructs Ezekiel to declare to Jerusalem all her abominable deeds that she is charged with. The city is indicted as 'the bloody city' Block interprets as a shocking expression, because this invites a comparison of the crimes perpetrated in the Judean capital with Assyria's brutal treatment of conquered people.[104] The charge relating to 'blood' occurs in v. 2, 3, 4, 6, 8, and 12. In v. 3, the indictment against Jerusalem is that she is a city that sheds blood that is repeated in vs. 6, 8, and 12. This theme was raised earlier by the Lord in 7:23, where the land is 'full of bloody judicial crimes' and in 9:9, where the land is 'filled with bloodshed.' In Ch. 24:6, 9, the charge 'woe to the bloody city' that means 'city of bloodshed' repeats the indictment of Ch. 22:1, in which blood represents murder.[105] The charge of shedding blood is linked with the indictment of making idols that leads to the accusation Jerusalem is guilty, because of the blood she has shed and is defiled because of the idols she has made – vs. 3-4. Previously the Lord charged the city because of her abominations, primarily idolatrous practices and sexual offences.

> Idolatry and bloodguilt are particularly grave crimes because they strike at the foundation of Israel's communal life. The former a violation of the first four terms of the covenant, undermine the nation's vertical relationship with Yahweh: the latter, shorthand for all kinds of social ills, undermines the members' horizontal relationships.[106]

Because of these covenantal violations the city is guilty and, 'the appointed time of her years has come' – v. 4, the day of the Lord's judgment. Because of the atrocities of bloodshed and idolatry, these twin abominations precipitate the mockery, and the taunts, and the reproach of other nations the Lord unleashed on the city. The Lord has made Jerusalem a disgrace and a mockery among all the nations. 'The ridicule is intensified because of the disconnection between what the people claimed to be and their behaviour in the eyes of outsiders...The final phrase, 'great in confusion/turmoil/tumult' – v. 5, aptly summarises a society that has lost both chart and compass. One is tempted to apply it to contemporary Western culture.'[107] Block perceives that because Jerusalem has been disgraced and mocked by the nations, 'she failed to achieve the Lord's vision in Deuteronomy for the nation, to be exalted over the nations for praise, fame and honour' – Deut. 26:19. Now she must prepare for the full force of the covenant curse: becoming the object of astonishment/horror, a proverb and a byword.[108] Jerusalem had become so polluted that in the Lord's vision he gives to Ezekiel in Ch. 48:35, Jerusalem is given a new name.

'Behold, the princes-rulers of Israel' – v. 6, is an ominous introduction in the oracle of the systematic presentation against the political leaders because of their abusive use of power that resulted in the social disintegration in Jerusalem. Ezekiel lists a catalogue of charges, specific crimes in which they are guilty of breaking the moral and religious obligations in the Ten Commandments in 6-12. They dishonour – treat with contempt their parents, violating Lev. 19. They take advantage of and victimise refugees, orphans and widows, violating Deut. 24:17, 19-21. They despise and profane the Lord's Sabbaths, violating Lev. 19. Block in effect says, the Hebrew plural indicates they also violate sacred days and years as well. These struck at the heart of the relationship between Yahweh and his people. The Sabbath was a gift to the nation, and a sign of her covenant relationship with the Lord – Exodus 31:13-17. The Sabbaths were a reminder of God's gracious provision and Israel's reliance on the Lord. As such keeping the Sabbaths served as tests of faith.[109] They also violate the sanctity of human life by spilling blood, and take part in pagan ritual meals at cultic centres on the hilltops. They violate a series of sexual taboos prohibited in Lev. 18 and 20. Ezekiel lists five specific sexual crimes. 1) They engage in sexual relations with their mother/stepmother – v. 10, violating Lev. 20:11, a capital crime punishable by death. 2). They engage in sexual intercourse with women during their menstrual period – v. 10, violating Lev. 20:18 resulting in both parties being cut off from their people. 3) They commit adultery with their neighbour's wife – v.11, violating Lev. 20:10 punishable by death. 4) They engage in sexual intercourse with their daughter-in-law – v. 11, violating Lev. 20:12 punishable by death. 5) They engage in sexual intercourse with their sister – v. 11, violating Lev: 20:17 punishable by death. 6) They engage in incestuous sexual intercourse with their sisters – v. 11, violating Lev. 20:17

punishable by death. 7) They abuse peoples' right for justice by
taking bribes for murder-shed blood – v. 12 violating Exodus
23:8. 8) They abuse their position of power by charging ext-
ortionate rates of interest – v. 12, violating Lev. 25:35-37. 'These
offences represent much more than the mere violation of specific
laws of a legal code (The Holiness Code – Lev. 17-26.). They
were symptomatic of the nation's, specifically the leaders'
spiritual decline.'[110] The Lord's damning conclusion at the end of
these indictments is that his people have forgotten him. Hummel
astutely says,

> The theological piece de resistance of the entire section
> comes in the final two Hebrew words of the bill of
> indictment, literally, 'me you have forgotten.' If one
> is not careful it is easy to overlook the tremendous
> significance of this last clause as merely the last in a
> list of discrete offences of various sorts. Instead, it is
> clearly a climatic and comprehensive charge, encomp-
> assing all of the individual ones preceding it. Under-
> lying the objective reality of broken laws is the
> personal offense of having forgotten the Lord and all
> his redemptive acts and promises,[111] as the Lord con-
> fronts an apostate city.

In Ch. 21 the Day of the Lord's judgment on Jerusalem was
graphically portrayed using the metaphor of the sword, with
terrifying allusions about the havoc and slaughter the sword would
inflict when Nebuchadnezzar attacks Jerusalem because of her
abominable sins of idolatry and alliances with foreign nations.
Now in Ch. 22 the Lord's oracle to Ezekiel denounces the
despicable sexual sins and social crimes that have been committed
and for which Jerusalem is charged. And in 13-16 the Lord
announces his sentence of judgment, as he exclaims, 'Behold,
therefore, I strike my hands together,' that signifies his indignation
at the social sins listed in 2-12. As the Lord claps his hands and
announces his judgment, in a rhetorical question he challenges
whether Jerusalem's confidence in herself can withstand his
sentence. Especially as the Lord makes an oath that he will carry

out his sentence. The Lord announces the people will be scattered among the nations, in fulfillment of the covenant curses in Lev. 26:33-39. Through the scattering of the people the Lord says, 'and I will consume your filthiness out of you' – v.15. Zimmerli says, 'In the removal of uncleanness we must think, according to the context, not of a reassuring statement in line with Ch. 36:25, but of the harsh destruction of those who are unclean in a remorseless judgment to annihilation.'[112] Alongside the Lord's catastrophic judgment he also declares, 'and I shall be profaned through you in the sight of the nations: and you shall know that I am the Lord' – v. 16. This sentence announces the climax of the Lord's judgment as the Lord is profaned through his people by their exile in Babylon. In their hearts they will know this was the Lord's sentence and acknowledge his judgment upon them.

GOD'S WRATH CONTINUED – 22: 17-31

'And the word of the Lord came to me, "Son of man, the house of Israel has become dross to me: all of them, silver and bronze and tin and iron and lead in the furnace. Therefore, thus says the Lord God, Because you have all become dross, therefore, behold, I will gather you into the midst of Jerusalem. As men gather silver and bronze and iron and lead and tin into a furnace, to blow the fire upon it in order to melt it: so I will gather you in my anger and in my wrath and I will put you in and melt you. I will gather you and blow upon you with the fire of my wrath and you shall be melted in the midst of it. As silver is melted in a furnace so you shall be melted in the midst of it: and you shall know that I the Lord have poured my wrath upon you."

And the word of the Lord came to me, "Son of man, say to her, You are a land that is not cleansed or rained upon in the day of indignation. Her princes in the midst of her are like a roaring lion tearing the prey: they have devoured human lives, they have taken treasure and precious things: they have made many widows happy in the midst of her. Her priests have done violence to my law and have profaned my holy things: they have made no distinction between the holy and the common, neither have they taught the difference between the unclean and clean, and they have disregarded my Sabbaths, so that I am profaned among them. Her princes in the midst of her are like wolves tearing prey, shedding blood, destroying lives to get dishonest gain. And her prophets have daubed for them with whitewash, seeing false visions and divining lies for them, saying, 'Thus says the Lord God,' when the Lord has not spoken. The people of the land have practiced extortion and committed robbery: they have oppressed the poor and needy, and have extorted from the sojourner without redress. And I sought for a man among them who should build up the wall and stand in the breach before me for the land, that I should not destroy it: but I found none. Therefore I have poured out my indignation upon them: I have consumed them with the fire of my wrath: their way have I requited upon their heads, says the Lord God.''

Verses 17-22 is one of the briefest oracles in the book of Ezekiel. 'The rhetorical force of this oracle is determined to a large extent by the use of repetition. *'Dross'* appears three times in 18-19 and six times the city of Jerusalem is the locus of the smelting event.'[113] Although Jerusalem was the Lord's chosen city where his presence dwelt in the Holy of Holies in the Temple, the peoples' abominable sins forfeited its special status and protection in God's eyes. The Lord begins his oracle about the house of Israel by likening the people to dross in the context of a metaphor about metals. All the people mingled with the silver, bronze, tin, iron and lead in the furnace, have become dross, and Israel is now a worthless pile of metallic slag in the eyes of the Lord. A number of verbs used in the smelting process – 20-21, cast the Lord in the role of the smelter extracting valuable metal from ore that likens the Lord's judgment to a refining furnace. The Lord is the smelter who in his anger and wrath gathers Israel as men gather metallic ore to go into the furnace that represents Jerusalem, to be melted down. As the house of Israel has already been likened to dross-waste material – v. 18, that has come from the smelting process, a further smelting process is alluded to with the people thrown into the furnace – 20-21, that implies they further experience the

Lord's refining judgment. The picture of divine wrath portrayed in this oracle is terrifying, the near obliteration of God's people.[114]

In the final oracle of Ch. 22 the Lord begins by addressing the land and the rain, but this is not referring to the rain being withheld. The allusion to the rain is as a means of judgment to cleanse the land. The inference of the oracle is this cleansing has long been overdue and that the Lord will pour out his fury – judgment on the land. Although the land is addressed, the Lord indicts the princes, the priests, the prophets and the people – the entire strata of society, and condemns them. The princes (leaders) are portrayed as roaring lions mauling their prey – devouring peoples' lives, seizing their wealth, shedding blood and making women widows, destroying lives with dishonest gain – v. 25 and 27. This describes a corrupt and avaricious royal house, colluding with an equally corrupt judiciary and resorting to murder.[115] The priests are charged with inflicting violence to God's law. The Hebrew verb to 'do violence,' is used only seven times in the OT.[116] In this context it means to breach, contravene or pervert or show a blatant disregard God's law that in effect violates it. 'They twisted and interpreted the law for their own end'[117] – the equivalent of doing it violence. The priests also despised and desecrated the Lord's holy things, making no distinction between the sacred and common, the clean and unclean. They also disregarded the Lord's Sabbaths – failed to observe them, and consequently profaned the Lord among them – v. 26. The violation of God's holy laws and the Sabbath reflected the failure to grasp that the torah-law was not just a set of rules – it was a gift to receive and observe with heartfelt obedience.

Earlier in Ch. 13:1-10 the Lord addressed the prophets, 'My hand will be against the prophets who see delusive visions and who give lying divinations: they shall not be in the council of my people, nor be enrolled in the register of the house of Israel, nor shall they enter the land of Israel: and you shall know that I am the Lord God. Because, yes, because they have misled my people, saying, 'Peace,' when there is no peace: and because when the people build a wall they daub it with whitewash.' The prophets offered the people false promises of peace. They whitewashed the truth giving false oracles and visions, and arrogantly claimed to speak God's word when the Lord had not spoken to them – 'A harsher assessment of the prophets is scarcely imaginable.'[118] In the midst of an atmosphere of corrupt princes, priests, and prophets, and their failure to provide any spiritual leadership, the people themselves were corrupt. They practice extortion, commit robbery, oppress the poor and needy and fleece the sojourner – v. 29, as the people imitate their amoral rulers. Such was the endemic corruption that the Lord could not even find one man to build up the wall and stand in the breach – v. 30. The metaphor of a breach in the wall surrounding a city describes an enemy who would soon rush through the breach to defeat the city. Someone who stood in the breach represented a person who repealed the enemy or mended the gap. Here the metaphor signifies the Lord could not find someone to stand for justice, challenge the corruption, and call for repentance, and such a person would have been an intercessor. As such a man was not to be found the Lord pours out his indignation upon the people and he consumes them with the fire of his wrath – v. 31. The Lord's judgment and wrath is not an intellectually cool detached theological response. His wrath is like the full force of a volcanic eruption that emits his righteous anger with the full force of his sentence.

GOD'S CAULDRON OF JUDGMENT – 24: 1-14

'In the ninth year, in the tenth month, on the tenth day of the month, the word of the Lord came to me: "Son of man, write down the name of this day, this very day. The king of Babylon has laid siege to Jerusalem this very day. And utter an allegory to the rebellious house and say to them Thus says the Lord God:

> Set the pot, set it on, pour in water also:
> put in the pieces of flesh, all the good pieces,
> the thigh and the shoulder, fill it with choice bones.
> Take the choicest one of the flock,
> pile the logs under it, boil its pieces,
> simmer also its bones in it.

"Therefore thus says the Lord God: Woe to the bloody city, to the pot whose rust is in it, and whose rust has not gone out of it. Take out of it piece after piece, without making any choice. For the blood she has shed is still in the midst of her: she put it on the bare rock, she did not pour it upon the ground to cover it with dust. To rouse my wrath, to take vengeance, I have set on the bare rock the blood she has shed that it may not be covered. Therefore, thus says the Lord God, Woe to the bloody city. I also will make the pile great. Heap on the logs, kindle the fire, boil well the flesh and empty out the broth, and let the bones be burned up. Then set it empty upon the coals that it may become hot, and its copper may burn that its filththiness may be burned in it, its rust consumed. In vain have I wearied myself, its thick rust does not go out it by fire. Its rust is your filthy lewdness. Because I would have cleansed you and you were not cleansed from your filthiness, you shall not be cleansed any more till I have satisfied my fury upon you. I the Lord have spoken: it shall come to pass. I will not go back, I will not spare, I will not repent: according to your ways and your doings I will judge you, says the Lord God."

In chs. 1-24 the Lord's oracles were messages of judgment. The Lord also spoke about the destruction of Jerusalem and he also challenged peoples' false hope the city was secure. Now, Ch. 24 not only marks the middle of the Book of Ezekiel it is also the pivotal chapter that marks a transition in his ministry, when his tongue was loosened and the Lord's oracles included messages of hope for the future. Ch. 24 also marks the fateful day when the Lord revealed to Ezekiel that Nebuchadnezzar began his siege of Jerusalem, coupled with the anticipation of its fall two and half years later recorded in 33:21. But, tragically for Ezekiel, this fateful day was much more than that. It is also the day when the Lord informed him his that wife would die. As such the Lord instructed Ezekiel to write down the 'name of this day, this very day' – v. 2, that marks a sense of urgency concerning the time when the king of Babylon laid siege to Jerusalem, recorded as being some time in January 587. (Fourteen dates appear in Ezekiel, and all of them except one in 1:1 figure from 597 BC, the first year of the captivity when Ezekiel was taken to Babylon).[119]

At the start of Ch. 24 five years had elapsed during which Ezekiel had announced the oracles from the Lord about the Lord's judgment and destruction of Jerusalem. Since however the exiles were skeptical about his announcements, having a precise record of the oracle about this momentous day of the beginning of the siege of Jerusalem, in retrospect would authenticate his calling as a true prophet. In the future when messengers confirmed the collapse of Jerusalem this would verify Ezekiel's oracle. 'The written dated oracle therefore provided a litmus test of Ezekiel's authenticity...Finally, in January 587, the fearful day of Yahweh had arrived.'[120] The siege of Jerusalem was also a poignant date as this marked the complete collapse of the monarchy instituted under David and Solomon.

Ch. 24 divides into two sections: the parable of the cooking pot and its interpretation – 1.14, and the death of Ezekiel's wife and the significance of her death for the exiles – 15-27. The oracle from the Lord addresses 'the rebellious house' that the Lord informed Ezekiel about at the inauguration of his ministry in Ch. 2. The Lord instructs Ezekiel to announce an allegory about a cooking pot whose rhyming lyrics are like a memorable song about a cooking pot. Block thinks the meaning of the song is determined form the context, 'which suggests either the quotation of a proverbial saying circulating in Jerusalem or the composition of an extended metaphor capturing prevailing thinking...A Jerusalem audience would have undoubtedly have received this song with great enthusiasm and interpreted it positively.'[121] The Lord instructs Ezekiel to interpret this song to the exiles as he announces an oracle of complete destruction as Jerusalem is cast into a cauldron of judgment. The allegory of the cooking pot signifies the preparation of a sumptuous meal with the choice ingredients – vs. 4-5, that represents the peoples' illusion of safety and superiority, as the Jerusalemites considered they were God's elect people safe in the vessel. The ingredients were generously thrown into the pot, a copper cauldron – v.11, not a clay pot for cooking ordinary meals. Hence, a special meal in a copper pot may imply a cultic meal with the allusion to issues of defilement and purity in 11-12.

The interpretation of the parable of the cooking pot begins with the citation formula, 'Therefore, thus says the Lord God: Woe to the bloody city' – v. 6, that announces the shocking news of the imminent catastrophe and tragedy because of the bloodshed, and violence first mentioned in Ch. 22. The moral and spiritual degeneration of Jerusalem is likened to the city being immersed in the cooking pot encrusted with scum, the pollution of the peoples' impurities and wickedness, which challenges the peoples' perception of themselves. The analogy of the people being choice cuts of meat now indicates they are putrid flesh only fit to be discarded as refuse and thrown out of the pot, and rejected piece by piece – v. 6.[122] The Jerusalemites were guilty of shedding the blood of victims – v. 7-8, an allusion to the sacrificial slaughter of their children and judicial murder. Consequently, the Lord's wrath will take vengeance on Jerusalem and on her inhabitants, as the blood they shed is a perpetual witness to the crimes they committed.

The Lord's first oracle of woe condemned the Jerusalemites, now the second oracle of woe speaks of the utter destruction of the city. The second oracle of woe of the Lord's judgment on 'the bloody city' – v. 9, increases in intensity as the image of the cooking pot finds Jerusalem and its inhabitants immersed in it. Logs are piled onto the fire to cook the broth and the liquid is poured out so ten the bones are burned up – cremated into a useless mass of carbon. The empty pot is once again heated on the intense heat of the fire that its filthiness may be consumed – v. 11. The filthiness represents the moral and spiritual degeneracy of Jerusalem: 'the magnitude of its corruption'[123] and their filthy lewdness – wickedness – v. 13. Wright says, 'the city itself was so corrupt the only fate that was now appropriate for it was the allconsuming meltdown of final destruction.'[124] When the Lord speaks of the rust of the pot not being consumed by the intense heat of the fire, the rust is the city's filthy lewdness that probably represents, 'the social and legal disintegration that follows violent political repression.'[125] The oracle reaches its climax as the Lord declares his judgment that will satisfy his fury-wrath – v. 13. The Lord declares that he has spoken and that his judgment will be fulfilled and he emphatically announces four personal oaths that 'I will do it.' 'I will not go back,' 'I will not spare,' I will not repent' – v. 14. 'The oracle concludes with the most emphatic affirmation of divine resolve in Ezekiel.'[126] The Lord's justifies the irrevocable nature of his judgment on Jerusalem as he declares the judgment is compatible with the wanton behaviour of the city.

DEATH AND DESTRUCTION – 24: 15-27

'Also the word of the Lord came to me: "Son of man, behold, I am about to take the delight of your eyes away from you at a stroke: yet you shall not mourn or weep nor shall your tears run down. Sigh, but not aloud: make no mourning for the dead. Bind on your turban, and put your shoes on your feet: do not cover your lips, nor eat the bread of mourners." So I spoke to the people in the morning, and at evening my wife died. And on the next morning I did as I was commanded.

And the people said to me, "Will you not tell us what these things mean for us, that you are acting out?" Then I said to them, 'The word of the Lord came to me: 'say to the house of Israel, Thus says the Lord God: Behold, I will profane my sanctuary, the pride of your power, the delight of your eyes, and the desire of your soul: and your sons and you daughters whom you left behind shall fall by the sword. And you shall do as I have done: you shall not cover your lips, nor eat the bread of mourners. Your turbans shall be on your heads and your shoes on your feet: you shall not mourn or weep, but you shall pine away in your iniquities and groan to one another. Thus shall Ezekiel be a sign to you: according to all that he has done, you shall do. When this comes, then you will know that I am the Lord God.'

"And you, son of man, on the day when I take from them their stronghold, their joy and their glory, the delight of their eyes and their heart's desire, and also their sons and daughters, on that day a fugitive will come to you to report the news. On that day your mouth will be opened to the fugitive, and you shall speak and be no longer dumb. So you will be a sign to them, and they will know that I am the Lord.''

Despite the Lord's stated intention for the death of Ezekiel's wife that was completely sprung on him, this must surely rank as the most extraordinary and tragic symbolic sign-act the Lord announced to Ezekiel that on a natural level is beyond comprehension: and which may be considered to be the most poignant moment in the lives of the OT prophets. Yet it is indisputable that in the ministry of these prophets each had their personal cup of suffering to bear. Jeremiah was commanded by the Lord not to marry and not to socialise – Jer. Ch. 16, and Hosea was commanded by the Lord to take back his unfaithful wife – Hosea chs. 1-3. Ezekiel and his wife 'the delight of his eyes' – v. 16 together suffered the hardship that accompanied his ministry. For five years he had been struck dumb by the Lord and could only speak when he had to utter an oracle as his wife endured his silence with him. Confined to his own home Ezekiel was commanded by the Lord to enact some of the most bizarre symbolic sign-acts imaginable while he was supported by his wife amongst the disbelieving exiles.

As surely as Ezekiel delighted in his wife, so his wife despite the hardship of his eccentric ministry surely delighted in him, as they consoled one another with their love amongst the exiles. It appears unnaturally cruel that in one devastating blow the Lord informed Ezekiel he was to take his wife's life away from her: and that he was not to observe the cultural ritual of mourning her death amongst his fellow exiles. Nothing prepared him for this heart-wrenching personal tragedy he accepted, without any lament to express his personal feelings, nor his sorrow or his loss: and no record of how he feels about her death is recorded by him. For Ezekiel, 'the why and wherefore of a divine intervention is not open to discussion: the Lord's sovereign freedom does not have to give any reason for what he does.'[127] Ezekiel is informed by the Lord to sigh, but not aloud – v. 17. He is only to mourn his wife inwardly, silently in his heart.

The relationship between Ezekiel and his wife functions as a surrogate for the relationship between the Lord and the temple and Jerusalem – the delight of the Lord's eyes. When the Lord informs Ezekiel he is not to engage in any external ceremonial mourning he does not actually tell him the reason for his wife's death. At this stage, all his is told by the Lord is to put on his turban which the Hebrew root means 'to beautify or glorify,'[128] that indicates it was not the usual turban but a festive one and not to eat any mourning food. On the next day Ezekiel's unquestioning obedience to the Lord instructions is truly extraordinary as he does not question the Lord taking his wife from him. As the text is silent about the matter, we can but speculate whether his fellow exiles comforted Ezekiel and what their reaction to her sudden death was as she was not gravely ill. Unsurprisingly, when his neighbours come to the mourning ceremony for his wife, as he is not dressed in his ritual mourning robes, they perceive his action has some meaning for them and ask what it is. At great personal cost to Ezekiel the Lord used the death of his wife as a tragic symbolic sign to convince the exiles about the coming destruction of the temple and Jerusalem and the death of the city's inhabitants.

When the exiles ask Ezekiel to explain to them why he isn't mourning the death of his wife – v. 19 he addresses them with an oracle the Lord had given to him, as the Lord had now informed him about the reason for her death and the meaning this had for the exiles. Ezekiel now knows the Lord laid claim to him and his wife's death as a prophetic sign to speak to the exiles. The word of the Lord to the exiles was a cataclysmic oracle that spoke of the Lord himself profaning-desecrating his sanctuary in the temple in Jerusalem by his judgment through Nebuchadnezzar. The temple, Jerusalem and their children – 'the pride of your power, the delight of your eyes, and the desire of your soul: and your sons and daughters whom you left behind shall fall by the sword' – v. 21. This bereavement would leave them overwhelmed with inexpressible grief just as Ezekiel had been by the death of his wife. The allusion to the exiles' 'delight of your eyes and the desire of your soul' was a poignant reminder of their yearning for these things, especially as their loss was symbolised by the death of Ezekiel's wife. 'Banished from their native lands, Ezekiel's compatriots were filled with an insatiable longing for the glorious symbol of Israelite pride and identity.'[129] Ezekiel prophesies the exiles will refrain from mourning just as he had done, and will groan and rot away because of their iniquities – v. 23.

> Here it is more of a spiritual and psychological dest-
> itution as each person sorrows silently. The picture is
> of overwhelming grief that no tears or lamentation
> can express adequately, with only an inner pain on
> account of the sins that had brought things to such
> a pass. The prophet's own silent groaning will be
> paralleled by the peoples' inarticulate, unritualised
> expression of bereavement beyond words.[130]

The Lord concludes his oracle to the exiles by confirming Ezekiel will be an incarnate sign to them and that they shall refrain from mourning as he had done, because of the death and destruction coming upon Jerusalem. Then they will know that the Lord is God – v. 24. After this oracle the Lord speaks to Ezekiel and informs him that on the day when the temple and Jerusalem are destroyed and their children murdered, a fugitive will come to him and report the news the atrocities have taken place. And on that day when this news reaches Ezekiel he will be released from being dumb and this news will also be a sign to the people to know he is the Lord – v. 27. Moshe Greenberg perceives that at this news the exiles' 'hostility to Ezekiel would be removed at a stroke. The calamity would be the start of his fortune – his and God's – as the people would eventually realise the redemptive signif-icance of Jerusalem's fall.'[131] As a result the exiles' belief in the theology of the inviolability of Jerusalem would once and for all come to an end. The opening of Ezekiel's mouth would signify a turning point in Israel's history. The era of judgment on the peoples' idolatry and sinful abominations had now come to a climatic end. The dawn of a new age of hope could be ushered in.

CHAPTER FIVE

HOPE FOR ISRAEL
33:1-9, 21-22, 34: 36: 37

EZEKIEL THE WATCHMAN – 33: 1-9

'The word of the Lord came to me, "Son of man, speak to your people and say to them: If I bring the sword upon the land and the people of the land take a man from among them, and make him their watchman, and if he sees the sword coming upon the land and blows the trumpet and warns the people, then if any one who hears the sound of the trumpet does not take warning and the sword comes and takes him away, his blood shall be upon his own head. He heard the sound of the trumpet and did not take warning his blood shall be upon himself. But if he had taken warning he would have saved his life. But if the watchman sees the sword coming and does not blow the trumpet so that the people are not warned, and the sword comes and takes any one of them, that man is taken away in his iniquity, but his blood I will require at the watchman's hand."

"So you, son of man, I have made a watchman for the house of Israel: whenever you hear a word from my mouth, you shall give them a warning from me. If I say to the wicked, O wicked man you shall surely die, and you do not speak to warn the wicked to turn from his way, that wicked man shall die in his iniquity, but his blood I will require at your hand. But if you warn the wicked man to turn from his way, and he does not turn from his way: he shall die in his iniquity, but you will have saved your life."

In Ch. 24 after Ezekiel declares the Lord's oracle that predicts the fall of Jerusalem, the news of its demise came six months after it took place that was two years from the date of the oracle. And after the fall of Jerusalem Ezekiel's ministry would span another fifteen years which was three times longer than his first phase. Hummel believes the fall of Jerusalem marks a turning point in the OT and also the history of Israel, just as Christ's death is the turning point and axis of the NT. The judgment of the law in Ezekiel 1-24, now gives way to the Gospel promise of hope and restoration in 33-48.[1] After Ch. 24, chs. 25-32 comprise oracles against other nations, and Ch. 33 is the major transition in the Book of Ezekiel that introduces a message of hope in 34-48. Ch. 33:1-9, which also reaffirms Ezekiel's call to his prophetic ministry as a watchman is remarkably similar to his inaugural call in 3:16-21. Ezekiel's commission as a watchman in Ch. 3 was a personal call, whereas his commission in Ch. 33 is the public call to this ministry. If Ezekiel thought his ministry had come to a natural end after he received the news of the fall of Jerusalem, he was mistaken. Because the Lord reiterates that as a watchman he holds Ezekiel responsible to warn the people with the words he gives him to speak – v. 7.

The Lord's oracle begins with an imaginary scenario in which he brings a sword against a land-country, which ends by declaring that if he warns the people and they ignore him they are responsible for their own death. But if the watchman they appoint fails to warn the people about the attack he will be guilty and held responsible for those who die. There is a double emphasis on the individual responsibility placed on both the watchman and those who hear his warning because each is accountable for their actions – vs. 3-6. Verses 7-9 in which the Lord confirms Ezekiel's call as a watchman are virtually the same as his inaugural call as a watchman in 3: 17-19. And the public portrayal of Ezekiel as a watchman reaffirms once and for all his 'prophetic self-consciousness.'[2] Moreover, the Lord reiterates that he holds him responsible for announcing to the people the words the Lord gives him, and if he fails to do this he will hold him guilty. Equally, if he does warn people and they do not listen they are responsible, but Ezekiel will save his own life.

INDIVIDUAL RESPONSIBILITY – 33: 10-20

"And you, son of man, say to the house of Israel, Thus have you said: 'Our transgressions and our sins are upon us and we waste away because of them, how can we live?' Say to them, As I live says the Lord God, I have no pleasure in the death of the wicked, but that the wicked may turn from his way and live: turn back, turn back from your evil ways: for why will you die, O house of Israel? And you, son of man, say to your people, The righteousness of the righteous shall not deliver him when he transgresses: and as for the wickedness of the wicked, he shall not fall by it when he turns from his wickedness: and the righteous shall not be able to live by his righteousness when he sins. Though I say to the righteous that he shall surely live, yet if he trusts in his righteousness and commits iniquity, none of his righteous deeds shall be remembered: but in the iniquity that he has committed he shall die. Again though I say to the wicked, 'You shall surely die,' yet if he turns from his sins and does what is lawful and right, if the wicked restores the pledge, gives back what he has taken by robbery, and walks in the statutes of life, committing no iniquity: he shall surely live, he shall not die. None of the sins that he has committed shall be remembered against him: he has done what is lawful and right, he shall surely live.

'Yet your people say, 'the way of the Lord is not just,' when it is their own way that is not just. When the righteous turns from his righteousness and commits iniquity, he shall die for it. And when the wicked turns form his wickedness, and does what is lawful and right, he shall live by it. Yet you say, 'the way of the Lord is not just.' O house of Israel, I will judge each of you according to his ways.''

Chapter 33:10-20 only differs slightly from Ch. 18:21-25, and in 10-20 for the first time in the Book of Ezekiel the people admit that the guilt of their sins is the cause of their suffering. Eichrodt says, 'The 'house of rebellion' which has so far maintained such an obstinately closed attitude in face of the charges brought by Ezekiel at last comes to confess its guilt.'[3] The Lord then addresses the peoples' proverbial lament that they are cursed because of their sins and transgressions and feel their situation is hopeless – v. 10. This reflects their demoralised state in exile. There was nothing left for them to hope for. They would die in an unclean land in Babylon far from their home in Jerusalem and far from their children. But the Lord replies by taking an oath on his own life that he has no pleasure in the death of the wicked, but rather that the person repents from their evil ways and lives: and he asks the question, 'for why will you die, O house of Israel?' – v. 11. The Lord instructs Ezekiel to address both the righteous and the wicked, highlighting that the former will not be saved when he sins, and the latter shall be saved if he repents. Verses 12-16 indicate the death sentence of the exiles may be avoided if the people repent from their rebellion against the Lord. The peoples' response to the Lord's announcements is to complain that his ways are not just, but the Lord counters this by insisting that actually their ways are the ones that are not just. The Lord reiterates that if a righteous person commits iniquity he shall die, but if the wicked turns from his sins he shall live: and that He will judge everyone according to their conduct – 17-20. Ezekiel was commissioned as a watchman to declare the Lord's judgment but also to point out the possibility of life for the people once they owned their sin and repented. For almost ten years the exiles heard Ezekiel declaring the Lord's oracles and his warnings of judgment, but the people still deluded themselves that they are not responsible for the crisis they are in and for their loss of hope, instead blaming it on the Lord. Hummel says, 'To the peoples' apparent complaint that the Lord is acting in irrational, inscrutable, or unpredictable ways, the Lord responds that their refusal to accept his offer of 'amazing grace' even in this very last hour is irrational and incredible.'[4]

NEWS OF JERUSALEM FALL – 33: 21-22

'In the twelfth year of our exile, in the tenth month, on the fifth day of the month, a man who had escaped from Jerusalem came to me and said, "The city has fallen." Now the hand of the Lord had been upon me the evening before the fugitive came: and he had opened my mouth by the time the man came to me in the morning: so my mouth was opened, and I was no longer dumb.'

Verses 21-22 were originally closely associated with 24:25-27 – 'on that day a fugitive will come to you to report the news. On that day, your mouth will be opened to the fugitive, and you shall speak and be no longer dumb. So you will be a sign to them: and they will know that I am the Lord.' Ch. 24 not only marks the centre of the Book of Ezekiel, it is also the pivotal chapter that marked a transition in his ministry. Equally, it was the fateful day that the Lord told Ezekiel Nebuchadnezzar would begin his siege of Jerusalem. Now, even though verses 21-22 are brief, their significance in the book of Ezekiel can hardly be overstated. News of the fall of Jerusalem has vindicated Ezekiel's prophetic oracles from the Lord and authenticated his ministry as a true prophet. While this was tragic news about Jerusalem for the exiles, it had immense significance, because it confirmed the fulfillment of the Lord's word that predicted the fall of the city – 24:25-27. For Ezekiel, it too was a pivotal moment in his ministry as it marked the time when the Lord opened his mouth and he was no longer dumb – v. 22. The evening before the messenger arrive he was aware the hand of the Lord was upon him – v. 22, and although the text is silent about this actual event, it indicates Ezekiel was aware that the Lord released him from being dumb. Wright says, 'He describes the experience in the same way as his original call – a profound sensation of the physically overwhelming grip of God.'[5]

It is striking that the narrative does not record the exiles' response to the news about Jerusalem that was of great importance from the messenger. The text also does not record their response to Ezekiel being able to speak again, nor record his response to receiving his speech. This profound change impacted Ezekiel in a deeper sense as now he is quite free to speak while previously the Lord had restrained his speech. His release from his dumbness released him into a new phase of his prophetic ministry. He was now able to fulfill the usual role of a prophet and intercede for his fellow exiles as well as announce the Lord's messages of hope for the future. His decade of symbolic nonverbal communication had ended. It is clear from vs. 23-33, that the hearts of God's people have not changed or repented despite the Lord's judgment on Jerusalem. For both the residents of Judah – 23-29 and those among the exile – 30-33, they still delude themselves and continue in their abominable sins. They are people who hear God's word and accept it with their lips, but their hearts are far from the Lord – v. 31. Their response has been spiritually superficial and they are condemned by their failure to response to Ezekiel's messages from the Lord. Therefore, the Lord says to him:

> As for you son of man, your people who talk together about you by the walls and at the doors of the houses, say to one another, each to his brother, 'Come hear what the word is that comes forth from the Lord.' And they come to you as people, and they hear what you say but they will not do it: for with their lips they show much love, but their heart is set on their gain. And, lo, you are to them like one who sings love songs with a beautiful voice and plays well on an instrument, for they hear what you say, but they will not do it. When this comes – and come it will – then they will know that a prophet has been among them – vs. 30-33.

ORACLE AGAINST THE SHEPHERDS – 34: 1-10

'The word of the Lord came to me: "Son of man, prophesy against the shepherds of Israel, prophesy and say to them, even to the shepherds, Thus says the Lord God: Listen, shepherds of Israel who have been feeding yourselves. Should not the shepherds feed the sheep? You eat the fat, you clothe yourselves with the wool, you slaughter the fatlings but you do not feed the sheep. The weak you have not strengthened, the sick you have not healed, the crippled you have not bound up, the strayed you have not brought back, the lost you have not sought, and with force and harshness you have ruled them. So they were scattered because there was no shepherd and they became food for all the wild beasts. My sheep were scattered over all the mountains and on every high hill: my sheep were scattered over all the face of the earth."

"Therefore, you shepherds, hear the word of the Lord: As I live says the Lord God, because my sheep have become a prey, and my sheep have become food for all the wild beasts since there was no shepherd, and because my shepherds have fed themselves and have not fed my sheep, therefore, you shepherds hear the word of the Lord: Thus says the Lord God, Behold, I am against the shepherds and I will require my sheep at their hand, and put a stop to their feeding the sheep, no longer shall the shepherds feed themselves. I will rescue my sheep from their mouths, that they may not be food for them.''

It is interesting to note, the metaphor of the shepherd was widespread not only in the Bible but in the entire ancient Near East. The picture of gods as shepherds is found in some of the earliest Mesopotamian (Sumerian) literature and in Egyptian literature as well. In Homer, Agamemnon, the leader of the Greeks against Troy, is regularly styled shepherd of the people. And in mythology it's sometimes hard to distinguish whether the shepherd is the god or his agent.[6] In the OT the Lord himself is often called Israel's Shepherd, and is alluded to as 'the Lord is my shepherd' in Psalm 23:1.

Ezekiel Ch. 34 is probably one of the more familiar chapters as people identify the theme of shepherd with Jesus the Good Shepherd in the NT in John 10:7-18. While in Ch. 33 the Lord spoke about people's individual responsibility, his oracle against the shepherds in Ch. 34 highlights the leaders were more responsible for provoking the Lord's judgment. Jeremiah, Ezekiel's older contemporary also denounced the shepherds of Israel – Jer. 23:1-6, and it is possible that Ezekiel was familiar with this material. The Lord condemned the leaders as they failed to provide the quality or integrity of leadership the covenant required. And for more than a century before the fall of Jerusalem the leadership of the kings of Judah led the people 'further into idolatry, injustice and social collapse.'[7] Their failure is described by the Lord using the shepherd metaphor – as a failure to care for the sheep, God's people. In the ancient Near East, the designation of shepherds as leaders is traditional. Also in Israel this designation had a long standing tradition in Num. 27:17, when Moses prayed that the Lord would appoint a man over the congregations as a shepherd. Joel Biwul says, 'When interpreted within its historical context following the fall of Jerusalem Ch. 34 functions as the historical-literary centre of the entire book.'[8] Block points out the content of Ch. 34 reflects a complex structure. 'The citation formula, *koh amar adonay yhwh* – 'Thus says the Lord God' appears five times (v. 2, 10, 11, 17, 20). The signatory formula – *ne'um adonay yhwh* – 'the declaration of the Lord Yahweh' appears four times (v. 8, 15, 30, 31). 'Hear the word of the Lord' – *sim'u* – appears twice (v. 7, 9). The recognition formula, *weyadeuki ani adonay yhwh* – 'And they shall know that I am Yahweh,' appears twice (27, 30): and the oath formula, *hay ani* – 'As I live' appears in v. 7.'[9] Ch. 34, initially has an oracle of judgment followed by an oracle of salvation – vs. 1-10, and vs. 11-24 is an oracle about the Lord fulfilling the role of the shepherd himself.

In 34:2-6 the Lord commands Ezekiel to prophesy against the shepherds of Israel about their failure to care for the sheep-God's people. These verses describe the negligent and abusive leadership of the shepherds who are condemned because they looked after their own interests and neglected God's people. They exploited them and did not care for the weak, the sick and the crippled and failed to bring back the lost, ruling them with harshness – 2-6. We have a picture of ruthless exploitation and self-interest.[10] The metaphor of the shepherds is one with pastoral allusions but the leaders' actions are highlighted as they have caused a crisis. God's people, the sheep-the flock, has been jeopordised because of the gross negligence of the leaders-shepherds, who have been irresponsible with disastrous consequences – the sheep have been scattered over all the face of the earth – v. 6. 'The rulers have taken excellent care of themselves, but they have not cared or the flock.'[11] The Hebrew for wandered–scattered in v.6 highlights that the straying was moral as well, which resulted in pagan worship and the exile in Babylon.[12] Chris Wright perceives the danger that leaders may succumb to in Christian ministry today concerns those entrusted to their care, by establishing a mini-empire – using their authority and power as a symbol of status or source of personal identity.[13] At the end of the first oracle in an oath taken on the Lord's name, the Lord announces his judgment on the shepherds-rulers – vs. 7-9, by reiterating the charges that he levelled against them in 2-6. The Lord denounces them by categorically stating, 'I am against the shepherds: and I will require my sheep at their hand'– v. 10, that indicates the Lord holds them accountable for what they have done, and in effect signals the removal of the shepherds. As a result, the Lord will rescue 'my sheep' as he takes over the ownership of the sheep from the shepherds – v. 10.

THE GOOD SHEPHERD – 34: 11-24

"For thus says the Lord God: Behold, I, I myself will search for my sheep and I will seek them out. As a shepherd seeks out his flock when some of his sheep have been scattered abroad, so I will seek out my sheep: and I will rescue them from all places where they have been scattered on a day of clouds and thick darkness. And I will bring them out from the peoples and gather them from the countries and will bring them into their own land: and I will feed them on the mountains of Israel by the fountains, and in all the inhabited places of the country. I will feed them with good pasture and upon the mountain heights of Israel shall be their pasture: there they shall lie down in good grazing land and on fat pasture they shall feed on the mountains of Israel. I myself will be the shepherd of my sheep and I will make them lie down, says the Lord God. I will seek the lost and I will bring back the strayed, and I will bind up the crippled, and I will strengthen the weak, and the fat and the strong I will watch over, I will feed them in justice.

As for you my flock, thus says the Lord God: Behold, I will judge between sheep and sheep, rams and he-goats. Is it not enough for you to feed on the good pasture, that you must tread down with your feet the rest of your pasture: and to drink of clear water that you must foul the rest with your feet? And must my sheep eat what you have trodden down with your feet and drink what you have fouled with your feet?'

Therefore, thus says the Lord God to them: Behold, I, I myself will judge between the fat sheep and the lean sheep. Because you push with side and shoulder and thrust at all the weak with your horns till you have scattered abroad I will save my flock, they shall no longer be a prey: and I will judge between sheep and sheep. And I will set over them one shepherd my servant David, and he shall feed them: he shall feed them and be their shepherd. And I, the Lord, will be their God and my servant David shall be prince among them: I the Lord, have spoken.''

Having dealt with the shepherds whom the Lord denounced, He now declares that he will take up the role of the shepherd to rescue his flock. A series of active verbs in 11-16 highlights the Lord's care and salvation for the sheep who, 'have been scattered on a day of clouds and deep darkness' – v. 12 which refers to the exile in Babylon. 'I will search for and seek out.' 'I will rescue.' 'I will bring them out.' 'I will feed them.' 'I will be the shepherd of my sheep.' 'I will make them lie down.' 'I will seek the lost.' 'I will bring back the strayed.' 'I will bind up the crippled.' 'I will strengthen the weak.' 'The fat and the strong I will watch over.' The repeated emphasis of the Lord on, 'I will' in these verses reverses the failure of the shepherds to care for the sheep. The oracle about the Lord as the Good Shepherd foretells the restoration of his people to the land of Israel. This is also a glorious picture of the Lord as the Good Shepherd that found its fulfillment in Christ that is alluded to when the Lord says he will appoint a shepherd 'my servant David' to care for his sheep–v. 23.

Having assumed the role of the shepherd the Lord will also provide leadership to govern-judge the affairs of the exiles in Babylon to establish justice. And he will deal with the leaders who are alluded to as rams and he-goats, 'the same class of rapacious and self-serving lay leaders of the community'[14] so the vulnerable weaker members are not victimised by their aggressive leaders. Yet the Lord does not announce judgment on the strong instead he declares his justice. His intention is the deliverance of those who have been oppressed. But then there comes a climatic and dramatic movement in the oracle as the Lord will raise up and appoint a shepherd who is a descendent of David, because of his unconditional covenant with David that a descendent of his would always be on the throne – 2 Samuel 7:12-16. 'The election and survival of the people of Israel was inextricably bound up with Yahweh's covenant with David.'[14] As NT believers we interpret the appointment of a shepherd in a messianic way as it clearly refers to Christ who was descended from David: God's servant in contrast to the self-serving leaders of God's people. The messianic hope of a ruler of Israel and servant of the Lord also finds expression in the eighth century prophet Isaiah and his portrayal of the 'Servant of the Lord in Isaiah 40-55. God also refers to Christ as a prince who will dwell with his people and who symbolises his presence amongst them. With astute perception Block has grasped the significance that the appointment of God's servant, was intended to instill new hope in the hearts of the exiles.[16] This oracle is affirmed by the Lord's divine self-formula, 'And I the Lord will be their God' – v. 24, which reinforces the Lord's irrevocable commitment to the house of David. Hummel sees the prophesy about the future concerning 'my servant David,' to be a striking element and a remarkable announcement.[17]

In vs. 25-31 after the Lord appoints a shepherd 'my servant David' he speaks about the restoration of his covenant relationship with his people: and the 'covenant of peace' – v. 25. The Hebrew word for peace is 'shalom' which means this new covenant will bring wholeness and harmony. This will involve the Lord's salvation in the land on a practical level where the earth is fruitful and the people enjoy security, and where they have been set free from their enemies who enslaved them – vs. 25-27. The new covenant will bring a whole series of rich blessings and bring about a remarkable change in the exiles fortunes. Hummel interprets the people's liberation and their restoration as a second exodus.[8] But the climax of the new covenant is the renewed relationship between the Lord and his people – 'the house of Israel' – as their salvation will be evidence the Lord is their God and that he is with them: and that they are his sheep and he is their shepherd – vs. 30-31. And, 'The true shepherd of God's people is the Lord himself.' Block captures the sublime significance of Ch. 34 when he says:

> The theological implications of Ezek. 34 are both pro-
> found and exhilarating. When Yahweh extends his
> grace to Israel again, the disintegrated deity-nation-
> land triangle is restored. Ezekiel's message of the
> messianic age recognises a measure of truth in his
> contemporaries' theological formulations. Yahweh had
> indeed entered into an eternal marriage covenant with
> them. His promise to David of an eternal title to the
> throne of Jerusalem still stands. These covenant hopes
> will all be fulfilled in the messianic age. At that time,
> when Yahweh's people live securely in their and are
> ruled by a divinely appointed David, and enjoy the
> shalom of God's presence and grace, they will finally
> acknowledge him astheir Saviour and covenant Lord.[19]

THE RESTORATION OF ISRAEL – 36: 8-21

'But you, O mountain of Israel, shall shoot forth your branches and yield your fruit to my people Israel for they will soon come home. For, behold, I am for you, and I will turn to you and you shall be tilled and sown, and I will multiply men upon you, the whole house of Israel, all of it. The cities shall be inhabited and the waste places rebuilt and I will multiply upon you man and beast: and I will cause you to be inhabited as in your former times, and will do more good to you than ever before. Then you will know that I am the Lord. Yes, I will let men walk upon you, even my people of Israel: and they shall possess you, and you shall be their inheritance, and you shall no longer bereave them children. Thus says the Lord God: Because men say to you, 'You devour men, and you bereave your nation of children,' therefore you shall no longer devour men and no longer bereave your nation of children, says the Lord God. And I will not let you hear any more the reproach of the nations, and you shall no longer bear the disgrace of the peoples and no longer cause your nation to stumble, says the Lord God.''

"The word of the Lord came to me: 'Son of man, when the house of Israel dwelt in their own land they defiled it by their ways and their doings: their conduct before me was like the uncleanness of a woman in impurity. So I poured out my wrath upon them for the blood which they had shed in the land, for the idols with which they defiled it. I scattered them among the nations and they were dispersed through the countries: in accordance with their conduct and their deeds I judged them. But when they came to the nations wherever they came, they profaned my holy name, in that men said to them, 'These are the people of the Lord, and yet they had to go out of his land.' But I had concern for my holy name, which the house of Israel caused to be profaned among the nations to which they came."

The deportation to Babylon was a shattering blow to the exiles as they were a displaced people who had lost their homeland. They were refugees in a foreign land far from Jerusalem whose national pride and status had been devastated. In the eyes of the foreign nations Israel had become a reproach, the target of mockery and abuse that brought emotional and spiritual trauma to the people.[20] This is the context Ezekiel Ch. 36 addresses and although the mountains of Israel are addressed in Ch. 36, the intended audience are the exiles who feel abandoned in Babylon. Leslie Allen in effect says, the desolated land that refers to 'the mountains and the hills, the ravines and the valleys, the desolate wastes and the deserted cities' – 36:4, represents an objective image of the how the exiles feel.[21] The Lord addresses the desolate mountains and the land and announces it will become fruitful and be inhabited once again: and this prophecy speaks about their restoration – 8-11. This oracle of salvation reverses the judgment oracle the Lord announced in Ch. 6:3: 'Thus says the Lord God to the mountains and the hills, to the ravines and the valleys: Behold I will bring a sword upon you and I will destroy your high places. Your altars shall become desolate, and your incense altars shall be broken: and I will cast down your slain before idols.'

The dominant feature of the land was its hilly and mountainous character which was not conducive to the large-scale cultivation of grains and vegetables, although trees and shrubs could flourish even on steep slopes as is still evidenced today. As the Lord addresses the land and blesses it he reverses its impact as a place that devours its population and the taunts of the other nations.[22] As the Lord addresses the mountains in v. 8 this marks a transition in the oracle which Block interprets as, 'an exciting and excited announcement of the reversal of the land's humiliation…the complete restoration of the deity-nation-land relationship.'[23] The Lord makes the most momentous declaration when he announces, 'For, behold, I am for you and will turn to you' – v. 9. Up until now, the Lord had been opposed to his people in judgment using the hostile formula 'I am against you.' The Lord had indeed turned his face against his people in judgment. Now turning his face turned toward his people reminds them of Aaron's blessing in Num. 6:24-26:

> The Lord bless you and keep you: The Lord make his face to shine upon you, and be gracious to you: The Lord lift up his face upon you, and give you peace.

In the Lord's oracles announced by Ezekiel to the exiles so sustained over a number of years was the emphasis on God's judgment, that a message of hope and renewal was difficult to dispel their devastation at the news of the fall of Jerusalem. In Ch. 36, the Lord seeks to reassure his people about their future restoration to Israel and that the time of judgment is over. Zimmerli says, 'The oracle obviously speaks to a hidden despondency on the part of the exiles who are concerned with the question: 'Will in fact a newly bestowed history in the land work out any differently from the first history?' Yahweh's word points to a future in which the threat from the land will be definitely removed.'[24] The Lord seeks to assure his people he will put an end to their reproach by other nations and that he will also end their oppression – v. 15. As the Lord declares he is now for the people and with them, the revival of the land and the peoples' restoration will testify to the fact, 'then you will know that I am the Lord' – v.11, when the word of the Lord has been fulfilled.

Understanding the meaning of vs. 20-21 is key to interpreting the second half of Ch. 36 as the attention now shifts from God's people and what the Lord will do for them, to the Lord himself. The theological issue the Lord addresses is that of his people profaning his holy name. Israel's election as God's people had set them apart and constituted them holy to the Lord so long as they were obedient to his commandments and laws. But because of their idolatry and abominable sins the Lord's judgment led to the exile in Babylon that resulted in other nations disrespecting God's name. To the foreign nations, Israel's deportation from her own land reflected negatively on the Lord's character and his reputation. Because to ancient Near Eastern theological perceptions the God of Israel was obligated to defend his land and his people. The foreign nations concluded either the Lord had willingly abandoned his people or he was unable to defend them against the superior might of Markduk, the god of Babylon. Therefore, the Lord's reputation has been profaned-defiled among the nations.[25]

> The expression 'profane God's name' was probably originally at home in liturgical contexts, since it first occurred in Lev. 18:21, 19:12, 20:3, 21:6, referring to child sacrifice, idolatry, false swearing, and improper behaviour in connections with offerings brought to the sanctuary (defile my sanctuary in Ezek. 5:11, 23:38). In ethical contexts to profane God, his name, or his holy things implies a deliberate flouting of his will, in violation of his commandments as in 13:9, 22:6. Yahweh tends to relate desecration of his name to historical events, and three times in 20:9, 14, 22, he explains how he acted for the sake of his name in ways that seem very similar to the language of 36:20 here. Unless he acted for the sake of his name he would be discredited by the misfortune of his people, when the nations to which they came drew negative and false conclusions about the Israelite 'god' (as they would view him), as though he were unable to protect his own

people or had been bested by the gods of the nations who conquered Israel.[26]

There is an alternative and complementary interpretation of 36:20-21, that hints at the possibility the Israelites had profaned the Lord's name by the way they behaved during their exile. Other passages in Ezekiel describe the exiles in terms of their depravity. In 12:15-16 the scattered survivors will confess all their abominable acts among the nations. Also, in 36:31 in retrospect the redeemed will loathe themselves for their sins and abominations, shocking even by Gentile standards – 5:6-7.[27]

A NEW HEART & NEW SPIRIT – 36: 22-32

'Therefore, say to the house of Israel, Thus says the Lord God: It is not for your sake, O house of Israel that I am about to act, but for the sake of my holy name which you have profaned among the nations to which you came. And I will vindicate the holiness of my name which has been profaned among the nations and which you profaned among them: and the nations will know that I am the Lord, says the Lord God, when through you I vindicate my holiness before their eyes. For I will take you from the nations and gather you from all the countries and bring you into your own land. I will sprinkle clean water upon you and you shall be clean from all your uncleannesses, and from all your idols I will cleanse you. A new heart I will give you, and a new spirit I will put within you: and I will take out of your flesh the heart of stone and give you a heart of flesh. And I will put my spirit within you, and cause you to walk in my statutes and be careful to observe my ordinances. You shall dwell in the land which I gave to your fathers, and you shall be my people, and I will be your God.''

Verse 22 marks the beginning of a new oracle to the house of Israel that initially appears to accuse God's people, but the vindication of the Lord's holy-sacred name is His purpose as they have profaned this among the nations: so the Lord categorically states that he is not acting for their sake, his name has been desecrated. He is acting for the sake of his holy name – 22-24.

The Lord will act to clear his name and restore his reputation and receive the honour due to him, and the nations will witness the manifestation of the Lord's holiness – v. 23. 'What is at stake is not an impressive position for Israel, but the justification of God's claim to reveal himself to the world...If Israel can still possess any sort of hope it must have as its sole basis the certainty that God's fidelity to his own intrinsic nature (and that is precisely what is ultimately meant by the hallowing of his name) must necessarily lead to his sanctifying and renewing the people whom he has rejected.'[28]

The Lord will vindicate his holy name among the nations by his saving restorative action on behalf of Israel as he gathers his people from among the nations where they were scattered. Just as the restoration in 36:24 will reverse the effect of the exile in 36:19, the Lord will cleanse his people in 36:25 and will affect the reversal of the impurities mentioned in 36:17-18. This probably alludes to the sprinkling of the blood and water cleansing ceremonies in Leviticus. The Lord's divine action is framed in terms of a new exodus motif as this is what in his sovereign power he will do for his people.

> 'I will take you from among the nations.' – v. 24
> 'I will gather you from all the countries.' – v. 24
> 'I will bring you into your own land.' – v. 24
> 'I will sprinkle clean water upon you.' – v. 25
> 'I will cleanse you from all your idols.' – v. 25
> 'I will give you a new heart.' – v. 26
> 'I will put a new spirit within you.' – v. 26
> 'I will take out your heart of stone.' – v. 26
> 'I will give you a heart of flesh. – v. 26
> 'I will put my spirit within you.' – v. 27
> 'I will be your God.' – v. 28

Block captures the essence of the Lord's remarkable salvation when he says, 'This passage (24-30), which expands on 11: 17-20, contains the most systematic and detailed summary of Yahweh's restorative agenda in Ezekiel, if not in all the prophetic books …The central core (25-28) deals with the internal spiritual dimension to Israel's restoration, framed by external promises for the return of the nation from exile (24) and the rejuvenation of their hereditary homeland.'[29]

Verses 25-28 speak about the transformation of Israel and the renewal of her relationship with the Lord, and the motif of a new heart and a new spirit in v. 26 is an allusion to Deut. 30:6, 8:

> And the Lord God will circumcise your heart and the heart of your offspring, so that you will love the Lord your God with all your heart and with all your soul, that you may live…And you shall again obey the voice of the Lord and keep his commandments which I command you this day.

However, as the Lord gives his people a new heart and a new spirit this is far more radical than Deut 30:6, 8, as this involves the removal of the old heart of stone that is to be replaced with a new heart of flesh along with a new spirit. The stubborn, hard hearted and unresponsive heart of God's people Ezekiel was warned about by the Lord in chapters 2 and 3 is resolved as the Lord removes their petrified heart 'with a warm, sensitive, and responsive heart of flesh.'[30] This will take place, because not only will the Lord give his people a new heart and a new spirit, he will also put his Spirit within his people. The promise of God's Spirit is also mentioned in 37:17, 'And I will put my spirit within you' and again in 39:29, when the Lord will pour out his Spirit upon the house of Israel. This emphasises that, 'nothing short of divine intervention will ever make it possible for God's intended covenant relationship to be implemented.'[31] As NT believers we can readily identify with receiving a new heart and a new spirit when by faith we receive God's Spirit – Acts 2:38.

THE VALLEY OF DRY BONES – 37: 1-14

'The hand of the Lord was upon me and he brought me out by the spirit of the Lord and set me down in the midst of the valley, it was full of bones. And he led me round among them, and behold, there were very many upon the valley, and lo they were very dry. And he said to me, "Son of man, can these bines live?" And I answered, "O Lord God, you know." Again he said to me, "Prophesy to these bones, and say to them, 'O dry bones hear the word of the Lord.' Thus says the Lord God to these bones, Behold I will cause breathe to enter you and you shall live. And I will lay sinews upon you, and will cause flesh to come upon you, and cover you with skin, and put breathe in you and you shall live, and you shall know that I am the Lord."

So I prophesied as I was commanded, and as I prophesied there was a noise, and behold, a rattling: and the bones came together, bone to bone. And as I looked there were sinews on them, and flesh had come upon them, and skin has covered them, but there was no breath in them. Then he said to me, "Prophesy to the breath, prophesy, son of man, and say to the breath, Thus says the Lord God: come from the four winds, O breath, and breathe upon these slain that they may live." So I prophesied as he commanded me and the breath came into them, and they lived and stood upon their feet, an exceedingly great host.

Then he said to me, "Son of man, these bones are the whole house of Israel. Behold, they say, 'Our bones are dried up, and our hope is lost: we are clean cut off.' Therefore prophesy, and say to them, Thus says the Lord God: Behold, I will open your graves and raise you from your graves, O my people: and I will bring you home into the land of Israel. And you shall know that I am the Lord when I open your graves, and raise you from your graves, O my people. And I will put my spirit within you, and you shall live, and I will place you in your own land: then you shall know that I, the Lord, have spoken and I have done it, says the Lord."

In Ezekiel Ch. 37 the famous allegory of the valley of dry bones, the Lord's salvation oracle unquestionably is a dramatic narrative. The bones represent the 'despair and anguish of abandonment.'[32] Alongside Ezekiel's inaugural vision in Ch. 1 this is probably the best know chapter in the book. Ch. 37 is a truly spectacular symbolic sign of breathtaking significance.

Through the allegory of the dry bones the Lord addresses the exiles who are devastated by the fall of Jerusalem and who have lost any hope of returning to their homeland from which they have 'been clean cut off' – v. 11. 'They have lost all hope in their future and all hope in God. The nation obviously needs deliverance not only from their exile but also from their own despondency.'[33]

Without mentioning a specific period of time the narrative begins with Ezekiel's autobiographical record of his ecstatic vision in which the hand of the Lord was upon him and he was brought out by the Spirit of the Lord to a valley full of dry bones – v. 1. The hand of the Lord features significantly on a number of occasions in Ezekiel's encounters with the Lord, and first appears in 1:3 and then subsequently in 3:14, 22, 8:1, 33:22 and in 40:1. He knows from past experience that the 'hand of the Lord' represents the overwhelming force which the Lord asserts over him and by his Spirit in 37:1 brings him to a valley. In Ch. 37 the repetition of key words impressively frames the narrative. In verses 1-14, the Hebrew *ruah* that can mean Spirit, breath or wind occurs ten times: the word 'bones' ten times: the verb 'prophesy' seven times: and to 'live again' and 'come to life' six times.[34] Block's translation of v. 2 reads: 'As he led me around among the bones, I was surprised to see how exceedingly numerous they were on the surface of the valley, and astonished at how exceedingly dry they were.' The Hebrew phrase at the end of v. 1, *wehinneh rabbot me'od* – highlights Ezekiel's amazement at the number of bones, which suggests the remains of a major catastrophe.[35] The bones on the surface resemble the remains of corpses denied a proper burial and their dryness indicates they had been there a very long time. The allegory of the dry bones represents the hopelessness of the exiles and is a picture, 'of death in all its horror, intensity and finality.'[36] As a priest Ezekiel knew that human bones left unburied was a horrific outcome and to be denied a burial was the ultimate degradation and a sign of being cursed and also one of divine judgment.[37]

As the Lord leads Ezekiel around the valley full of bones, he asks him a question, ''Son of man can these bones live?'' Such a possibility is clearly ludicrous and as Ezekiel has no clue what the Lord's intention is by asking this question, he is non-committal to this enigmatic question and replies, 'O Lord only you know the answer' – v. 3. During his prophetic ministry, the Lord had asked Ezekiel to do some bizarre things and to enact some strange symbolic signs, but nothing comes close to the Lord's command to now prophecy to a valley full of a colossal amount of dead, decaying bones. The command is to speak to the bones and specifically declare God's word to them. The Lord's command is truly remarkable as he states the bones will come to life, have breath and in effect become living persons once again. Ezekiel has learned not to challenge or question the Lord's oracles so he is obedient and prophesies to the bones and commands them to hear the word of the Lord – v. 7. And as he prophesies this is the fulfillment of 'the prophetic word and the event,'[38] as the bones came to life but had no breath – v.8. Zimmerli eloquently captures the drama of the occasion when he says:

> The prophet is suddenly transformed from being the spokesman of human impotence into the spokesman of divine omnipotence. He receives the commission to proclaim over the dry bones the prophetic word, which, with the summons to attention, calls the dead to pay attention, and as the authorised messenger delivers the divine message in which the 'God of the spirits of life for all flesh,' himself proclaims that he will bring his spirit of life and make the dead bones come to life.[39]

GOD'S NEW COVENANT – 37: 15-28

'The word of the Lord came to me: "Son of man, take a stick and write on it, 'For Judah and the children of Israel associated with him.' Then take another stick and write upon it, 'For Joseph (the stick of Ephraim) and all the house of Israel associated with him.' And join them together into one stick that they may become one in your hand. And when your people say to you, 'Will you not show us what you mean by these?' Say to them, Thus says the

Lord God: Behold, I am about the take the stick of Joseph (which is in the hand of Ephraim) and the tribes of Israel associated with him, and I will join it with the stick of Judah and make them one stick that they may be one in my hand. When the sticks on which you write are in your hand before their eyes, then says to them, Thus says the Lord God: Behold, I will take the people of Israel from the nations among which they have gone and will gather them from all sides, and bring them to their own land, and I will make one nation in the land upon the mountains of Israel. And one kind shall be king over them all and they shall be no longer two nations, and no longer divided into two kingdoms. They shall not defile themselves any more with their idols and their detestable things or with any of their transgressions: but I will save them from all their backslidings in which they have sinned, and will cleanse them, and they shall be my people and I will be their God.

My servant David shall be their king over them and they shall all have one shepherd. They shall follow my ordinances and be careful to observe my statutes. They shall dwell in the land where their fathers dwelt that I gave to my servant Jacob, they and their children's children shall dwell there for ever: and David my servant shall be their prince for ever. I will make a new covenant of peace with them it shall be an everlasting covenant with them: and I will bless them and multiply them, and will set my sanctuary in the midst of them for evermore. My dwelling place shall be with them, and I will be their God and they shall be my people. Then the nations will know that I the Lord sanctify Israel, when my sanctuary is in the midst of them for evermore.''

The oracles concerning the restoration of Israel that began in Ch. 36 continue with the Lord's promise of a new covenant with his people in Ch. 37. At last the Lord's compassion and mercy shine through as he announces their restoration and salvation and that again they will be his people and he will be their God – v. 23, 27. Once again, the Lord instructs Ezekiel to perform a symbolic sign-act using two sticks that represent the northern kingdom of Israel and southern kingdom of Judah. (The northern kingdom had been destroyed around 150 years before the fall of Jerusalem and the people dispersed among the nations). Ezekiel is instructed to write the name of the house of Israel on one stick and Judah on the other and then join them together. The usual translation of 'a stick of wood' could mean a piece in almost any shape or form and these sticks may have been staffs or staves. Block suggests this may have been a small wooden writing tablet which could be bound together to make a folder. He points out that these boards were made of flat pieces of wood and occasionally ivory covered on the writing surface with a compound of beeswax and 25 percent of orpiment on which a message would be etched.[40] Whatever form the sticks that Ezekiel took were, the key issue is in interpreting their symbolic significance that is clearly stated by the Lord in his command to Ezekiel: 'join them together into one stick, that they may become one in your hand' – v.17. The two sticks represent the reunification of God's people and that once again they will be untied in his hand. This focus on unity is found throughout this section with the emphasis on the word 'one' in v. 17, and in v. 19, 'that they may be one stick, that they may be one in my hand.' 'I will make them one nation in the land…and one king shall be over them' – v. 22, and 'They shall have one shepherd' – v. 24.

We can assume the symbolic sign-act of the two sticks is a public demonstration as the Lord also informs Ezekiel the people will say to him, 'Will you not show us what you mean by these?' – v. 18. The Lord instructs Ezekiel to speak an oracle to explain to them the meaning of his parabolic action and there is a four-fold significance to the Lord's oracle. 1) The union of the two kingdoms represents the descendents of Israel. Bearing in mind the northern tribes of Israel were dispersed by the Assyrians in upper Mesopotamia this reunification signifies the Lord extraordinary salvation. 2) The reunification of the two kingdoms on its own did not restore the national integrity of Israel so the Lord promises to restore his people to their own homeland. Jerusalem was the land they identified as a place of belonging as God's people and which gave them their identity in the land that the Lord had given to them. 3) The unification and restoration of

God's people will be complemented by their political establish-ment as the Lord promises one king shall rule over them. Bearing in mind the destruction of the monarchy by the dispersion of the two kingdoms, the appointment of a king will symbolise the restoration of Israel and their identity as a nation. 4) The restoration of the two kingdoms as one entity will be complete as the Lord establishes a new covenant with his people that symbolises their spiritual restoration. Their national identity was closely aligned to their spiritual inheritance as God's covenant people. The first sign of this renewed covenant would be the Lord's salvation from all their past sins and abominable practices associated with idols, because the Lord promised to cleanse them from all these things – v. 23. Their spiritual restoration would be complete as the Lord declares, 'they shall be my people and I will be their God' – v. 23. 'This declaration signals the full restoration of Israel's relationship with Yahweh.'[41]

Verses 15-24 include blessing upon blessing that are piled on top of one another as the Lord reaffirms the covenant renewal. He also promises, 'My dwelling place shall be with them, and I will be their God, and they shall be my people' – v. 27. In vs. 24-28 the Lord announces blessing upon blessing on his people. As the Lord gives them a new heart and a new spirit and puts his Spirit within them (Ch. 36), they will be obedient to the covenant he makes with them. This covenant will be one that is characterised by peace – but more than that, it will be an everlasting covenant as once again they thrive and multiply as a nation – v. 26. An additional blessing will be the appointment of a leader who is referred to as, 'My servant David shall be king over them and they will have one shepherd' – v. 24, and 'David my servant shall be their prince for ever' – v. 25. The allusion to David as the Lord's servant and prince is based on the unconditional covenant the Lord made with him – 2 Samuel 7:16 that one his descendents would always be on the throne. This speaks of 'the perpetuity of the Davidic dynasty through the eternal Son of David…The true special relationship of David with the Lord is summarised by 'my servant' a title of great honour in the ancient near East.'[42]

The climatic blessing of the oracle in Ch. 37:26-28 concerns the Lord's sanctuary he will set in their midst for ever. Commenting on these verses Hummel says: 'The discussion of the 'sanctuary' (37:26, 28) is inseparable from the alternate term used in 37:27 'tabernacle.' Yahweh often uses 'sanctuary' in the book for the Solomonic temple in Jerusalem which the Israelites defiled, whereas he speaks of 'my tabernacle' only in 37:27. 'Sanctuary' and 'tabernacle' complement one another. Initially here, the accent is that Yahweh will dwell among his people as the one who is 'holy' of which 'sanctuary' is a nominal derivative parallel to the connection of the 'sanctuary' with the Latin *sanctus* – holy. At the beginning of the Book of Ezekiel there was great accent on Yahweh's presence as his 'Glory.' As stressed there God's holiness and his glory tend to be correlative, and if, as the formula goes, 'God's glory is his holiness revealed,' the implication would be that now in the end time, the distinction will be erased, as God will be fully and forever revealed among his people.'[43] The remarkable conclusion of God's renewed covenant at the end of Ch. 37 is that God's presence that was in the Holy of Holies in the temple in Jerusalem before it was destroyed, will now in a new way be with his people after their restoration. Therefore, the sanctuary and the tabernacle that the Lord speaks about in 37:36, 38 is assimilated in the vision of the sanctuary in Ezekiel 40-48, that figuratively represents God dwelling in the midst of his people.[44] The promises in 37:25- 28, bear a striking resemblance to Lev: 26:1-13 in which the Lord promises to dwell among his people, that he will be their God and they will be his people, if they walk in his commandments and observe his statutes. Ch. 37:25-28 are also a fulfillment of Deut. 4:30-31: 'When you are in tribulation and all these things come upon you in the last days, you will return to the Lord your God and obey his voice, for the Lord your God is a merciful God: he will not fail you, or destroy you, or forget this covenant with your fathers which he swore to them.' Finally, Ch. 37 has significant messianic allusions. The main features of the Messiah are found in the titles/ roles he bears as God's servant, shepherd and prince of his people.

As New Testament Christians in the 21st century, we can readily relate to the Lord giving his people Israel in the Old Testament, a new heart and a new spirit and also putting his Spirit within them, that is reminiscent of Joel Ch. 2. The context of this chapter is the Day of the Lord's judgment that sees the people responding to the Lord, who promises a future blessing on the land and on the people with the Lord saying in Joel 2: 27-29:

> You shall know that I am in the midst of Israel, and that I the Lord, am your God and there is none else. And my people shall never again be put to shame. And it shall come to pass afterward, that I will pour out my spirit on all flesh: and your sons and you daughters will prophecy, your old men shall dream dreams, and your young men shall see visions. Even upon menservants and maidservants in those days, I will pour out my spirit.

This promise was fulfilled on the Day of Pentecost in Acts 2 and God's presence and the presence of Christ can now dwell in us by his Spirit, so that Christians are now the temple of the Holy Spirit – 1 Cor. 6:19. Therefore, God's presence with his people in his sanctuary that referred originally to the temple in the OT has been superseded by his indwelling presence in our hearts by the Holy Spirit. As we reflect on God's glory and his holiness that his people defiled and desecrated in the temple in Jerusalem before the exile by their idolatry and abominable sins, God's glory and holiness that were associated with his presence in the Holy of Holies in the temple are now associated with his indwelling presence in the Church – the body of Christ.

The concept of God's shekinah glory – the glory of the Lord's divine presence, and God's holiness, with a heightened awareness of God's presence dwelling among us, are attributes of the Lord we should be able to encounter in our corporate worship. And the allusion to God's sanctuary in Ezek. 37 that is the dwelling place of God's presence, which can be likened to the Lord's indwelling presence in Christians, means that God's sanctuary can also be interpreted as the context of our corporate worship, where the Lord manifests his presence in a powerfully tangible way amongst us. The concepts of God's holiness, God's glory, and God's presence, and the potential of experiencing these attributes of the Lord, challenge us to reflect on our approach, our attitudes and our values in our corporate worship. Is there a sense of awe and an awareness of God's holiness and glory and presence amongst us in our corporate worship? Or have we imposed our cultural and denominational values on our corporate worship, and as a result deposed the Lord because of our subjective preferences that we prioritise in our worship? God's people whom the Lord addressed through Ezekiel's prophetic ministry were indicted because of their idolatry and abominable sins many of which were actually introduced into their temple worship. While their practices appear alien to us and realistically are not applicable to us, we do well to reflect on the more insidious idols that may have infiltrated our corporate worship, through our cultural and denominational biases – and repent of them.

As the first half of the book of Ezekiel comprising 24 chapters relentlessly focuses on God's judgment – the 'Day of the Lord's Judgment' in his covenant relationship with Israel, in conclusion it is appropriate to reflect on this topic in the 21st century. The supreme difference since the incarnation of Christ is that God is no longer in a covenant relationship with nations in the way that he was with Israel, so the Lord does not judge each nation in the way he held Israel accountable in his covenant relationship with her. Therefore, the challenge facing the Church is for its leaders, the clergy, the Bishops and the Archbishops, to be the Lord's 'watchmen' and 'spokesmen' and speak out on his behalf to address the nation and promote God's Ten Commandments as the basis of our national life to address the sin and evil in society. And to remind the nation there is a Judgment Day that Christ himself also spoke about, when everyone will have to give an account to God of how they lived.

Christ himself referred to the 'Day of Judgment' in his ministry: for example in Math. 10:14-15, 11:20-24, 12:38-42 and 25:31-46. In Matthew 25:31-46 Christ clearly speaks about sitting on his throne when all nations will be gathered before him and he will judge all the people. The Church has a calling and an obligation to speak out to remind people about their personal accountability to God and to remind the nation about the Day of Judgment. In Romans Ch. 1 Paul speaks about the Gospel being the power of God for salvation and in Ch. 2 he talks about God's judgment and knowing God's truth in our hearts through our conscience God has given us. But, he also speaks about God's kindness and patience that people might respond to this and avoid God's punishment on the Day of Judgment. As we declare the Gospel of Salvation in and through Christ alone, are we more concerned to make it 'accessible' or do we have the courage and integrity to speak about God's holy character and his judgment, as an integral aspect of the Gospel? In our day, do we nullify the 'Day of Judgment' by avoiding it, as we declare the Gospel of Christ?

FOOTNOTES

BACK COVER

1.   D. Block Ezekiel Eerdmans 1997 128
2.   35-36
3.   Ibid 128

PREFACE

1.   P. M. Joyce After Ezekiel – The Library Of Hebrew Old Testament Studies T. & T. Clark 2014 3-5
2.   D. Block ibid 107
3.   Ibid 35-36
4.   W. Zimmerli Fortress Press 1979 58
5.   D. Block Ibid 42-43
6.   D. Block Ibid 137
7.   C. Wright Ezekiel IVP 2001 28
8.   L. C. Allen Ezekiel 1-19 Zondervan 1987 24
9.   C. Wright ibid 28--29
10. H. D. Hummel Ezekiel 1-20 Concordia Publishing 2005 38
11. K. Stevenson M Glerup Editors Ezekiel & Daniel IVP 2008 xx
12. S. Tuell Ezekiel Paternoster 2009 1
13. J. Biwul A Theological Examination of Symbolism In Ezekiel with Emphasis on the Shepherd Metaphor Langham Monographs 2013 32
14. J. Blenkinsopp Ezekiel John Knox 1990 33
15. D. Block ibid

CHAPTER ONE

1.   P. M. Joyce Ezekiel – The Library Of Hebrew Old Testament Studies T & T Clark 2009 3
2.   J. Blenkinsopp ibid 3
3.   D. Block ibid 2
4.   Ibid 2-3
5.   I. M. Duguid Ezekiel Zondervann 1999 22-23
6.   Ibid 22
7.   P. M. Joyce ibid 4-5
8.   C. Wright Ezekiel IVP 2001 41

9.   Ibid 51
10.   Ibid 51
11.   Ibid 40-41
12.   D. Block ibid 9
13.   C. Wright ibid 21
14.   Ibid 21
15.   D. Block ibid 1997
16.   Ibid 22, 25, 27
17.   C. Wright ibid 28
18.   L. C. Allen ibid 24
19.   C. Wright ibid 28--29
20.   D. Block ibid 144
21.   Ibid 10-11
22.   W. Zimmerli ibid 20-21
23.   Ibid 19
24.   Ibid 20
25.   D. Block ibid 14
26.   W. Zimmerli ibid 57
27.   Ibid 58
28.   J. Biwul ibid 32
29.   J. Blenkinsopp ibid 33
30.   J. Biwul ibid 35-36
31.   J. Blenkinsopp ibid 34
32.   D. Block ibid 166
33.   W. Zimmerli ibid 156
34.   W. Eichrodt ibid 81-82
35.   J. Biwul ibid 44
36.   H. Hummel Ezekiel 1-20 Concordia Publishing 2005 4-5
37.   D. Block ibid 15, 17
38.   J. Biwul ibid 47
39.   Ibid 50-52
40.   Ibid 55
41.   Ibid 61
42.   D. Block ibid 64
43.   Ibid 64
44.   C. Wright ibid 214, 216

45.   D. Block ibid 27, 31
46.   Ibid 20-21
47.   Ibid 30-31
48.   P. Joyce ibid 27
49.   Ibid 29
50.   Ibid 27
51.   D. Block Ibid 39-40
52.   Ibid 32-33
53.   Ibid 33
54.   Ibid 35-36
55.   W. Zimmerli ibid 132
56.   Ibid 133
57.   D. Block ibid 33
58.   W. Eichrodt ibid 62-63
59.   Ibid 63
60.   W. Zimmerli ibid 137
61.   D. Block ibid 124
62.   Ibid 128
63.   H. Hummel ibid 87, 115

CHAPTER TWO

1.   W. Eichrodt ibid 53
2.   M. Odel ibid 14
3.   W. Eichrodt ibid 53
4.   W. Zimmerli ibid 98
5.   D. Block ibid 90
6.   Ibid 90
7.   S. Tuell ibid 10
8.   D. Block ibid 89
9.   Ibid 89-90
10.   Ibid 96
11.   I. Duguid ibid 58
12.   C. Wright ibid 48-49
13.   D. Block ibid 98
14.   M. Odell ibid 18
15.   H. Hummel ibid 139

16. D. Block ibid 101
17. H. Hummel ibid 64
18. Ibid 64-66
19. D. Block ibid 106
20. C. Wright ibid 50
21. D. Block ibid 103
22. C. Wright ibid 51
23. D. Block ibid 106-7
24. Ibid 105
25. Ibid 113
26. Ibid 112
27. H. Hummel ibid 70-71
28. D. Block 35
29. C. Wright 58
30. D. Block ibid 117
31. Ibid 118
32. S. Tuell ibid 13
33. W. Eichrodt ibid 62
34. D. Block ibid 118
35. H. Hummel ibid 87
36. D. Block Ibid 124-125
37. Ibid 125
38. W. Eichrodt ibid 62
39. H. Hummel ibid 113
40. D. Block ibid 126
41. W. Eichrodt ibid 65
42. H. Hummel ibid 112-113
43. D. Block ibid 128
44. H. Hummel ibid 116
45. C. Wright ibid 62
46. W. Zimmerli ibid 138
47. H. Hummel ibid 117
48. W. Eichrodt ibid 66
49. Ibid 66
50. D. Block ibid 136
51. Ibid 136

52.   Ibid 136-137

53.   H. Hummel ibid 119

54.   W. Eichrodt ibid 66

55.   D. Block ibid 137-138

56.   C. Wright ibid 63

57.   D. Block ibid 143

58.   W. Eichrodt ibid 75

59.   D. Block ibid 140-141

60.   Ibid 144

61.   C. Wright ibid 65

62.   D. Block 150

63.   Ibid 153

64.   W. Eichrodt ibid 74-75

65.   Ibid 76

66.   C. Wright ibid 69

67.   D. Block ibid 161

68.   Ibid 161

69.   C. Wright ibid 73

70.   D. Block Ibid 156

71.   Ibid 156

72.   R. Albertz A History Of Israelite Religion in the Old
        Testament SCM 1994 373

CHAPTER THREE

1.   H. Hummel ibid 148-150

2.   D. Block ibid 164

3.   Ibid 162

4.   Ibid 163

5.   J. Blenkinsopp ibid 34

6.   D. Block ibid 166

7.   J. Biwul ibid 144

8.   W. Zimmerli ibid 156

9.   D. Block ibid 17

10.   H. Hummel ibid 137-138

11.   W. Zimmerli ibid 162

12.   I. Duguid ibid 88

13.   C. Wright ibid 75
14.   D. Block ibid 173
15.   Ibid 167
16.   W. Zimmerli ibid 162
17.   D. Block ibid 176
18.   H. Hummel ibid 158
19.   W. Zimmerli ibid 164-165
20.   D. Block ibid 178
21.   Ibid 180
22.   Ibid 180
23.   Ibid 185
24.   Ibid 185
25.   Ibid 186
26.   W. Zimmerli 145-146
27.   D. Block ibid 187
28.   Ibid 188-189
29.   C. Wright ibid 82-83
30.   D. Block ibid 192
31.   Ibid 193
32.   W. Eichrodt ibid 87
33.   D. Block ibid 191
34.   Ibid 194
35.   Ibid 196
36.   Ibid 197
37.   Ibid 199
38.   Ibid 200
39.   Ibid 201
40.   W. Zimmerli 197
41.   C. Wright ibid 87
42.   W. Zimmerli ibid 183
43.   D. Block ibid 216
44.   Ibid 211
45.   Ibid 211
46.   M. Greenberg ibid 138
47.   R. Jenson Ezekiel SCM 2009 64
48.   D. Block 224

49.   Ibid 225
50.   Ibid 226
51.   H. Hummel ibid 193
52.   W. Zimmerli ibid 201
53.   Ibid 201
54.   H. Hummel ibid 207
55.   D. Block ibid 250
56.   M. Greenberg ibid 163
57.   R. Jenson ibid 70
58.   D. Block ibid 248
59.   D. Block By The River Chebar James Clarke
        & Co Ltd 2014 22
60.   Ibid 22
61.   Ibid 47-48
62.   W. Zimmerli 209
63.   D. Block ibid 244
64.   Ibid 256
65.   Ibid 256
66.   W. Zimmerli 213
67.   W. Eichrodt ibid 102-104

CHAPTER FOUR

1.   H. Hummel ibid 245
2.   C. Wright ibid 97
3.   D. Block ibid 279
4.   H. Hummel ibid 245
5.   Ibid 246
6.   C. Wright ibid 98
7.   Ibid 101
8.   D. Block ibid 282
9.   C. Wright ibid 101
10.   M. Odell ibid 105
11.   J. Blenkinsopp ibid 54
12.   D. Block ibid 283
13.   H. Hummel 251

14.   Ibid 241
15.   W. Eichrodt ibid 123
16.   D. Block ibid 291
17.   H. Hummel ibid 254
18.   D. Block ibid 288
19.   J. Blenkinsopp ibid 55
20.   H. Hummel ibid 238
21.   D. Block ibid 295
22.   H. Hummel ibid 257-258
23.   I. Duguid ibid 133
24.   J. Blenkinsopp ibid 55
25.   W. Eichrodt ibid 127
26.   C. Wright ibid 107
27.   H. Hummel ibid 260
28.   Ibid 241
29.   T. A. Dearborn & S. Coil Worship At The Next Level
        Baker 2004 25
30.   The Liturgical Commission Transforming Worship Church
        House Publishing 2007 8-9
31.   C. Cocksworth Holding Together Cant. Press 2008 158
32.   Ibid 167
33.   Ibid 168
34.   C. Cocksworth Lecture on The Liturgy and the Spirit
        given at The Oase Conference in Norway in Feb 2007
35.   D. Block ibid 329
36.   C. Wright ibid 123
37.   W. Zimmerli ibid 260
38.   D. Block ibid 341
39.   C. Wright ibid 124
40.   D. Block ibid 349-350
41.   Ibid 356
42.   H. Hummel ibid 324
43.   R. Jenson ibid 98
44.   H. Hummel ibid 325
45.   D. Block ibid 365
46.   W. Eichrodt ibid 150

47.   Ibid 150

48.   W. Zimmerli ibid 271

49.   W. Eichrodt ibid 153

50.   D. Block ibid 383

51.   Ibid 381

52.   Ibid 385

53.   W. Eichrodt ibid 155-156

54.   D. Block ibid 467-469

55.   C. Wright ibid 130

56.   D. Block ibid 465

57.   C. Wright ibid 130

58.   D. Block ibid 467

59.   H. Hummel ibid 423

60.   D. Block ibid 282-283

61.   Ibid 486-487

62.   C. Wright ibid 136

63.   H. Hummel ibid 460

64.   Ibid 421, 460

65.   D. Block ibid 472

66.   Ibid 487

67.   H. Hummel ibid 478

68.   D. Block ibid 494

69.   C. Wright ibid 143

70.   D. Block ibid 501-502

71.   H. Hummel ibid 483

72.   C. Wright ibid 144

73.   W. Eichrodt ibid 215

74.   D. Block ibid 510

75.   H. Hummel ibid 489

76.   D. Block ibid 513-514

77.   Ibid 517

78.   H. Hummel ibid 512

79.   D. Block ibid 525

80.   Ibid 526

81.   H. Hummel ibid 516

82.   D. Block ibid 551

83.   W. Eichrodt ibid 251
84.   H. Hummel ibid 558-559
85.   D. Block ibid 595
86.   Ibid 604
87.   Ibid 659
88.   H. Hummel ibid 645-646
89.   Ibid 646
90.   D. Block 675
91.   W. Eichrodt ibid 290-291
92.   D. Block ibid 671
93.   W. Eichrodt ibid 29394.
95.   W. Zimmerli ibid 425
96.   H. Hummerl ibid 653
97.   D. Block ibid 685
98.   Ibid 686
99.   Ibid 689
100.   I. Duguid ibid 277
101.   H. Hummel ibid 658
102.   Ibid 679
103.   Ibid 679
104.   D. Block ibid 704
105.   H. Hummel ibid 680
106.   D. Block ibid 704
107.   H. Hummel ibid 681
108.   D. Block ibid 706
109.   Ibid 709
110.   Ibid 711
111.   H. Hummel ibid 685
112.   W. Zimmerli ibid 459
113.   D. Block ibid 716
114.   H. Hummel ibid 688
115.   Ibid 690
116.   Ibid 675
117.   Ibid 691
118.   Ibid 692
119.   H. Hummel ibid 740

120. D. Block ibid 774
121. Ibid 774-776
122. Ibid 778
123. Ibid 781
124. C. Wright ibid 214
125. R. Jenson ibid 201
126. D. Block 781
127. W. Eichrodt ibid 343
128. H. Hummel ibid 750-751
129. D. Block ibid 792
130. H. Hummel ibid 766
131. M. Greenberg Ezekiel 21-37 Anchor 1997 516

CHAPTER FIVE

1.   H. Hummel ibid 970
2.   D. Block Ezekiel 25-48 Eerdmans 1998 243
3.   W. Eichrodt ibid 453
4.   H. Hummel ibid 975
5.   C. Wright ibid 223
6.   H. Hummel ibid 996-997
7.   C, Wright ibid 274
8.   J. Biwul ibid 202
9.   D. Block ibid 273
10. C. Wright ibid 275
11. H. Hummel ibid 998-999
12. D. Block ibid 283
13. C. Wright ibid 276
14. D. Block ibid 293
15. H. Hummel ibid 1004
16. D. Block ibid 300
17. H. Hummel ibid 218
18. Ibid 1008
19. D. Block ibid 308
20. C. Wright ibid 286
21. L. C. Allen Ezekiel 20-48 Send The Light 1990 174
22. C. Wright ibid 287

23.   D. Block ibid 333
24.   W. Zimmerli ibid 239
25.   D. Block ibid 347-348
26.   H. Hummel ibid 1048-1049
27.   Ibid 1049
28.   W. Eichrodt ibid 96-497
29.   D. Block ibid 352-353
30.   Ibid 355
31.   H. Hummel ibid 1056
32.   M O'Dell ibid 192
33.   D. Block ibid 372
34.   H. Hummel ibid 1075
35.   D. Block ibid 374
36.   Ibid 374
37.   C. Wright ibid 304
38.   D. Block ibid 376
39.   W. Zimmerli ibid 260
40.   D. Block ibid 400
41.   Ibid 414
42.   H. Hummel ibid 1091
43.   Ibid 1095
44.   Ibid 1096-1097

BIBLIOGRAPHY

R. Albertz A History Of Israelite Religion in the Old Testament SCM 1994

L. C. Allen Ezekiel 1-19 Zondervan 1987

L. C. Allen Ezekiel 20-48 Send The Light 1990

J. Biwul A Theological Examination of Symbolism In Ezekiel, with Emphasis on the Shepherd Metaphor Langham Monographs 2013

J. Blenkinsopp Ezekiel John Knox 1990

R. E. Clements Ezekiel John Knox Press 1996

D. Block By The River Chebar Historical, Literary, and Theological Studies in the Book of Ezekiel James Clarke & Co Ltd 2014

D. Block Ezekiel 1-24 Eerdmans 1997

D. Block Ezekiel 25-38 Eerdmans

D. Bodi Ezekiel & The Poem Of Erra Freiburg 1991

C. Cocksworth Holding Together Canterbury Press 2008

C. Cocksworth Lecture on The Liturgy and the Spirit given at The Oase Conference in Norway in Feb 2007

T. A. Dearborn & S. Coil Worship At The Next Level Baker 2004

I. M. Duguid Ezekiel Zondervann 1999

W. Eichrodt Ezekiel Westminster Press 1970

M. Greenberg Ezekiel 1-20 Anchor 1983

M. Greenberg Ezekiel 21-37 Anchor 1997

H. D. Hummel Ezekiel 1-20 Concordia Publishing 2005

H. D. Hummel Ezekiel 21-48 Concordia Publishing 2007

R. W. Jenson Ezekiel SCM Press 2009

P. M. Joyce After Ezekiel – The Library Of Hebrew Old Testament Studies T. & T. Clark 2014

P. M. Joyce Ezekiel – The Library Of Hebrew Old Testament Studies T & T Clark 2009

The Liturgical Commission Transforming Worship Church House Publishing 2007

M. O'Dell Ezekiel Smyth & Helwys 2005

K. Stevenson, M Glerup Editors Ezekiel & Daniel IVP 2008

S. Tuell Ezekiel Paternoster 2009

C. Wright Ezekiel IVP 2001

W. Zimmerli 1-24 Fortress Press 1979

W. Zimmerli 25-38 Fortress Press